asian kitchen

asian kitchen

MURDOCH
BOOKS

contents

in the asian kitchen

Asian cooking is fresh, colourful and full of flavour. With its emphasis on grains and vegetables, it is also healthy, often inexpensive and quick to prepare. However, it wasn't that long ago that the most contact many of us ever had with Asian food was a trip to the local Chinese or Indian restaurant. Gradually, things have changed—immigration of Asian nationalities throughout the world has helped to develop a general awareness of Asian cuisine and culture, restaurant chefs are including Asian ingredients and cooking techniques in their repertoire, and new restaurants are opening up, introducing an array of exciting cooking styles from not only China and India, but also Sri Lanka, Nepal, Thailand, Vietnam, Japan, Malaysia and Indonesia, to name a few.

With these changes came a greater accessibility to Asian ingredients. Herbs such as fresh coriander (cilantro) and lemon grass are now commonplace in many suburban greengrocers and supermarkets, as well as all types of dried lentils and beans, noodles in many thicknesses and shapes, and a variety of rices.

Asian food is astonishingly multi-faceted. While cooking techniques and styles are based on years of tradition, many cuisines have been influenced by neighbouring countries, or have evolved as a result of the introduction of new foods and spices from migrants and missionaries, or by the occupation of one country by another. Thai cooking has strong Chinese influences as many of its population are of Chinese origin. Chillies are not native to Thailand but were introduced by Portuguese missionaries, and adopted, with much enthusiasm, into the cuisine. The simple fresh cuisine of Vietnam was complemented by skills in bread- and pastry-making acquired after its period of French occupation, while stir-frying and steaming techniques are the result of the influence of neighbouring China in the north.

where to buy asian food

In non-Asian countries, there has been a rise in the number of market gardens growing the fresh herbs, fruit and vegetables used in Asian cooking. This means that ingredients such as Thai sweet basil, chillies, lemon grass, ginger, garlic and Asian vegetables, including the great variety of delicious greens, are readily available. Demand from restaurants and home cooks has led to Asian-style seasonings and flavourings in the form of spices such as star anise and turmeric, and sauces such as soy and hoisin, becoming commonplace.

To find the best fresh Asian ingredients, visit your local Chinatown or find an Asian supermarket closest to you that has a quick turnover. If you have a local shop that specializes in Asian food, it is often the best place to find the more unusual ingredients.

If you are lucky enough to have access to produce markets, where small quantity farmers and producers sell their fresh foods directly to the public, you have the best source of all. Some of these producers specialize in Asian food.

how to use this book

The aim of this book is to introduce you to just some of the vast array of Asian ingredients you might come across, either when browsing through your local Asian supermarket or in recipes for Asian food.

The book has been divided into five chapters, and the items in each chapter are listed alphabetically.

store cupboard: Flours, rice, lentils and noodles—these are just a few of the store cupboard basics you will find here.

pastes and sauces: This chapter includes some of the basic Asian seasonings and sauces such as soy sauce, bean pastes and fish sauce.

seasonings, herbs and spices: Fresh and dried herbs, garlic, lemon grass and ginger—these are some of the colourful and fragrant seasonings used in Asian cooking.

fresh produce: Included here are some of the commonly used Asian fruit and vegetables along with the more unusual—durian, snake gourds and longans.

speciality shopping: Sea cucumber, shark's fin, edible silver leaf and kamaboko are just a few of the more unusual ingredients that you will find here. Bean curd is also listed here, and although this is often used in Asian cooking, this entry also covers some of the less well known by-products, such as mouldy and fermented bean curd.

Each entry has a colour photograph to help you identify it. Many of the entries also feature a recipe, which will give you an idea of how the particular ingredient is used. All herbs or seasonings, such as ginger or chilli, used in the recipes should be fresh, unless specified otherwise.

When looking for a particular ingredient, find it within its chapter, or refer to the subject index. Where there are alternative names or spellings for an entry, these will be found in the index as well. In addition to the subject index there is a recipe index.

cooking equipment

Besides the staple equipment required in a kitchen, a few cooking implements especially suited for Asian cooking are a good investment and are not expensive.

wok

No-one contemplating cooking a range of Asian dishes should be without a wok. With its large surface area and high sides it is ideal for stir-frying, and for deep-frying it requires less oil than a straight-sided pan. A wok is also ideal for steaming. Its sloping sides allow bamboo and metal steamers to fit firmly into place.

buying a wok There are many types available, varying in size and shape and the materials from which they are made. Inexpensive carbon steel or pressed steel woks—sold in Chinese and Asian stores—are good conductors of heat. Woks are also made from stainless steel, cast iron and aluminium, and some have nonstick surfaces. Not all woks come with lids, which are necessary when making soups or curries or when steaming, so check before you buy.

Woks are available with either a round or flat bottom. Round-bottom woks are best suited to cooking on a gas stove, as the flames can be regulated to reach up and hit the exterior of the wok. A wok stand can be used to ensure that the wok remains stable on the stove. Flat-bottom woks are a better option if cooking on an electric stove, as this ensures the surface is in constant contact with the heat source.

While all woks are based on the same basic design there are some variations, including size. For general domestic cooking, a 30–35 cm (12–14 inch) diameter wok is the most versatile size, as it is easier to cook small batches of food in a large wok than vice versa.

Two-handled woks are more stable, which is valuable when steaming or deep-frying, whereas one-handled woks are better for stir-frying, as the handle can be held in one hand and the charn (a spade-like scoop used for stir-frying) in the other to create the constant movement required when stir-frying.

cleaning and seasoning your wok New carbon steel woks are coated with a thin film of lacquer to stop them rusting. This film has to be removed before the wok can be used. This procedure is not necessary for stainless steel, cast-iron or nonstick woks.

To do this, place the wok on the stove top, fill it with cold water and add 2 tablespoons of bicarbonate of soda. Bring the water to the boil and boil rapidly for 15 minutes. Drain, scrub off the varnish with a plastic scourer, and repeat the process if any lacquer remains. Rinse and dry the wok.

The wok is now ready to be seasoned. This is done to create a smooth surface that stops the food sticking to it. Place the wok over low heat. Have a small bowl of oil, preferably peanut oil, nearby and scrunch a paper towel into a wad. When the wok is hot, wipe it with the wadded paper dipped into the oil. Repeat the process with fresh paper until it comes away clean and without any trace of colour. This coating builds up over time and provides a nonstick effect.

care and maintenance A seasoned wok should not be scrubbed. To wash a wok after cooking, use hot water and a sponge. Dry it well after washing by heating it gently over low heat, and rubbing it all over with an oiled paper towel. Store the wok in a dry, well-ventilated place. Long periods in a dark, warm, airless cupboard can cause the oil coating to turn rancid. Using the wok frequently is the best way to prevent it from rusting. If you do need to use detergent and a piece of fine steel wool to clean your wok, it will then need re-seasoning.

mortar and pestle

No Asian kitchen would be without some sort of grinding apparatus, usually a mortar and pestle. Pounding the ingredients in a mortar and pestle is the best way to make curry and spice pastes, but if the paste is wet enough, a blender or food processor can be used.

Ground spices quickly lose their flavour and aroma, so it is best to grind small amounts of whole spices when needed. You can also use a spice grinder or an electric coffee grinder. If you cannot set aside a coffee grinder just for spices, grind a little rice to remove coffee flavours, and again after the spices have been processed.

steamers

These are usually made from bamboo or aluminium. Bamboo stackable steamers are useful for a whole range of foods, from dumplings to whole fish, and can go straight from the wok to the table. It is best to line bamboo steamers with baking paper or banana leaves to stop pieces of food from falling into the wok.

clay pot

Glazed on the inside and used for slow cooking as it heats up evenly all over. The lid is sloped and forces condensation back into the dish.

knives

Sharp, good-quality knives are essential as so much Asian cooking involves cutting up raw ingredients. For most jobs, a Western chef's knife is the easiest to handle.

chopper/cleaver

Used for chopping through bones, as well as an all-purpose knife. Buy a good heavy one for chopping and a lighter one for slicing. They can prove indispensable when chopping up lots of ingredients for a stir-fry.

wire mesh spoon

For deep-frying in a wok, a wire mesh ladle is useful for lifting and draining fried food. The spoons are available in many different sizes. Alternatively, use a slotted spoon or tongs. A pair of long wooden chopsticks is also good for turning deep-fried food over to brown and crisp evenly. Metal or bamboo tongs are very useful for turning over things, or lifting things into or out of boiling liquids.

charn

The one essential tool if you do a lot of stir-frying is a 'charn' or wok turner. This is a spade-like scoop that is ideal for the continuous, fast scooping and turning required when stir-frying.

Pictured from top: mortar and pestle, bamboo steamers, wire mesh spoon.

cooking techniques

steaming

Food that is steamed is cooked by the moist heat given off by steadily boiling water. To get the best results:

Fill your wok or pan about one-third full with water. Stand the steamer over the water to check that it is the correct height before you bring the water to the boil. It is important that you have enough, and not too much water, in your wok. If there is too much water, it will boil up into the food; too little water, and it will quickly boil dry during cooking.

When the water is boiling, arrange the food in the steamer and place it carefully in the wok. Cover the wok and maintain the heat so the water boils rapidly, allowing the steam to circulate evenly around the food.

When lifting the lid on a wok while steaming is in progress, always lift it up and away from you like a shield so the skin on your wrist is not exposed to a blast of scalding steam.

stir-frying

Stir-frying involves cooking small pieces of food over medium to high heat for a short period of time. To get the best results:

Prepare all the ingredients before you start to cook. Slice the meat and vegetables, and have noodles (if using) ready to be added. All the ingredients for the sauce should be measured out.

Heat the wok before adding the oil, then heat the oil before adding the food. This ensures that the cooking time will be short and that the ingredients, especially meat, will be seared instantly, sealing in the juices and the flavour.

Toss and turn the food carefully while it cooks. Keeping the food constantly moving ensures even cooking and prevents burning. Stir-fried vegetables should be crisp and the meat tender and succulent.

deep-frying

It is very important to make sure that the wok or pan you are using for deep-frying is stable and secure on the stove top, and you should never leave the kitchen while the oil is heating as it can quickly overheat and ignite. To get the best results:

Add the oil, never filling the pan or wok more than half full, and heat over high heat. When the oil is the required temperature for deep-frying, 180°C (350°F), it will start to move and a 3 cm (1 ¼ inch) cube of bread lowered into it will brown in just 15 seconds. Lower the heat to medium if that is all that is needed to maintain the right temperature.

Carefully add the food to the hot oil, taking care as the oil may spatter. Using tongs, move the pieces of the food around (if small), gently turning them to ensure even cooking. When the food is cooked, carefully lift it out with a wire mesh strainer, tongs or a slotted spoon and drain it on a tray covered with several layers of paper towels.

When frying food in batches, make sure you reheat the oil to the required temperature after each batch. Use a slotted spoon to remove any small fragments of food left in the oil as these will burn.

store cupboard

agar-agar

Agar-agar is a flavourless gelling agent made from boiled and dried seaweed. It can be used to set ice creams, make jellies or desserts, and to make the sweet Indian drink, falooda. Unlike gelatine, agar-agar is not derived from animals and is therefore suitable for vegetarians. Foods that are set with agar-agar will set at room temperature, unlike those that contain gelatine, which only set on chilling. Agar-agar flakes, strands, powder or blocks are sold in health food shops, some supermarkets and Asian or Indian supermarkets.

Also known as — agar, Japanese gelatine, kanten, seaweed gelatine

Agar-agar can be used to make jellies (pictured above, with agar-agar strands).

falooda with rose syrup

250 g (9 oz) white sugar
2 teaspoons rosewater, or
  to taste
pink food colouring
2 teaspoons agar-agar
yellow food colouring
30 g (1 oz) basil seeds

1 tablespoon icing
  (confectioners') sugar
1 litre (4 cups) milk, chilled
6 tablespoons cream,
  whipped, or ice cream
almonds, chopped, for garnish
  (optional)

put the sugar and 250 ml (1 cup) water in a large, heavy-based saucepan, bring to the boil and boil for 2 minutes. Add rosewater, to taste, and enough colouring to make a pink syrup. Cool.

to prepare the falooda, dissolve the agar-agar in 250 ml (1 cup) boiling water in a small saucepan. Stir constantly over medium heat for 15 minutes. Add a little yellow food colouring. Pour into a large, flat dish and refrigerate until set. Turn out onto a cutting board and slice into thin strips (thin enough to be sucked up a straw).

soak the basil seeds in a little water for 1 hour, then drain. Stir the icing sugar into the milk. To prepare six large glasses of falooda, pour 2 tablespoons rose syrup into each glass. Add a helping of falooda and 2–3 teaspoons basil seeds to each, and top with the milk and 1 tablespoon cream or ice cream. Garnish with almonds if you wish. Serves 6.

Although both bitter and sweet almonds are cultivated, it is sweet almonds that are most often used in cooking. Almonds feature in Asian cuisines, particularly in northern India where they are ground and used in drinks, such as almond sarbat, or sweets such as barfi, or to thicken sauces in braised meat dishes. Almonds are sold whole, blanched, ground, chopped or flaked, or as almond extract. Store unshelled almonds in a cool place for up to a year. Shelled almonds will keep in the refrigerator for up to 6 months.

cooking

toasting Spread almonds in an even layer on a baking tray. Cook in a 180°C (350°F/Gas 4) oven for 8–10 minutes. Use a timer as the almonds will burn very quickly after they start to brown.

grinding Grind with a food processor or mortar and pestle. Use either blanched almonds or those with skins on. Add a little sugar to help absorb the oil and prevent an oily paste forming.

almond sarbat

250 g (2½ cups) freshly ground almonds
1 kg (4½ cups) sugar
12 cardamom pods
almond essence, to taste

put the almonds, sugar and 250 ml (1 cup) water in a heavy-based saucepan and stir over low heat until the sugar dissolves. Remove the cardamom seeds from the pods and grind with 1 tablespoon water in a mortar and pestle. Add to the almond syrup. Stir the mixture; remove any scum from the top. Cook until the syrup thickens. Remove from the heat, strain through a sieve lined with muslin; cool. Add the essence. Serve in glasses, with water, over crushed ice. Makes 250 ml (1 cup).

almonds

candlenuts

Candlenuts are hard, oily, tropical nuts. Because of their high oil content, candlenuts were once used to make candles. The nuts are usually crushed and added to soups, or ground and used as a thickening agent in Indonesian and Malaysian cooking. The raw nuts are slightly toxic, so they must be cooked before they are safe to eat. Buy candlenuts in Indian and Asian supermarkets and store them in the refrigerator. If candlenuts are unavailable, use macadamia or brazil nuts instead.

cashew nuts

These curious nuts are encased in a kidney-shaped hard shell and develop inside a fruit called the cashew apple. Each apple only produces one nut and, when the nut is ripe, the nut and shell protrude below the fruit. The shell contains a toxic oil, which can irritate the skin and eyes. The whole nuts are removed from the apples and heated before the nut can be safely extracted. Cashew nuts can be eaten roasted and salted, or added raw to Thai curries or stir-fries. In southern India, cashews are used to thicken stews, and in recipes for Indian cakes and sweets. Store in the refrigerator to prevent them turning rancid.

chicken with chilli jam and cashews

10 dried long red chillies
4 tablespoons peanut oil
1 red capsicum (pepper), chopped
1 head (50 g/1¾ oz) garlic, peeled and roughly chopped
200 g (7 oz) Asian shallots, chopped
100 g (3½ oz) palm sugar, grated

2 tablespoons tamarind purée
1 tablespoon peanut oil, extra
6 spring onions (scallions), cut into 3 cm (1¼ inch) lengths
500 g (1 lb 2 oz) chicken breast fillet, cut into slices
50 g (⅓ cup) roasted unsalted cashews
1 tablespoon fish sauce
15 g (½ cup) Thai sweet basil

to make the chilli jam, soak the chillies in boiling water for 15 minutes. Drain, remove the seeds and chop. Put in a food processor, then add the oil, capsicum, garlic and shallots and blend until smooth.

heat a wok over medium heat and add the chilli mixture. Cook, stirring occasionally, for 15 minutes. Add the sugar and tamarind and simmer for 10 minutes, or until it darkens and reaches a jam-like consistency. Remove.

clean and reheat the wok over high heat, add the oil and swirl to coat. Stir-fry the spring onion for 1 minute. Add the chicken and stir-fry for 5 minutes, or until tender. Add the cashews, fish sauce and 4 tablespoons of the chilli jam. Stir-fry for 2 minutes, then stir in the basil. Serves 4.

coconut milk/cream

From left: coconut cream powder, coconut cream, block of creamed coconut, and coconut milk.

Coconut cream and coconut milk are standard ingredients in much of the cookery of Southeast Asia and parts of India, and are a store cupboard essential. Coconut milk and cream are extracted from the flesh of fresh coconuts (see page 165). The cream is pressed out first and is thicker than the milk. The milk is extracted after the cream has been pressed out and is thinner. The quality and consistency of the different brands vary enormously. Although coconut cream is sold separately, all coconut milk, if left to sit long enough, will separate and the remaining cream will rise to the top. Once opened, the milk or cream does not keep longer than a day, so freeze any leftovers.

Coconut cream powder is a powdered form of coconut which, when mixed with water, makes coconut cream or milk. Creamed coconut is a solid block of coconut, which can be added straight to a dish to give a strong coconut flavour, or reconstituted with water. Coconut oil contains 90 per cent saturated fat but is good for frying as it contains natural lecithin, which makes it nonstick.

thai green curry with chicken

1 Add the chicken and stir for a few minutes.

2 Add the mixed eggplants, such as Thai and pea eggplants.

60 ml (¼ cup) coconut cream
2 tablespoons ready-made Thai green curry paste
350 g (12 oz) skinless chicken thigh fillets, sliced
440 ml (1¾ cups) coconut milk
2½ tablespoons fish sauce
1 tablespoon palm sugar
350 g (12 oz) mixed Thai eggplants (aubergines), cut into quarters, and pea eggplants (aubergines)
50 g (1¾ oz) galangal, julienned
7 makrut (kaffir) lime leaves, torn in half
a handful of Thai sweet basil leaves, for garnish
1 long red chilli, seeded and finely sliced, for garnish

put the coconut cream in a wok or saucepan and simmer over medium heat for 5 minutes, or until the cream separates and a layer of oil forms on the surface. Stir the cream if it starts to brown around the edges. Add the curry paste, stir well to combine and cook until fragrant.

add the chicken and stir for a few minutes. Add nearly all of the coconut milk, the fish sauce and palm sugar and simmer over medium heat for another 5 minutes.

add the eggplants and cook, stirring occasionally, for about 5 minutes, or until the eggplants are cooked. Add the galangal and makrut lime leaves. Taste, then adjust the seasoning if necessary. Spoon into a serving bowl and sprinkle with the last bit of coconut milk, as well as the basil leaves and chilli slices. Serves 4.

coconut vinegar

Vinegars can be made with any sugar or starch that can be fermented in a process that first produces alcohol, then a vinegar. Vinegars can be made from wine, cider, malt and rice, as well as from ethyl alcohol (synthetic white vinegar), cane sugar, molasses, millet, sorghum, dates, stone fruit and citrus. To make coconut vinegar, the coconut tree is tapped by cutting off the tip of a flower stem. The sap is released and quickly ferments. This is then allowed to turn into vinegar.

In India, the vinegars used in cooking are based on sugar cane molasses (dark) or coconut (clear). If these are unavailable, substitute balsamic (for dark) or white vinegar (for clear).

sri lankan fish fillets in tomato curry

60 ml (¼ cup) lemon juice
60 ml (¼ cup) coconut vinegar
2 teaspoons cumin seeds
1 teaspoon ground turmeric
1 teaspoon cayenne pepper
1 kg (2 lb 4 oz) firm white fish fillets, such as snapper or ling
60 ml (¼ cup) vegetable oil
1 large onion, finely chopped
3 large garlic cloves, crushed

2 tablespoons grated ginger
1 teaspoon black mustard seeds
3 x 400 g (14 oz) tins diced tomatoes
3 tablespoons finely chopped coriander (cilantro) leaves
2 small green chillies, seeded and finely chopped
2 tablespoons grated palm sugar

to make the marinade, put the lemon juice, coconut vinegar, cumin seeds, ground turmeric, cayenne pepper and 1 teaspoon salt in a shallow, non-metallic container and mix together thoroughly.

carefully remove any remaining bones from the fish with tweezers and cut the flesh into 2.5 x 10 cm (1 x 4 inch) pieces. Add the fish pieces to the marinade and gently toss until they are well coated. Cover with plastic wrap and refrigerate for 30 minutes.

heat a nonstick wok over high heat, add the oil and swirl to coat the side of the wok. Reduce the heat to low, add the onion, garlic, ginger and mustard seeds and cook, stirring frequently, for 5 minutes.

add the fish and marinade, diced tomatoes, coriander, chilli and sugar to the wok and cover with a lid. Simmer gently, stirring occasionally, for 10–15 minutes, or until the fish is cooked and just flakes when tested with the tines of a fork. Serve with basmati rice. Serves 6.

dashi granules

Made from dried fish (bonito) and dried kelp (kombu), dashi is the basic stock base used in Japanese cooking. It is available as instant granules (dashi-no-moto) or as a powder, both of which are dissolved in hot water. As brands vary in their concentration, follow the manufacturer's instructions as to the amount of water required.

miso soup

1.25 litres (5 cups) dashi
3 tablespoons shinshu-miso (see page 89)
250 g (9 oz) silken firm bean curd (tofu), diced
4 spring onions (scallions), sliced diagonally, for garnish

bring the dashi to the boil. Mix the shinshu-miso with 3 tablespoons of the hot dashi, then add to the rest of the dashi.

bring to a simmer but do not allow to boil. Add the bean curd and simmer for 2 minutes. Serve in bowls and garnish with spring onion slices. Serves 4.

dried beans, peas and lentils

There are thousands of plants whose seed pods split open down both seams when ripe, and it is these seed pods that are known as legumes. Some of the most common are beans, peas and lentils. When dried, the seeds of legumes are usually referred to as pulses.

Legumes grow worldwide and are among the earliest food crops cultivated by humans. Individual countries place differing degrees of importance on certain types of legumes. India, for example, makes much use of lentils. Here, pulses are further split into 'gram', which are whole seeds, and dal, which are split skinned seeds. Dal is used to describe not only an ingredient but a dish made from it. The dal relates to any type of dried split pea, bean or lentil. In China, Japan and Southeast Asia, it is soya beans that are widely used. This versatile bean is processed and made into a variety of products, such as soy sauce, black bean sauce and soya bean pastes.

Legumes provide a cheaper source of protein than meat, and are also a good source of fibre as well as iron, zinc, calcium, magnesium and B vitamins. With the exception of lentils and split peas, which do not need to be pre-soaked, legumes should be soaked to help soften them and reduce the cooking time. Soaking also helps reduce the levels of some carbohydrates that cause flatulence. Some legumes, such as black beans, are sold preserved in brine. When time is short, you will find some legumes are available pre-cooked in cans or vacuum-sealed packets. A selection of some of the most common legumes are featured in the following pages.

storage

Pulses keep for long periods but do not keep indefinitely. They get harder as they get older and do not cook as well. Keep them in an airtight container away from light.

Adzuki beans are small, red, slightly sweet beans, popular in Japan, Korea and China, and are an important source of protein. They are sold dried or in tins. In Japan, they are made into red bean paste, which has a characteristic grainy flavour, and are used in desserts, steamed breads or dumplings, sweet cakes, confectionery, and sometimes as a filling in rice cakes. They may also be used whole in soups. The bean paste is used in China as a filling for mooncakes and dumplings. In the Philippines, they are cooked in sugar and served with fruit and shaved ice in a refreshing dessert called *halo-halo*.

Also known as — azuki beans

adzuki beans

japanese sweet red bean soup with rice cakes

220 g (1 cup) dried adzuki beans
160 g (²/₃ cup) caster (superfine) sugar
pinch of salt
4 squares of mochi (Japanese rice cakes)

rinse the beans, put them in a large saucepan of water and bring to the boil. Drain, then return the beans to the pan with 1 litre (4 cups) fresh water. Bring to the boil, cover, reduce the heat to low and cook for 2 hours, or until the beans are tender and almost all the water has been absorbed. Check the beans occasionally as you may need to add a little water.

add the sugar and 1.5 litres (6 cups) water and stir to combine. Increase the heat to high and cook for about 40 minutes, or until the beans are soft but not mushy. You should have a thin but chunky soup. If you prefer a thicker soup, mash some of the beans, or if you prefer it thinner, add water. Remove from the heat, cover and set aside.

preheat the grill (broiler) to high. Line a baking tray with foil, put the rice cakes on it and grill (broil), turning frequently, until mottled golden and puffed up and doubled in size. This should take about 10 minutes.

put the mochi rice cakes in the bases of four small, deep serving bowls and ladle the soup into the bowls. Traditionally the chewy mochi are eaten with chopsticks, then the soup is drunk directly from the bowl. Serves 4.

In India, black-eyed beans are called lobhia. Here they are combined with mushrooms and tomatoes to make an excellent vegetarian main course, or serve it on the side with meat and vegetables.

black-eyed beans

These are actually dried cow peas, and have been grown and eaten in parts of Asia for many centuries, even though they are commonly associated with the food of the deep south in America. They are small and cream coloured with a distinctive black spot. In India, they are also known as *chowli dal* when split. Black-eyed beans need to be soaked before they are cooked.

Also known as — black-eyed peas

black-eyed beans with mushrooms

put the black-eyed beans in a large saucepan with 1 litre (4 cups) water and bring to the boil. Cover and simmer for 2 minutes. Remove from the heat and leave to stand for 1 hour. Alternatively, soak the black-eyed beans overnight in cold water.

bring the beans back to the boil, then simmer for 20–30 minutes until tender. Drain well.

meanwhile, heat the oil in a deep, heavy-based frying pan or saucepan. Add the cumin seeds and cinnamon stick, let them sizzle for 10 seconds, then add the onion and garlic. Stir over medium heat until soft and starting to brown. Add the mushrooms and fry for 2–3 minutes. Add the tomato, ground coriander, cumin, turmeric and cayenne pepper. Cover and cook over low heat for 10 minutes. Add the black-eyed beans and season with salt, to taste. Stir in the coriander leaves and simmer, uncovered, for 30 minutes. Serves 6.

200 g (1 cup) black-eyed beans
125 ml (1/2 cup) oil
1 teaspoon cumin seeds
3 cm (1 1/4 inch) piece of
   cinnamon stick
150 g (5 1/2 oz) onion, chopped
4 garlic cloves, finely chopped
250 g (9 oz) mushrooms, sliced
400 g (14 oz) tin chopped
   tomatoes
2 teaspoons ground coriander
1 teaspoon ground cumin
1/2 teaspoon ground turmeric
1/4 teaspoon cayenne pepper
2 tablespoons chopped
   coriander (cilantro) leaves

black gram

Black gram (called sabat urad) are a pulse, similar to mung beans, and are black or green when whole. When split and skinned they are creamy white (see entry under 'black lentil', page 29). Whole black gram need to soaked or precooked before use. Black lentils may be cooked to make dal, and feature in celebratory dishes of the Punjab.

Also known as — urad, urd

kali dal

250 g (1 cup) whole black gram (sabat urad)
1 onion, roughly chopped
2 garlic cloves, chopped
5 cm (2 inch) piece of ginger, roughly chopped
1 green chilli, roughly chopped

125 ml (½ cup) oil
2 tablespoons ground cumin
1 tablespoon ground coriander
2 teaspoons salt
¼ teaspoon chilli powder
3 tablespoons garam masala
125 ml (½ cup) cream

put the black gram in a large, heavy-based saucepan, add 2 litres (8 cups) water and bring to the boil. Reduce the heat and simmer for 1 hour, or until the dal feels soft when pressed between the thumb and index finger. Most of the dal will split to reveal the creamy insides. Drain, reserving the cooking liquid.

blend the onion, garlic, ginger and chilli together in a food processor to form a paste, or finely chop them together with a knife. Heat the oil in a frying pan and fry the onion mixture over high heat, stirring constantly, until golden brown. Add the cumin and coriander and fry for 2 minutes. Add the dal and stir in the salt, chilli powder and garam masala. Pour 300 ml (10½ fl oz) of the reserved dal liquid into the pan, bring to the boil, then reduce the heat and simmer for 10 minutes. Just before serving, stir in the cream and simmer for another 2 minutes to heat through. Serves 6.

This Indian dish, kali dal, is named for the colour of the gram—'kali' means black. The gram for this dish do not need to be soaked before use.

chickpeas

Chickpeas are a very important food across a large part of the world, including India, Europe and the Middle East. Chickpeas are called 'channa' in India where they form the basis of many vegetarian dishes. In India, white or pale yellow chickpeas are called kabuli channa, and black chickpeas (which are actually dark brown in colour) are called kala channa. Chickpeas are usually sold whole, but may also be sold split. Soak dried chickpeas in cold water for 8 hours before use (they will double in size after soaking). Tinned chickpeas can be used in recipes but add them at the end of cooking as they are already very soft.

Also known as — channa, garbanzo

sweet and sour chickpeas

500 g (1 lb 2 oz) chickpeas
2 tablespoons oil or ghee
2 large red onions, thinly sliced
2 cm (3/4 inch) piece of ginger, finely chopped
2 teaspoons sugar
2 teaspoons ground coriander
2 teaspoons ground cumin
pinch of chilli powder (optional)
1 teaspoon garam masala
3 tablespoons tamarind purée
4 ripe tomatoes, chopped
4 tablespoons coriander (cilantro) or mint leaves,
**   finely chopped**

soak the chickpeas overnight in 2 litres (8 cups) water. Drain, then put the chickpeas in a large saucepan with 2 litres (8 cups) water. Bring to the boil, spooning off any scum from the surface. Cover and simmer over low heat for 1–1 1/2 hours until soft. It is important they are soft at this stage as they won't soften any more once the sauce has been added. Drain.

heat the oil in a heavy-based frying pan. Fry the onion until soft and brown, then stir in the ginger. Add the chickpeas, sugar, coriander, cumin, chilli powder, garam masala and a pinch of salt. Stir, then add the tamarind and tomato and simmer for 2–3 minutes.

add 500 ml (2 cups) water, bring to the boil and cook until the sauce has thickened. Stir in the coriander leaves. Serve with Indian bread such as rotis. Serves 6.

lentils

Lentils are tiny, flat and lens-shaped. They grow in pods and vary in size and colour, the most common colours being yellow, red, green and brown. Lentils have a high food value—they are high in protein, fibre and B vitamins. Lentils are one of the most important foods in the Indian diet. Lentils are referred to as dal in India and dal is also used to describe a dish made from lentils, which accompanies almost every meal. A dal dish can be a thin soup or more like a stew. Some of the common lentils used in Indian cooking are listed on the following page.

preparation

Contrary to popular belief, not all lentils need to be soaked before they are cooked and, in fact, soaking may cause some varieties to break up. Follow the instructions in your recipe. Pick through lentils to remove any discoloured ones or pieces of grit, then rinse well. Discard any lentils that float, as these may have been partially eaten by bugs. The cooking times vary as do the texture and flavour.

types of lentils

black lentils (urad dal)   Whole black lentils (sabat urad), also known as black gram, are used whole in the north of India, and split in the south. The split variety (chilke urad) is cream in colour with black skin. The skinned variety (urad dal) is cream coloured, and is sometimes referred to as white gram. Urad dal does not usually need to be soaked although some recipes do suggest it. The dal is used when making dosa (rice and lentil pancakes) and idli (steamed rice cakes) and it becomes glutinous and creamy when cooked.

gram lentils (channa dal)   These are husked, split, polished, yellow Bengal gram, the most common type of gram lentil in India. They are often cooked with asafoetida to make them easier to digest.

red lentils (masoor dal)   When whole, these are dark brown or green. When split, they are orange in colour. The split ones are the most common as they cook more easily and do not usually need soaking as the whole ones do.

yellow lentils (toor dal)   These come oiled and plain. Oiled ones look slightly greasy and need to be soaked in hot water to remove the oil. Soak for a few hours before cooking.

mung lentils (moong dal)   Whole mung beans, also called green gram, must be soaked before use. Split and skinned mung beans, which are pale yellow, are quick to cook and do not always need to be soaked before use.

split peas (matar dal)   These are split dried peas, which need to be soaked before they are cooked and have a slightly chewy texture. Green and yellow ones are available.

Test to see if the lentils are cooked by gently squeezing them between your thumb and index finger. They should be soft.

From left: yellow lentils (toor dal); split, unskinned black lentils (chilke urad); split peas (matar dal).

soya beans

Cultivated in their native China for thousands of years, soya beans are the most nutritious and versatile of all beans. Soya beans contain a higher proportion of protein than any other legume, even higher than that of red meat, making them an important part of vegetarian diets and in Japanese, Chinese and Southeast Asian cooking where little meat is used. Soya beans can be red, green, yellow, black (see opposite page) or brown.

Soya beans are an extremely versatile and essential ingredient in Chinese cooking. Although rarely eaten whole, the beans are used for sprouting, to make soy sauce, bean curd (tofu), soy milk, and vegetable oil, as well as fermented beans and bean pastes. The fresh beans are eaten as a vegetable, cooked in their fuzzy pods and served as a snack. In Japan, soya beans are used in miso and are fermented to make the dish called natto, which is usually served with rice. In Indonesia, they are made into a 'cake' called tempeh.

preparation

Dried soya beans contain a trypsin inhibitor that is destroyed by soaking and cooking the beans for a long time. If the beans are not soaked for long enough, they are indigestible and most of the valuable protein in the beans passes straight through the digestive system. Soak dried beans for at least 6 hours before use. Yellow soya beans need longer soaking than black. Discard the soaking water before cooking.

cooking

Soya beans have little flavour and a slightly oily texture and benefit from being cooked with strong flavours such as chilli, garlic and soy sauce.

soya beans, black

Black soya beans are small, dark and shiny. They may be mashed and used as a filling for sweet Chinese pastries and sometimes are used in salads, but their most common association is with black bean sauce, made from puréed fermented black soya beans, and used in Chinese stir-fries with vegetables, beef or seafood. Soak dried black soya beans for 6 hours before cooking. The fermented beans are usually sold tinned in brine and need to be drained and rinsed thoroughly before use. Mash whole beans a little before use.

scallops with black bean sauce

1 kg (2 lb 4 oz) large scallops
2 tablespoons salted, fermented black beans, rinsed and mashed
2 garlic cloves, crushed
3 teaspoons finely chopped ginger

2 teaspoons sugar
2 teaspoons light soy sauce
2 tablespoons oyster sauce
2 tablespoons oil
2 spring onions (scallions), cut into 2 cm (¾ inch) lengths

slice the small, hard white muscle off the side of each scallop and pull off any membrane. Rinse the scallops and drain them. Pull off the roes if you prefer.

put the black beans, garlic, ginger, sugar, and soy and oyster sauces in a bowl and mix together.

heat a wok over high heat, add the oil and heat until very hot. Stir-fry the scallops and roes for 2 minutes, or until the scallops are cooked through and opaque. Just before the scallops are cooked, add the spring onion. Transfer the mixture to a sieve to drain.

reheat the wok over medium heat. Stir-fry the black bean mixture for 1–2 minutes, or until aromatic. Return the scallops and spring onion to the wok and toss together to combine. Serves 6.

Black beans are sold in tins or in packets. The tinned version (above, left) is saltier, so drain and rinse before use. Vacuum-packed black beans need to be rehydrated in a little hot water and rinsed before use.

flours

Flours made from wheat, as well as various seeds, legumes, vegetables and grains are used throughout Asia. They are used not only as a base for noodles, as well as in cakes, bread, pastries and batters, but also as thickeners and flavourings. Originally the flours were made manually by grinding the wheat, or other ingredients, in large wooden mortars using wooden pestles. There is a wide range of flours available in supermarkets and specialist stores. Some of them are described on the following pages.

Clockwise from top: rice flour, besan flour, tempura flour, atta flour, maida flour.

atta flour

Atta is made from finely ground whole durum wheat. Sometimes, a proportion of white flour is added, and the flour is labelled as 80/20 or 60/40. Atta is much finer and softer than wholemeal flour so, if you can't find it, use half wholemeal and half maida or plain (all-purpose) flour instead. Atta flour is used to make Indian flat breads, such as spinach (saag) roti.

saag roti

cook the spinach briefly in a little simmering water until it is just wilted, then refresh in cold water. Drain thoroughly, then finely chop. Squeeze out any extra water by putting the spinach between two plates and pushing them together.

sift the atta and salt into a bowl and make a well in the centre. Add the spinach, ghee and about 250 ml (1 cup) tepid water and mix to form a soft, pliable dough. Turn out the dough onto a floured work surface and knead for 5 minutes. Put in an oiled bowl, cover and allow to rest for 30 minutes.

divide the dough into 20 balls. Working with one portion at a time and keeping the rest covered, on a lightly floured surface evenly roll out each portion to a 12 cm (5 inch) circle about 1 mm (1/16 inch) thick.

heat a tava (a specially shaped hotplate used to cook Indian flat breads) or heavy-based frying pan until hot, oil it lightly with ghee or oil and cook one roti at a time. Cook each on one side, covered with a saucepan lid (this will help keep them soft), for about 1 minute. Turn it over, cover again and cook the other side for 2 minutes. Check the roti a few times to make sure it doesn't overcook. The roti will blister a little and brown in some places. Remove the roti and keep it warm under a tea towel. Cook the remaining roti. Makes 20.

200 g (7 oz) baby English spinach leaves, stalks removed
500 g (1 lb 2 oz) atta flour
1 teaspoon salt
1 teaspoon ghee or oil
ghee or oil, for cooking

Also known as — chapati flour

1 Add the spinach, ghee and about 250 ml (1 cup) water.

2 Ensure the spinach is evenly distributed throughout the dough.

3 The roti will begin to brown in places when cooked.

besan flour

This pale yellow flour is made by finely milling hulled and split chickpeas. The flour has a nutty flavour, is high in protein, and is used in Indian cooking as a thickener in curries, as well as in batters, dumplings, sweets and breads.

Also known as — chickpea flour, gram flour

spinach koftas in yoghurt sauce

yoghurt sauce
375 g (1½ cups) thick natural yoghurt
4 tablespoons besan flour
1 tablespoon oil
2 teaspoons black mustard seeds
1 teaspoon fenugreek seeds
6 curry leaves
1 large onion, finely chopped
3 garlic cloves, crushed
1 teaspoon ground turmeric
½ teaspoon chilli powder

spinach koftas
500 g (1 lb 2 oz) frozen English spinach, thawed and drained
170 g (6 oz) besan flour
1 red onion, finely chopped
1 ripe tomato, finely diced
2 garlic cloves, crushed
1 teaspoon ground cumin
2 tablespoons coriander (cilantro) leaves
oil, for deep-frying

to make the yoghurt sauce, in a large bowl whisk the yoghurt, besan flour and 750 ml (3 cups) water to a smooth paste. Heat the oil in a heavy-based saucepan or deep frying pan over low heat. Add the mustard and fenugreek seeds and the curry leaves, cover and allow the seeds to pop for 1 minute. Add the onion and cook for 5 minutes, or until soft and starting to brown. Add the garlic and stir for 1 minute, or until soft. Add the turmeric and chilli powder and stir for 30 seconds. Add the yoghurt mixture, bring to the boil and simmer over low heat for 10 minutes. Season with salt, to taste.

to make the spinach koftas, combine the spinach with the remaining kofta ingredients and up to 60 ml (¼ cup) water, a little at a time, adding enough to make the mixture soft but not sloppy. If it becomes too sloppy, add more besan flour. Season with salt, to taste. (To test the seasoning, fry a small amount of the mixture and taste it.) Shape the mixture into balls by rolling it in dampened hands, using 1 tablespoon of mixture for each.

fill a heavy-based saucepan one-third full with oil and heat to 180°C (350°F), or until a cube of bread browns in 15 seconds. Lower the koftas into the oil in batches and fry until golden and crisp. Don't overcrowd the pan. Remove the koftas as they cook, shake off any excess oil and add them to the yoghurt sauce.

gently reheat the yoghurt sauce. Serves 6.

maida flour

This is a plain white flour used for making naan bread and in other Indian dishes. Plain (all-purpose) flour is a suitable substitute.

naan

500 g (4 cups) maida or plain (all-purpose) flour
300 ml (1 ¼ cups) milk
2 teaspoons easy-blend dried yeast or 15 g (½ oz) fresh yeast
2 teaspoons nigella seeds (optional)
½ teaspoon baking powder
½ teaspoon salt
1 egg, beaten
2 tablespoons oil or ghee
185 ml (¾ cup) thick natural yoghurt

sift the maida into a large bowl and make a well in the centre. Warm the milk over low heat in a saucepan until it is hand hot (the milk will feel the same temperature as your finger when you dip your finger into it). If you are using fresh yeast, mix it with a little milk and a pinch of maida and set it aside to activate and go frothy.

add the yeast, nigella seeds, baking powder and salt to the maida. In another bowl, mix the egg, oil and yoghurt. Pour into the maida with 250 ml (1 cup) of the milk and mix to form a soft dough. If the dough seems dry, add the remaining milk. Turn out onto a floured work surface and knead for 5 minutes, or until smooth and elastic. Put in an oiled bowl, cover and leave in a warm place to double in size. This will take several hours.

preheat the oven to 200°C (400°F/Gas 6). Place a roasting tin half-filled with water at the bottom of the oven. This provides moisture in the oven, which prevents the naan from drying out too quickly.

punch down the dough, knead it briefly and divide it into 10 portions. Using the tips of your fingers, spread out one portion of dough to the shape of a naan bread. They are traditionally tear-drop in shape, so pull the dough on one end. Put the naan on a greased baking tray. Bake on the top shelf for 7 minutes, then turn the naan over and cook for another 5 minutes. While the first naan is cooking, shape the next one. If your tray is big enough, you may be able to fit two naan at a time. Remove the cooked naan from the oven and cover with a cloth to keep it warm and soft.

repeat the cooking process until all the dough is used. You can only use the top shelf of the oven because the naan won't cook properly on the middle shelf. Refill the baking tray with boiling water when necessary. Makes 10.

1 Knead the dough for 5 minutes, or until smooth and elastic.

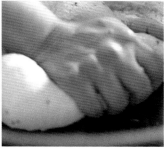

2 Punch down the dough and then knead it briefly.

3 Shape the dough into its traditional tear-drop shape.

1 Pour a ladleful of batter into the centre of the pan.

2 Quickly spread it out with the back of the ladle.

3 Cook the dosa until small holes appear on the surface.

rice flour

Rice flours are ground from long-grain rice and are used to make noodles, rice cakes and various food 'wrappers'. Some rice flours are more finely ground than others and specific rices are chosen according to what they are to be used for. In India, finely ground rice is used for making dosas—large spongy pancakes with a crisp surface. Buy rice flours at specialist food shops.

dosas

110 g (4 oz) skinned, split black lentils (urad dal)
1 teaspoon salt
300 g (1²/₃ cups) rice flour
oil, for cooking

put the lentils in a bowl and cover with water. Soak for 4 hours, or overnight. Drain, then grind the lentils with the salt and a little water in a food processor, blender or mortar and pestle to form a fine paste. Mix the paste with the rice flour, add 1 litre (4 cups) water and mix well. Cover with a cloth and leave in a warm place for 8 hours, or until the batter ferments and bubbles. The batter will double in volume.

heat a nonstick frying pan over medium heat. Don't overheat it—the heat should always be medium. Lightly brush the surface of the pan with oil. Stir the batter and pour a ladleful into the middle of the pan and quickly spread it out with the back of the ladle to form a thin pancake. Don't worry if the dosa is not perfect, they are hard to get exactly right. Drizzle a little oil around the edge to help it crisp up. Cook until small holes appear on the surface and the edges start to curl. Turn over with a spatula and cook the other side. (The first dosa is often a disaster but it will season the pan for the following ones.)

repeat with the remaining mixture, oiling the pan between each dosa. Roll the dosas into big tubes and keep warm. Dosas are often filled with cooked vegetables and served with chutneys, or served with curries. Makes 20.

cooking

Tempura batter is made with ice-cold water and only lightly mixed to combine the ingredients. The lumps are not beaten out.

The secret of crisp tempura is to have the food and batter as cold as possible prior to cooking. Maintain the oil at a temperature of 180°C (350°F)—if the temperature drops, the tempura may lose its featherlight crispness.

tempura flour

Tempura flour is a very fine flour used to make tempura batter. Tempura is not, as is commonly believed, a Japanese dish, but was actually introduced by Portuguese missionaries in Japan in the sixteenth century. The Japanese adopted their techniques, and today, tempura restaurants flourish throughout Japan. The dish consists of bite-sized pieces of vegetable or seafood, such as prawns (shrimp) or white fish, coated in a light batter and deep-fried until crisp. The batter is a paste made from tempura flour, water and sometimes egg. Tempura flour is sold in Japanese food stores and large supermarkets.

prawn tempura

combine the tempura flour with the ice-cold water. Heat the oil in a large deep-fryer to 180°C (350°F), or until a piece of bread fries golden brown in 15 seconds. Dip 3–4 prawns in the batter and cook in batches until crisp and golden. Drain on paper towels.

to make a dipping sauce, put the mirin, soy sauce, 250 ml (1 cup) water and bonito flakes in a saucepan. Bring to the boil, then strain and cool.

squeeze the grated daikon to remove any liquid. Serve the prawns with the dipping sauce and a small pile of grated daikon and pickled ginger. Serves 4.

90 g (3/4 cup) tempura flour
170 ml (2/3 cup) ice-cold water
oil, for deep-frying
12 large raw prawns (shrimp), peeled and deveined, tails intact
60 ml (1/4 cup) mirin
60 ml (1/4 cup) soy sauce
10 g (1/4 oz) bonito flakes
grated daikon, to serve
pickled ginger, to serve

fungi/ mushrooms

The term 'fungus' refers to any of a large group of simple plants that also includes mushrooms, toadstools, yeast and moulds. All mushrooms are fungi, but only some mushrooms are actually called fungi, such as black fungus. Fungi are more likely to be found dried but can be bought fresh when in season. Most dried fungi need to be soaked in cold water for about 20 minutes, or until they swell up and soften. Some, such as shiitake, are soaked in hot water. Dried fungi can reconstitute up to six or eight times their original weight. Store all dried fungi in a sealed container in the pantry. Tinned fungi and mushrooms should be drained and rinsed before use. See also fresh mushrooms and fungi, page 185.

types of fungi

chinese mushrooms These are usually sold dried, as drying intensifies their flavour and aroma. They need to be soaked to reconstitute them before use. Soak in boiling water for 20–30 minutes, or simmer with a little sugar for 15 minutes. Cut off the stalk and chop the caps. The soaking water will be flavourful, so strain it and add to stock or a sauce.

shiitake mushrooms Closely related to Chinese mushrooms, this is the most commonly used mushroom in Japanese cooking. Soak in boiling water for 20–30 minutes before use. Also available fresh.

bamboo fungus Also known as staghorn fungus. A lacy fungus that grows on bamboo. It has a musty, earthy taste and is used in Asian soups and stir-fries. Usually bought dried and reconstituted. Soak in salted water until tender, blanch to tenderize further, then rinse.

black fungus Known by many other names, such as wood ear, wood fungus, cloud ear fungus, rat's ear fungus (translated from its name in Thai) and tree ears. This small, black crinkly fungus is tiny when dried but puffs up after being soaked. Soak in water until soft and jelly-like, then remove any hard woody bits of stem. Used in stir-fries for a smoky flavour, as well as texture and contrasting colour. Available dried and fresh.

white fungus A crinkly white fungus used in Chinese cooking, related to the black, or cloud ear, fungus. It is used mainly for its texture as it doesn't have much flavour. Soak the dried fungus in warm water, draining a couple of times and re-soaking before use. White fungus is also available fresh.

Pictured above, this page: black fungus. Pictured above, opposite page: shiitake mushrooms (left), bamboo fungus (right, top) and white fungus (right, bottom).

hot and sour soup

4 dried Chinese mushrooms
2 tablespoons dried black
  fungus
100 g (3½ oz) lean pork,
  thinly shredded
1 tablespoon cornflour
  (cornstarch)
120 g (4 oz) firm bean curd
  (tofu), drained
55 g (2 oz) fresh or tinned
  bamboo shoots, rinsed and
  drained
1 litre (4 cups) chicken stock

1 teaspoon salt
1 tablespoon Shaoxing rice
  wine
2 tablespoons light soy
  sauce
1–2 tablespoons Chinese black
  rice vinegar
2 eggs, beaten
1–2 teaspoons freshly ground
  white pepper
chopped spring onion
  (scallion), for garnish

This Chinese soup should not contain chillies. The hotness comes from ground white pepper, which, for the best flavour, should be freshly ground.

soak the dried Chinese mushrooms in boiled water for 30 minutes, then drain and squeeze out any excess water. Remove and discard the stems and shred the caps. Soak the black fungus in cold water for 20 minutes, drain and squeeze out any excess water, then shred it.

combine the shredded pork, a pinch of salt and 1 teaspoon of the cornflour. Thinly shred the bean curd and bamboo shoots to the same size as the pork.

bring the stock to the boil in a large clay pot or saucepan. Add the pork and stir to separate the meat, then add the mushrooms, fungus, bean curd and bamboo. Return to the boil and add the salt, rice wine, soy sauce and vinegar. Slowly pour in the egg, whisking to form thin threads, and cook for 1 minute.

combine the remaining cornflour with enough water to make a paste, add to the soup and simmer until thickened. Put the pepper in a bowl, pour in the soup and stir. Garnish with spring onion. Serves 4.

ghee

A highly clarified butter (or pure butter fat) made from cow or water buffalo milk, ghee can be heated to a high temperature without burning and has an aromatic flavour. It is often used in Indian meat dishes. Vegetable ghees are also available but don't have the same aromatic qualities. Ghee is sold in tins or tubs from large supermarkets and from Indian speciality shops, or you can make your own, as explained below.

making ghee

To make your own ghee, melt unsalted butter in a saucepan, bring it to a simmer and cook for about 30 minutes to evaporate out any water. Skim any scum off the surface, then drain the clarified butter off, leaving the white sediment behind. Leave to cool.

ginkgo nuts

eight-treasure rice

12 whole blanched
   lotus seeds
12 jujubes
20 fresh or tinned ginkgo
   nuts, shelled
225 g (8 oz) glutinous (sticky)
   white rice

2 tablespoons sugar
2 teaspoons oil
30 g (1 oz) slab sugar
8 glacé cherries
6 dried longans, pitted
4 almonds or walnuts
225 g (8 oz) red bean paste

These are the nuts of the maidenhair tree. The hard shells are cracked open and the inner cream-coloured nuts are soaked to loosen their skins. Ginkgo nuts are known for their medicinal properties and are one of the eight 'treasures' in Chinese dishes such as eight-treasure rice. The Japanese and Koreans like to roast the nuts on skewers made from pine needles, or they are used as an ingredient in savoury custards. Shelled nuts can be bought in tins in Asian speciality shops and are easier to use.

soak the lotus seeds and jujubes in bowls of cold water for 30 minutes, then drain. Remove the seeds from the jujubes. If using fresh ginkgo nuts, blanch in a pan of boiling water for 5 minutes, then refresh in cold water and dry thoroughly.

put the glutinous rice and 310 ml (1 ¼ cups) water in a heavy-based saucepan and bring to the boil. Reduce the heat to low and simmer for 10–15 minutes. Stir in the sugar and oil. Dissolve the slab sugar in 185 ml (¾ cup) water and bring to the boil. Add the lotus seeds, jujubes and ginkgo nuts and simmer for 1 hour, or until the lotus seeds are soft. Drain, reserving the liquid.

grease a 1 litre (4 cup) heatproof bowl and decorate the base with the lotus seeds, jujubes, ginkgo nuts, cherries, longans and almonds. Smooth two-thirds of the rice over this to form a shell on the surface of the bowl. Fill with the bean paste, cover with the remaining rice and smooth the surface. Cover the rice with a piece of greased foil and then put the bowl in a steamer. Cover and steam over simmering water in a wok for 1–1 ½ hours, replenishing with boiling water during cooking.

turn the pudding out onto a plate and pour the reserved sugar liquid over the top. Serve hot. Serves 8.

jaggery

Jaggery is an Indian unrefined sugar obtained from sugar cane or various date palms. It has a caramel flavour and alcoholic aroma. Jaggery is sold in lumps, is slightly sticky and varies in colour depending on the quality of the sugar cane. A full-flavoured soft brown sugar or molasses can be used as a substitute. Store in a cool, dry place.

Also known as — gur

The kokum gives this Indian dish a sour, fruity flavour, which is balanced by the sweetness of the jaggery.

toor dal

500 g (1 lb 2 oz) yellow lentils (toor dal)
5 x 5 cm (2 inch) pieces of kokum
2 teaspoons coriander seeds
2 teaspoons cumin seeds
2 tablespoons oil
2 teaspoons black mustard seeds
10 curry leaves
7 cloves
10 cm (4 inch) piece of cinnamon stick
5 green chillies, finely chopped
1/2 teaspoon ground turmeric
400 g (14 oz) tin chopped tomatoes
20 g (3/4 oz) jaggery or 10 g (1/4 oz) molasses
coriander (cilantro) leaves, for garnish

soak the lentils in cold water for 2 hours. Rinse the kokum, remove any stones and put the kokum in a bowl of cold water for a few minutes to soften. Drain the lentils and put them in a heavy-based saucepan with 1 litre (4 cups) water and the pieces of kokum. Bring slowly to the boil, then simmer for about 40 minutes, or until the lentils feel soft when pressed between the thumb and index finger.

place a small frying pan over low heat and dry-roast the coriander seeds. Remove and dry-roast the cumin seeds. Grind the roasted seeds to a fine powder using a spice grinder or mortar and pestle.

heat the oil in a small pan over low heat. Add the mustard seeds and allow to pop. Add the curry leaves, cloves, cinnamon, chilli, turmeric and the roasted spice mix and cook for 1 minute. Add the tomato and cook for 2–3 minutes, or until the tomato is soft and can be broken up easily and incorporated into the sauce. Add the jaggery, then pour the spicy mixture into the simmering lentils and cook for 10 minutes. Season with salt, to taste. Garnish with coriander leaves. Serves 8.

jellyfish

The edible parts of some varieties of jellyfish are highly prized in Asian cuisines, particularly in China where it is prepared for banquets or served as an appetizer. Jellyfish is sold either dried (when it needs to be soaked, blanched and shredded before use), or ready to use in a vacuum pack. Semi-translucent in colour with a delicate flavour, jellyfish is appreciated mostly for its crunchy, chewy texture.

jellyfish salad

150 g (5 1/2 oz) packet of shredded jellyfish
1/4 iceberg lettuce, shredded
1/2 cucumber, peeled and julienned
2 teaspoons toasted sesame seeds
1 tablespoon light soy sauce
2 tablespoons Chinese rice vinegar
1 teaspoon sesame oil
1 tablespoon sugar

put the shredded jellyfish in a colander and allow to drain. Transfer to a large bowl and add the lettuce, cucumber and sesame seeds. Mix the light soy sauce, rice vinegar, sesame oil and sugar in a bowl, pour over the salad and toss well. Serves 4.

If you buy jellyfish that isn't cut up, it is easiest to use a pair of scissors to cut it into strands. Make them roughly the same width.

jujubes

Jujubes are an olive-sized dried fruit with red, wrinkled skin. In China, where they are mainly used, they are thought to build strength. They need to be soaked before use in eight-treasure dishes, soups or desserts. They are thought to be lucky because of their red colour.

Also known as — Chinese red dates

steamed pears in honey

100 g (3½ oz) jujubes
6 nearly ripe pears
6 tablespoons honey

soak the jujubes in hot water for 1 hour, changing the water twice. Drain, remove the stones and cut crosswise into strips.

cut a slice off the bottom of each pear so that it will sit flat. Cut a 2.5 cm (1 inch) piece off the top and set it aside. Using a fruit corer or knife, remove the cores without cutting right through to the bottom.

arrange the pears upright on a heatproof plate. Put 1 tablespoon of the honey and some jujubes into the cavity of each pear. Replace the tops and, if necessary, fasten with toothpicks.

put the plate in a steamer. Cover and steam over simmering water in a wok for 30 minutes, or until tender when pierced with a knife. Serve hot or cold. Serves 6.

Krupuk are commonly served as an accompaniment to Southeast Asian meals, such as the Indonesian vegetable salad gado gado, and with drinks. They are deep-fried crisps made from a batter of dried prawn (shrimp) and flavoured rice flour or tapioca flour, which puff up into light and crunchy foam-like crackers. In Indonesia and Malaysia they are called *krupuk udang*, and in Vietnam they are called *bahn phong*. Chinese prawn crackers come in an assortment of vivid colours but do not have the intense flavour of the Indonesian version.

Also known as — prawn crackers

krupuk

gado gado

100 g (3¹/₂ oz) shredded cabbage
200 g (7 oz) green beans
250 g (9 oz) carrots, cut into batons
110 g (4 oz) cauliflower florets
1 potato, sliced
100 g (3¹/₂ oz) fried bean curd (tofu), cut into cubes
2 hard-boiled eggs, quartered
1 cucumber, sliced
100 g (3¹/₂ oz) soya bean sprouts
ready-made satay sauce, to serve
crispy fried onions, to serve
krupuk, to serve

steam the cabbage, beans, carrots, cauliflower and potato until they are tender.

arrange them on a plate with the bean curd. Top with the quartered eggs, cucumber and bean sprouts. Dress with satay sauce and crispy fried onions. Serve with krupuk. Serves 4.

Mirin (left) and cooking sake (right).

mirin/sake

Mirin is a sweet spirit-based rice liquid used predominantly in Japanese cooking in basting sauces and marinades, in salad dressings and stir-fries. Its high sugar content adds a sheen to the food. Mirin, when mixed with soy sauce, sake and sugar forms the basis of yakitori and teriyaki marinades. The real thing, hon mirin (pictured), contains 14 per cent alcohol and is far superior to the low-alcohol imitation mirin. It is used exclusively in cooking and not as a beverage.

Some recipes suggest that if mirin is not available it can be replaced with either sweet sherry or dry sherry (add a little extra sugar if using dry sherry), but this will alter the flavour considerably.

Sake is an alcoholic (15–17 per cent) liquid made by fermenting cooked, ground rice. It has a dry, sherry-like taste and is used in cooking, particularly in sauces and marinades. In its more refined form, sake is drunk as a drink, either hot or cold. Sake does not last for long once the bottle has been opened.

msg

MSG is the abbreviated term for monosodium glutamate. This flavour enhancer was discovered in the 1900s, extracted from plants such as seaweed and sugar beet. Although MSG is a flavour-enhancing compound, it has little flavour of its own but helps to bring out the flavour of soups, as well as meat, vegetable and fish dishes.

As an additive, MSG has the number 621. However, ingredients that naturally contain MSG, which is present in very small amounts in foods such as tomatoes and eggplants (aubergine), do not have to be labelled. The addition of MSG in food is thought to cause allergic reactions or discomfort such as headaches or chest pains in some people.

Also known as — accent, aji no moto, ve-tsin

mustard oil/powder

Mustard is a condiment made from the ground seeds of the mustard plant. There are many species, but it is usually the black (the hottest and most pungent), brown and white seeds (sometimes called yellow) that are commonly used. Mustard paste is made by macerating the seeds in liquid, such as water, vinegar or wine, then grinding them to a fine paste. The pungency, colour, flavour and texture of the mustard will depend on the type of seeds used and the style of mustard. Commercially prepared mustards common in the West are not widely used in the Asian kitchen.

Mustard oil, made by pressing brown mustard seeds, is a strongly flavoured oil used in Indian cooking, usually in curries. As it is an excellent preservative, it is also used in pickles. Mustard powder is simply ground mustard seeds and may be mixed with water and used as prepared mustard. See also mustard seeds, page 134.

bengali fried fish

600 g (1 lb 5 oz) rainbow trout or salmon cutlets
1½ tablespoons lemon juice
½ teaspoon ground turmeric
½ teaspoon salt
3 green chillies, chopped
3 ripe tomatoes, chopped
5 cm (2 inch) piece of ginger, chopped
4 tablespoons mustard oil or vegetable oil
2 teaspoons panch phoron
½ teaspoon garam masala

sprinkle the fish with the lemon juice and leave for 10 minutes, then wash under cold water and pat dry. Rub the fish with the combined turmeric and salt.

put the chilli, tomato and ginger in a food processor and chop until smooth, or finely chop together with a knife.

heat the oil in a heavy-based frying pan over low heat and fry the fish a few pieces at a time until brown on both sides. Drain on paper towels. Add more oil if necessary, add the panch phoron and fry for 1 minute until aromatic. Add the tomato mixture and fry for another 2 minutes. Add 185 ml water (¾ cup) and bring slowly to the boil. Simmer for 3 minutes, add the fish, slowly return to the boil, then simmer for another 3 minutes. Sprinkle with the garam masala and season with salt, to taste. Serves 4.

noodles

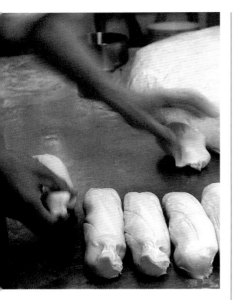

Noodles have been part of Asian cuisine for over 2000 years, and they play a vital role in the cuisines of many countries, from China, Japan and Vietnam, to Indonesia, Myanmar and Cambodia. The types of noodles available, their flavour and texture, shape and thickness vary enormously, but noodles can be generally classified by their main ingredient—rice flour, wheat flour, mung bean starch or potato starch—although some are named for their appearance, such as the Japanese transparent noodles, shirataki, meaning 'white waterfall'. Noodles are nutritious and easy to prepare, and they can be used in soups, salads, stir-fries and hotpots, so keep a good stock of dried noodles in your store cupboard, or fresh noodles in the refrigerator. On the following pages, some of the main varieties are described.

In China, wheat noodles are still made by hand.

bean thread noodles

These are translucent noodles that vary in thickness and are popular in China and Vietnam. They are usually made from mung bean starch and become transparent when cooked. Before using bean thread noodles, soak in boiling water for a few minutes until soft. Don't leave them too long as they will start to break up. When soft, rinse in cold water, then drain. If you want to use them as a garnish, deep-fry them straight from the packet until they puff up, then remove and drain on paper towels.

Harusame, a Japanese word meaning 'spring rain', are noodles made from mung bean, soya bean, potato or corn starches. Sold dried in small packets, these may be used as for bean thread noodles.

Bean thread noodles are made of mung bean starch and used as an ingredient in soups or braises. They need to be soaked before use.

***Also known as —
cellophane noodles,
glass or jelly noodles,
mung bean vermicelli***

Buckwheat noodles are usually sold dried, and known either as Japanese soba noodles or the slightly more chewy Korean buckwheat noodles called *naeng myun*. They are made from plain buckwheat flour, or mixtures of buckwheat and wheat flours. Some also have cornflour (cornstarch) and eggs to bind the noodles. Buckwheat noodles retain their texture when boiled and are usually eaten cold with a dipping sauce in summer, or hot in soups. Another type popular in Japan, *chasoba*, is made from buckwheat and green tea powder.

buckwheat noodles

These Korean buckwheat noodles (above), made from buckwheat flour and potato starch, are a little more chewy than the Japanese soba noodles (left).

to cook

add soba noodles to a large saucepan of boiling water and stir to separate. Return to the boil, adding 250 ml (1 cup) cold water, and repeat this step three times, as it comes to the boil. Drain and rinse under cold water. Cooked soba noodles are served with broths, which have flavourings such as soy, poured over them, or with a thin sauce served on the side for dipping the noodles into. They can also be used in salads.

egg noodles

Made from wheat flour and eggs, these noodles are sold in both fresh and dried forms. The thin, round noodles are used in soups, stir-fries and for deep-frying, while the flatter, wider noodles are used mainly in soups.

Chinese e-fu noodles are referred to as 'birthday' or 'long life' noodles—the longer the noodle, the longer the eater's life, so cutting them is seen to be unlucky. They are pressed into a cake and need to be boiled for 2–3 minutes to soften.

1 Traditionally egg noodles are made by hand.

2 The dough is quite stiff and is worked into a flaky mass.

3 The dough is passed through rollers, then fed through a cutter.

Hokkien noodles (above, left) are thick, fresh egg noodles that have been cooked and lightly oiled before packaging. To prepare them, first cover with boiling water for 1 minute to separate them and then drain and rinse. Hokkien noodles are used in Malaysia, Singapore and Indonesia in stir-fries, soups and salads.

Shanghai noodles (above, right) come from northern China, and are thick round egg noodles, similar to Hokkien noodles, but have not been cooked or oiled. They are sold loosely packed and dusted with flour. Cook in boiling water for 4–5 minutes, then drain and rinse.

Hokkien noodles are also known as — egg noodles

hokkien/shanghai noodles
crispy duck with hokkien noodles

4 duck breasts (200 g/7 oz each)
1 tablespoon five-spice powder
400 g (14 oz) Hokkien (egg) noodles
100 g (3½ oz) snow peas (mangetout)
1 tablespoon peanut oil
2 garlic cloves, crushed
2 teaspoons finely chopped ginger
1 small red chilli, seeded and finely chopped
3 tablespoons soy sauce
1 tablespoon hoisin sauce
2 tablespoons plum sauce
1 tablespoon honey
50 g (1¾ oz) soya bean sprouts
3 spring onions (scallions), cut into thin strips
150 g (5½ oz) cucumber, cut into thin strips

preheat the oven to 230°C (450°F/Gas 8). Put the duck breasts in a roasting tin, skin-side up. Combine the five-spice powder and 2 teaspoons salt and press onto each breast. Roast for 35 minutes. Rest for 5 minutes, then cut into thin slices.

soak the noodles in boiling water for 1 minute. Drain and put in a bowl. Blanch the snow peas for 15 seconds.

heat the peanut oil in a saucepan and cook the garlic, ginger and chilli for 30 seconds. Combine the soy, hoisin and plum sauces, honey and 2 tablespoons water, add to the pan and cook for 1 minute.

combine the duck, noodles, snow peas, bean sprouts, spring onion, cucumber and the warm sauce and serve. Serves 4.

ramen/somen noodles
pork and corn ramen soup

**200 g (7 oz) Chinese barbecue pork (char siu)
  fillet in one piece**
2 small fresh corn cobs
200 g (7 oz) dried ramen noodles
2 teaspoons peanut oil
1 teaspoon grated ginger
1.5 litres (6 cups) chicken stock
2 tablespoons mirin
2 spring onions (scallions), sliced on the diagonal
20 g (³/₄ oz) unsalted butter
1 spring onion (scallion), extra, sliced on the diagonal

cut the pork into thin slices and remove the corn kernels from the cob using a sharp knife.

cook the ramen noodles in a large saucepan of boiling water for 4 minutes, or until tender. Drain, then rinse in cold water.

heat the oil in a large saucepan over high heat. Stir-fry the ginger for 1 minute. Add the chicken stock and mirin and bring to the boil. Reduce the heat and simmer for 8 minutes.

add the pork slices to the liquid and cook for 5 minutes, then add the corn kernels and spring onion and cook for another 4–5 minutes, or until the kernels are tender.

separate the noodles by running them under hot water, then divide among four deep bowls. Ladle on the soup, then put 1 teaspoon butter on each serving. Garnish with the extra spring onion and serve at once. Serves 4.

Ramen noodles originated in China, but are now popular all over Japan. They are a wheat noodle bound together with egg and are traditionally served in a hot broth. They are available fresh, dried or as instant noodles. Before use, they need to be boiled. Fresh noodles take about 2 minutes to cook and dried noodles take 4 minutes. For instant noodles, just add boiling stock. Fresh ramen can be kept refrigerated for up to 4 days.

Somen noodles are delicate, thin Japanese noodles made from wheat flour. They also need to be cooked in boiling water for 2 minutes, then rinsed. They are traditionally eaten cold with a dipping sauce, but may also be served in a broth.

rice noodles

Dried noodles such as rice sticks and vermicelli are made from a dough of rice flour and water, and are popular in China and Vietnam. These are softened in hot water, then used in soups and stir-fries, or deep-fry the thread-like rice vermicelli until crispy. Thicker rice sticks are used in Thailand to make phad Thai.

Fresh rice noodles may be shaped into sheets, ribbons or long, round strands, such as laksa noodles. Rice sheets can be cut to the desired width, and can be filled or rolled around other ingredients, and steamed. Fresh noodles are best eaten the day they are made (they will harden and will be difficult to separate if refrigerated).

bean curd puffs with mushrooms and rice noodles

8 dried shiitake mushrooms
500 g (1 lb 2 oz) fresh round rice noodles
3 litres (12 cups) good-quality chicken stock
1 carrot, thinly sliced on the diagonal
100 g (3½ oz) bean curd (tofu) puffs, cut in half
800 g (1 lb 12 oz) bok choy (pak choi), trimmed and quartered
1–1½ tablespoons mushroom soy sauce
6 drops roasted sesame oil
ground white pepper, to season
100 g (3½ oz) enoki mushrooms, ends trimmed

put the shiitake mushrooms in a heatproof bowl, cover with boiling water and soak for 30 minutes. Drain and remove the stems, squeezing out any excess water.

meanwhile, put the noodles in a heatproof bowl, cover with boiling water and soak briefly. Gently separate the noodles with your hands and drain well.

put the chicken stock in a large saucepan, cover and bring to a simmer. Add the noodles to the simmering stock along with the carrot, bean curd, shiitake mushrooms and bok choy. Cook for 1–2 minutes, or until the carrot and noodles are tender and the bok choy has wilted slightly. Stir in the soy sauce and sesame oil and season to taste with white pepper.

divide the noodles, vegetables, bean curd puffs and enoki mushrooms among four serving bowls, ladle the broth on top and serve immediately. Serves 4.

sevian noodles

These are very fine vermicelli noodles made from wheat flour. They have a biscuity flavour and are used in Indian cookery to make dishes such as the popular milk pudding sevian kheer, or to make savoury dishes such as sevian kheema, which is made with minced (ground) meat. Sold as skeins of noodles or as bunches of straight noodles.

sevian kheema

place a small frying pan over low heat, dry-roast the cumin until aromatic, then grind to a fine powder using a spice grinder or mortar and pestle. Heat 1 tablespoon ghee in a heavy-based frying pan and fry the onion, garlic and ginger for 3–4 minutes. Add the cumin, cook for 1 minute, then add the meat and cook for 8 minutes, or until the meat is dry, breaking up any lumps with the back of a fork. Season with the black pepper and salt, to taste, and remove from the pan.

heat the remaining ghee in the frying pan and fry the sevian for 2 minutes. Add the meat and fry for 1 minute. Add 185 ml (3/4 cup) water and cook until the sevian are tender, adding more water if necessary. The dish should be dry, so don't add too much at once. When cooked, sprinkle with the juice. Serves 4.

1 teaspoon cumin seeds
3 tablespoons ghee or oil
1 red onion, finely chopped
3 garlic cloves, crushed
2 cm (3/4 inch) piece of ginger, grated
225 g (8 oz) minced (ground) lamb or beef
1 teaspoon ground black pepper
225 g (8 oz) sevian noodles, broken into small pieces
3 tablespoons lime or lemon juice

shirataki noodles

Japanese for 'white waterfall', shirataki noodles are thin, jelly-like noodles made from konnyaku, which is made from a starchy root called konjac (sometimes called devil's taro). Shirataki are indispensable in the Japanese dish, sukiyaki. The noodles are usually sold packaged in liquid in the refrigerated section in Japanese supermarkets. They don't need to be cooked—just drop them into hot liquid, then rinse well. If unavailable, use reconstituted harusame (see page 51).

After soaking shirataki noodles in boiling water, rinse under cold running water, then drain well.

sauce

½–1 teaspoon dashi granules
80 ml (⅓ cup) soy sauce
2 tablespoons sake
2 tablespoons mirin
1 tablespoon caster
  (superfine) sugar

300 g (10½ oz) shirataki
  noodles
50 g (1¾ oz) lard
5 large spring onions
  (scallions), cut into 1 cm
  (½ inch) slices on the
  diagonal
16 fresh shiitake mushrooms
  (180 g/6 oz), cut into
  smaller pieces if too large
800 g (1 lb 12 oz) rump
  steak, thinly sliced across
  the grain (see note)
100 g (3½ oz) watercress,
  trimmed
4 eggs (optional)

sukiyaki

to make the sauce, dissolve the dashi granules in 125 ml (½ cup) water in a bowl. Add the soy sauce, sake, mirin and caster sugar and stir until combined. Drain the noodles (they are usually sold packaged in water), put in a large heatproof bowl, cover with boiling water and soak for 2 minutes. Rinse in cold water, and drain well.

melt the lard in a large frying pan over medium heat. Cook the spring onion, shiitake mushrooms and beef in batches, stirring continuously, for 1–2 minutes each batch, or until just brown. Return all the meat, spring onion and shiitake to the pan, then add the sauce and watercress. Cook for 1 minute, or until heated through and the watercress has wilted—the sauce needs to just cover the ingredients but not drown them.

divide the noodles among four serving bowls and spoon the sauce evenly over the top. If desired, crack an egg into each bowl and break up through the soup using chopsticks until it partially cooks. Serves 4.

note: Freeze the beef for 40 minutes before cutting it. This will enable you to cut it into very thin slices.

Also known as — devil's tongue noodles

sweet potato noodles

These are made from sweet potato starch and come dried in bundles. They are often labelled as Korean vermicelli: check the ingredients for 'sweet potato starch' to make sure you are buying the right thing.

The noodles are used in soups and stir-fries because they soak up the sauce. Before using them, soak in boiling water for 10 minutes until softened, or cook in boiling water for 3 minutes, then drain and rinse. They become plump and gelatinous when cooked—take care not to overcook or they can become gluggy.

kim chi with omelette on noodles

cook the noodles in a saucepan of boiling water for 3 minutes, or until softened. Drain and rinse under cold, running water.

heat a wok over high heat, add 2 teaspoons of the oil and swirl to coat. Lightly beat the egg yolks, season and cook, undisturbed, for 30 seconds, then turn to cook the other side for 30 seconds. Transfer to a plate. Lightly beat the egg white, season and cook the same way as the yolks. Slice the egg yolk and egg white into thin strips, about 3 cm (1 1/4 inches) long.

heat the remaining oil in the wok, add the noodles, sugar, soy sauce, sesame oil and spring onion and stir-fry for 1 minute. Top with the egg strips and pickled vegetables and serve immediately. Serves 6 (as a side dish).

note: Kim chi is a Korean hot, fermented pickle, popular also in Japan. It is sold in packets or tubs in the refrigerated section of Asian grocery stores.

200 g (7 oz) sweet potato starch noodles
1 1/2 tablespoons vegetable oil
2 eggs, separated
1 teaspoon sugar
1 tablespoon light soy sauce
1 teaspoon sesame oil
2 spring onions (scallions), thinly sliced on the diagonal
150 g (5 1/2 oz) prepared kim chi (see note)

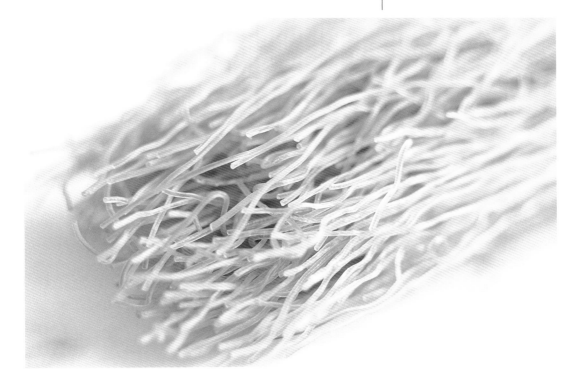

udon noodles

Udon noodles are thick, white, wheat flour noodles used in Japanese cooking. They can be round or flat, in a variety of widths, and in fresh, frozen, dried and instant varieties. After boiling, drain and rinse before use. Udon noodles are used in Japanese soups and simmered dishes, or they can be stir-fried or braised and served with a sauce.

warm pork and udon noodle salad with lime dressing

dressing
- **80 ml (1/3 cup) lime juice**
- **1 tablespoon roasted sesame oil**
- **2 tablespoons ponzu sauce (see note, page 215)**
- **90 g (1/4 cup) honey**

- **400 g (14 oz) fresh udon noodles**
- **500 g (1 lb 2 oz) pork fillet**
- **1 tablespoon roasted sesame oil**
- **200 g (7 oz) roasted unsalted peanuts**
- **2 teaspoons finely chopped ginger**
- **2 large red chillies, seeded and finely diced**
- **1 large cucumber, peeled, halved, seeds removed and julienned**
- **200 g (7 oz) soya bean sprouts**
- **25 g (1/2 cup) chopped coriander (cilantro) leaves**

preheat the oven to 200°C (400°F/Gas 6). To make the dressing, put the lime juice, sesame oil, ponzu and honey in a screwtop jar and shake to combine.

cook the noodles in a saucepan of boiling water for 1–2 minutes, or until tender. Drain, rinse and set aside.

trim the fat and sinew off the pork and brush with the sesame oil. Season. Heat a non-stick frying pan until very hot and cook the pork for 5–6 minutes, or until browned on all sides and cooked to your liking. Remove from the pan and rest for 5 minutes.

combine the noodles, peanuts, ginger, chilli, cucumber, bean sprouts and coriander and toss well. Cut the pork into thin slices, add to the salad with the dressing and toss before serving. Serves 4.

wheat noodles

These are thin, round noodles made simply with wheat flour and water. They are usually sold dried, but also fresh, and in varying thicknesses. Before wheat noodles can be used, boil them (2 minutes for fresh, 4 minutes for dried), then drain and rinse. Wheat noodles are good in stir-fries (such as dan dan mian, a popular snack in China) as they are strong and also absorb the delicious flavours of their sauce.

dan dan mian

1 tablespoon Sichuan
   peppercorns
200 g (7 oz) minced (ground)
   pork
50 g (1¾ oz) preserved
   turnip, rinsed and finely
   chopped
4 tablespoons light soy sauce
2 tablespoons oil

2 garlic cloves, crushed
2 tablespoons grated ginger
4 spring onions (scallions),
   finely chopped
2 tablespoons sesame paste
   or smooth peanut butter
2 teaspoons chilli oil
185 ml (¾ cup) chicken stock
400 g (14 oz) wheat noodles

dry-fry the Sichuan peppercorns in a wok or pan until brown and aromatic, then crush lightly. Combine the pork with the preserved turnip and half the soy sauce and leave to marinate for a few minutes. Heat a wok over high heat, add the oil and heat until very hot. Stir-fry the pork until crisp and browned. Remove and drain well.

add the garlic, ginger and spring onion to the wok and stir-fry for 30 seconds, then add the sesame paste, remaining soy sauce, chilli oil and stock and simmer for 2 minutes.

cook the noodles in a pan of salted boiling water for 4–8 minutes, then drain well. Divide among four bowls, ladle the sauce over the noodles, then top with the pork and peppercorns. Serves 4.

In China, wheat noodles are made by pulling them by hand. The noodles are made fresh for each customer and cooked immediately.

palm sugar

Palm sugar is a dark, unrefined sugar obtained from the sap of various palm trees, including the palmyra palm and some sugar palms, which grow in Indonesia, Malaysia, the Philippines, Thailand and other parts of Southeast Asia. The sap is collected, boiled until it turns into a thick, dark syrup, then poured into moulds where it dries to form dense, heavy cakes. Palm sugar is widely used in Southeast Asian dishes, not only in sweet dishes but also to balance the flavours in savoury dishes. It can also be used as an alternative to raw or brown sugar. The easiest way to use it is to shave the sugar from the cake with a sharp knife.

Buy in blocks or in jars from Asian shops. Thai palm sugar is lighter in colour, softer and more refined than the Indonesian or Malaysian versions. If palm sugar is unavailable, a full-flavoured brown sugar can be used instead.

peanuts

Not in fact a nut, the peanut is a member of the legume family, like peas. Its 'nut' is encased in pale-brown brittle pods. Peanuts are an important ingredient in the cooking of Southeast Asia, where they are used in sauces, salads and the well-known dish, satay. Peanut oil is extracted from the nut. Peanuts can be bought shelled or unshelled, raw, roasted, salted or boiled. Once opened, store in an airtight container in the refrigerator and use within 3 months. Raw peanuts deteriorate more quickly than roasted. Some people are allergic to peanuts and, for them, eating just one can be fatal.

Also known as — groundnut

larb gai

heat a frying pan over low heat. Add the rice and dry-fry for 3 minutes, or until lightly golden. Transfer the rice to a mortar and pestle and grind to a fine powder.

heat a wok over medium heat. Add the oil and swirl to coat. Add the mince and cook for 4 minutes, or until it changes colour, breaking up any lumps with the back of a wooden spoon. Add the fish sauce, lemon grass and stock and cook for a further 10 minutes. Remove the wok from the heat and allow to cool.

stir in the lime juice, spring onion, shallots, coriander, mint and ground rice and mix together thoroughly.

to serve, arrange the lettuce on a serving platter and top with the chicken mixture. Sprinkle with the nuts and chilli, and serve with lime wedges. Serves 6.

1 tablespoon jasmine rice
2 teaspoons vegetable oil
400 g (14 oz) minced (ground) chicken
2 tablespoons fish sauce
1 stem lemon grass, white part only, chopped
80 ml (1/3 cup) chicken stock
60 ml (1/4 cup) lime juice
4 spring onions (scallions), thinly sliced on the diagonal
4 Asian shallots, sliced
25 g (1/2 cup) finely chopped coriander (cilantro) leaves
25 g (1/2 cup) shredded mint
200 g (7 oz) lettuce leaves, shredded
40 g (1/4 cup) chopped roasted unsalted peanuts
1 small red chilli, sliced
lime wedges, to serve

Larb gai, or minced chicken salad, is a popular dish in the north and northeast of Thailand. The dish is characterized by flavours of chilli and lime juice, combined with fresh herbs.

pickles

Available in tins and jars, pickles are often used in Asian cuisine and are especially popular in India, China, Japan and Thailand. Pickles were devised as a way of preserving seasonal fruits and vegetables in vinegar, oil or brine. Eggplants (aubergine), tomatoes, cabbages, mangoes and limes are all used to make pickles. Flavourings, such as spices, garlic, ginger and chilli, make pickles a good accompaniment to meals, and they are also used as an ingredient in some dishes. Garlic and ginger are sometimes made into pickles by themselves. Chinese pickles can be made from several types of vegetables preserved in a clear brine solution, or in a soy-based solution. Both types can be used where Chinese pickles are called for in a recipe.

Pickles for sale in an Indian market.

A pickle stall in Sichuan, China.

Pine nuts are the small edible seeds that grow at the base of the cone of certain varieties of pine tree. There are many types of pine nuts: those used in Asian cooking generally come from Korea or the Himalayan region. The 'nut' is enclosed in a hard shell, which is always removed before the pine nuts are ready for sale. Pine nuts have quite a soapy texture with a slight 'piney' taste. They may be eaten raw but the flavour is enhanced when they are roasted or fried. Because the nuts are high in oil, they burn quickly when heated. They also go rancid quickly so buy in small quantities.

Pine nuts are used in Korean cooking as a garnish for desserts, or they may be used in kim chi, pickled cabbage. In China, they may be sprinkled over vegetarian dishes, and in India, particularly in Kashmir in the north, they are used whole or ground as a flour in meat, rice and vegetable dishes. Store in an airtight container in a cool, dark place or freeze for up to 6 months.

Also known as — Indian nut, pine kernel

Pine nuts are actually the seed of a pine cone. Pine nut oil (far right) is extracted from the seeds.

rice

Rice is central to both the culture and cuisines of many Asian countries. Here, different varieties of rice are on display in a Thai market.

storing

Once you have opened a packet of rice, store it in a cool, dry place in an airtight container. Rice bought in large sacks is best stored in a dry, clean container with a lid. An unopened packet will keep for up to a year. Brown rice still contains the oil-rich germ or bran layer, so it will turn rancid if left in a warm place for too long; store it in an airtight container in the refrigerator. You also need to take extra care with cooked rice. If it is not consumed immediately, cover it, then chill it quickly as harmful bacteria can grow rapidly. Cooked rice will store in the refrigerator for up to 2 days.

Rice is the foundation of the meal in Asian countries. It is the dietary staple of over half the world's population and has shaped the cuisines and cultures of billions of people. High in carbohydrate, iron and protein, rice is a powerhouse of nutrition. In places such as China, Japan and Korea, where chopsticks are used, medium- or short-grain rices, which tend to stick together, are preferred. In India, Sri Lanka and Malaysia, a rice that cooks into separate fluffy grains is more sought after. The Vietnamese eat both glutinous (sticky) rice and fluffy, dry rice. In Thailand, long-grain jasmine rice is eaten, with the exception of some parts of the north where glutinous rice is preferred.

There are more than 2000 types of rice. Mostly, rice is classified by the shape, or size, of the grain. However, texture, fragrance and colour also distinguish one type from another. We describe just a few of the many types of rice used in the Asian kitchen in the following pages.

types

long-grain rice   has long and slender grains that usually stay separate and fluffy after cooking. This is the best choice for serving as a side dish, as a bed for sauces, or for dishes such as pilafs and curries. This group includes rices such as basmati, and the aromatic rices such as jasmine rice, used mainly in Southeast Asian cooking.

medium-grain rice   is shorter and plumper and usually more absorbent than long-grain rice. This rice is popular in Chinese cookery.

short-grain rice   is almost round and has moist grains that stick together. It is used in Europe for risottos and paellas, and in Japan for sushi (see page 236) and in China. Short-grain rice is also used to make puddings. Brown rice is a short-grained rice, more nutritious than white, and takes longer to cook.

glutinous rice   may be short or long grained, black or white. When it is cooked it compresses into a sticky mass, hence its alternative name of sticky rice.

coloured rice   includes varieties prized for their brilliant colour. This category of rice covers all grains that are not white (or brown) after the husk has been removed. Bhutanese red rice, grown in the Himalayas, is tender and slightly sticky when cooked, so it is easy to eat with chopsticks. Thai red rice (grown among jasmine rice) has similar qualities, as does Vietnamese red cargo.

cooking

Packaged rice generally does not require rinsing before use, but rice bought in sacks needs to be washed to remove dust and stones. Rice can be cooked in many ways, including absorption, boiling or steaming techniques, which are described below.

absorption method   This is an efficient and nutritious way to cook rice, as nutrients are not discarded with the cooking water. Generally, long-grain rices suit this method. Put the rice in a saucepan and add enough water so it comes up to the first finger joint. Bring the water and rice to the boil, cover, then reduce the heat to a simmer. The rice is cooked by the hot water and by the remaining steam once the water has been absorbed. Simply fluff up the grains with a fork and serve immediately.

rapid boiling   Many rices, including parboiled rices, cook well in plenty of water. Bring a large saucepan of water to the boil, uncovered. Sprinkle in the rice and keep an eye on it so it does not stick or overcook. Drain the rice in a sieve (if using jasmine or Japanese rice, rinse it with a little tepid water to prevent it cooking any further).

steaming   This is the preferred method for glutinous (sticky) rice or can be used for long-grain rice. Soak the rice overnight, then drain. Spread out the grains in a steamer lined with cheesecloth or muslin, put the steamer over a wok or pan of boiling water. The rice does not touch the water—it is cooked only by the steam.

Absorption: The rice for this Indian dish has been boiled, then left to simmer for 15 minutes.

Rapid boiling: After the rice has boiled, drain it in a sieve.

Steaming: After steaming the rice, fluff up the grains with a fork to separate them.

basmati rice

Basmati rice is a long-grained rice with a distinct aroma and flavour, used predominantly in Indian cooking. Basmati rice cooks into long, slender grains that are dry, separate and fluffy, ideal for use in pilafs and north Indian pulaos and biryani, and as an accompaniment to curries. Basmati rice grows in the foothills of northern India and Pakistan. Basmati is often sold as Punni, Patna, Dehra Dun, Jeera-Sali or Delhi, named for the region or town in which it is grown.

khichhari

60 g (2¼ oz) yellow lentils (toor dal)
300 g (1½ cups) basmati rice
3 tablespoons ghee or unsalted butter
1 teaspoon cumin seeds
6 cloves
½ cinnamon stick
2 onions, finely chopped
2 garlic cloves, finely chopped
2 cm (1 inch) piece of ginger, finely chopped
1 teaspoon garam masala
3 tablespoons lemon juice

soak the lentils in 500 ml (2 cups) water in a large saucepan for 2 hours. Wash the rice in a sieve under cold running water until the water runs clear. Drain. Heat the ghee in a heavy-based saucepan over low heat and fry the cumin seeds, cloves and cinnamon for a few seconds. Increase the heat to medium, add the onion, garlic and ginger, and cook until they soften and begin to brown.

add the rice and lentils, and toss to thoroughly coat in ghee. Add the garam masala, lemon juice, 1 teaspoon of salt and 750 ml (3 cups) boiling water. Bring to the boil, then reduce the heat to very low, cover tightly and cook for 15 minutes. Remove from the heat and gently fluff up the grains with a fork. Cover the pan with a clean cloth and leave for 10 minutes. Fluff up again and season with salt. Serves 6.

Khichhari, or kitcheri, is the precursor to kedgeree, a dish taken up with much enthusiasm by the British in India. Serve with yoghurt or chutneys, and bread.

glutinous rice, white

This rice may be either long or short grained, black (see page 70) or white. Unlike other rice, glutinous rice cooks to a sticky mass. Its name is purely a description of its texture as rice does not contain gluten. Sticky-textured rices absorb less water during cooking and, once cooked, the grains stick together, making the rice suitable for use in some sweet dishes or for eating with chopsticks.

In Thailand, long-grain glutinous rice is preferred, mostly served with savoury dishes, but may also be sweetened. Short-grain glutinous rice is also used to make mochi, Japanese rice cakes, while in China it may be mixed with flavourings such as pork and wrapped in a lotus leaf.

Also known as — sticky rice

steamed glutinous rice in lotus leaves

put the rice in a bowl, cover with cold water and leave to soak overnight. Drain in a colander and place the rice in a bamboo steamer lined with a tea towel. Steam, covered, over simmering water in a wok for 30–40 minutes, or until the rice is cooked. Cool slightly before use.

soak the lotus leaves in boiling water for 1 hour, or until softened. Shake dry and cut the leaves in half to give eight equal pieces.

to make the filling, soak the dried shrimp in boiling water for 1 hour, then drain. Soak the dried mushrooms in boiling water for 30 minutes, then drain and squeeze out any excess water. Remove and discard the stems and finely chop the caps.

heat a wok over high heat, add half the oil and heat until very hot. Stir-fry the chicken for 2–3 minutes, or until browned. Add the shrimp, mushrooms, garlic, sausage and spring onion. Stir-fry for 1–2 minutes, or until aromatic. Add the oyster sauce, soy sauce, sugar and sesame oil and toss well. Combine the cornflour with 200 ml (7 fl oz) water, add to the sauce and simmer until thickened.

with wet hands, divide the rice into 16 balls. Place the lotus leaves on a work surface, put a ball of rice in the centre of each leaf and flatten the ball slightly, making a slight indentation in the middle. Spoon one eighth of the filling onto each rice ball, top with another slightly flattened rice ball and smooth into one ball. Wrap up firmly by folding the leaves over to form an envelope.

put the parcels in three steamers. Cover and steam over simmering water in a wok, reversing the steamers halfway through, for 30 minutes. To serve, open up each leaf and eat straight from the leaf while hot with some chilli sauce. Makes 8.

600 g (1 lb 5 oz) white
    glutinous (sticky) rice
4 large lotus leaves

filling
2 tablespoons dried shrimp
4 dried Chinese mushrooms
2 tablespoons oil
350 g (12 oz) skinless
    chicken breast fillet, cut
    into 1 cm (1/2 inch) cubes
1 garlic clove, crushed
2 Chinese sausages (lap
    cheong), thinly sliced
2 spring onions (scallions),
    thinly sliced
1 tablespoon oyster sauce
3 teaspoons light soy sauce
3 teaspoons sugar
1 teaspoon roasted sesame
    oil
1 tablespoon cornflour
    (cornstarch)
chilli sauce, to serve

Black rice is actually a variety of long-grain glutinous white rice coated in a black-coloured bran. The rice is not milled, so the outer (black) bran layers are left on the grain, but underneath is a sticky white rice. When cooked, the rice becomes a beautifully rich purple colour (sometimes it is cooked with glutinous white rice, and that, too, is 'dyed' purple). Black rice is popular in desserts and as snacks in Thailand, Singapore and Malaysia, where it is often cooked with coconut milk and palm sugar.

Because black rice is unmilled, like brown rice, it can take up to 30–60 minutes to cook, depending on whether a tender or more chewy texture is preferred. Most recipes suggest soaking the rice overnight in cold water to reduce the cooking time.

glutinous rice, black
sticky black rice pudding

400 g (2 cups) black glutinous (sticky) rice
3 fresh pandanus leaves
500 ml (2 cups) coconut milk
85 g (3 oz) palm sugar, grated
3 tablespoons caster (superfine) sugar
coconut cream, to serve
mango or papaya cubes, to serve

put the rice in a large glass or ceramic bowl and cover with water. Leave to soak for at least 8 hours, or preferably overnight. Drain, then put in a saucepan with 1 litre (4 cups) water and slowly bring to the boil. Cook at a slow boil, stirring frequently, for 20 minutes, or until tender. Drain.

shred the pandanus leaves into strips with your fingers, then tie them in a knot. Pour the coconut milk into a large saucepan and heat until almost boiling. Add the palm sugar, caster sugar and pandanus leaves and stir until the sugar is dissolved.

add the rice to the pan and cook, stirring, for about 8 minutes without boiling. Remove from the heat, cover and leave for 15 minutes to absorb the flavours. Remove the pandanus leaves.

spoon the rice into individual bowls and serve warm with coconut cream and fresh mango or papaya cubes. Serves 6.

Also known as — sticky black rice, Thai black rice

jasmine rice

Jasmine rice is a fragrant rice, usually long-grained, and named after the sweet-smelling jasmine flower of Southeast Asia because, on cooking, it releases a similar floral aroma (however, it is not related to the jasmine plant). Jasmine rice cooks to a soft, slightly clingy grain and its taste enhances the traditional spices of Thai dishes. It is also served plain as it requires no seasoning.

thai basil fried rice

2 tablespoons oil
3 Asian shallots, sliced
1 garlic clove, finely chopped
1 small red chilli, finely
   chopped
100 g (3½ oz) snake or green
   beans, cut into short pieces
1 small red capsicum
   (pepper), cut into strips
90 g (3¼ oz) button
   mushrooms, halved

470 g (2½ cups) cooked
   jasmine rice
1 teaspoon grated palm sugar
3 tablespoons light soy sauce
10 g (¼ cup) Thai sweet basil
   leaves, shredded, plus extra
   for garnish
1 tablespoon coriander
   (cilantro) leaves, chopped
fried Asian shallot flakes,
   for garnish

heat a wok over high heat, add the oil and swirl. Stir-fry the shallots, garlic and chilli for 3 minutes, or until the shallots start to brown. Add the beans, capsicum and mushrooms, stir-fry for 3 minutes, or until cooked, then stir in the cooked jasmine rice and heat through.

dissolve the palm sugar in the soy sauce, then pour over the rice. Stir in the herbs. Garnish with the shallot flakes and basil. Serves 4.

rice vinegars

Made from fermented rice, these vinegars are used in China, Japan and Korea. Chinese and Japanese vinegars are milder and a little sweeter than Western vinegars. Japanese rice vinegars are used in dressings and sushi. In China, clear rice vinegar is used for pickles and sweet-and-sour dishes. Black rice vinegar is used in soups, sauces and noodles. Red vinegar is used as a dipping sauce or is served with shark's fin soup. Rice vinegars can last indefinitely but may lose their aroma, so buy small bottles. If unavailable, use cider vinegar instead of clear rice vinegar, and balsamic vinegar instead of black.

crispy shredded beef

400 g (14 oz) rump or sirloin steak, trimmed
2 eggs, beaten
1/2 teaspoon salt
4 tablespoons cornflour (cornstarch)
oil, for deep-frying
2 carrots, finely shredded
2 spring onions (scallions), shredded
1 garlic clove, finely chopped
2 red chillies, shredded
4 tablespoons caster (superfine) sugar
3 tablespoons Chinese black rice vinegar
2 tablespoons light soy sauce

cut the beef into thin shreds. Combine the eggs, salt and cornflour, then coat the shredded beef with the batter. Mix well.

fill a wok one-quarter full of oil. Heat the oil to 180°C (350°F), or until a piece of bread fries golden brown in 15 seconds. Cook the beef for 3–4 minutes, stirring to separate, then remove and drain. Cook the carrot for 1 1/2 minutes, then remove and drain. Pour the oil from the wok, leaving 1 tablespoon.

reheat the reserved oil over high heat until very hot and stir-fry the spring onion, garlic and chilli for a few seconds. Add the beef, carrot, sugar, vinegar and soy and stir to combine. Serves 4.

Chinese black vinegar and clear rice vinegar.

rock/
slab sugar

Yellow rock sugar comes as uneven lumps of sugar, which may need to be further crushed before use if the lumps are very big. It is a pure sugar that gives a clear syrup and is added to sauces to make them shiny and clear. Buy from Asian stores. If unavailable, use sugar lumps.

Slab sugar (pictured) is a dark brown caramel-flavoured sugar sold in either thick slabs or in thin layers in packets. If unavailable, use soft brown sugar.

rosewater

Rosewater, made from a distillation of rose petals, is used in India to perfume sweets, desserts and drinks such as lassi, a refreshing yoghurt-based drink. It gives a sweet fragrance to curries and rice dishes when sprinkled over the finished dish. Rosewater is also used to make gulab jamun (literally translated as 'rose-flavoured plum'), a very popular Indian sweet.

gulab jamun

440 g (2 cups) sugar
4–5 drops rosewater
100 g (1 cup) low-fat
  powdered milk
2 tablespoons self-raising
  flour

2 teaspoons fine semolina
2 tablespoons ghee
4 tablespoons milk, to mix
24 pistachio nuts (optional)
oil, for deep-frying

put the sugar in a large, heavy-based saucepan with 875 ml (3 1/2 cups) water. Stir over low heat to dissolve the sugar. Increase the heat and boil for 3 minutes to make a syrup. Stir in the rosewater and remove from the heat.

to make the gulab jamun, mix the powdered milk, flour, semolina and ghee in a bowl. Add enough milk to make a soft dough, mix until smooth, then divide into 24 portions. Press each piece of dough in the centre to make a hole, fill with a pistachio, then roll into a ball. If not using pistachios, just roll each piece into a ball.

fill a deep saucepan one-third full with oil. Heat to 150°C (300°F) (a cube of bread will brown in 30 seconds) and fry the balls over low heat until golden brown. Remove with a slotted spoon and transfer to the syrup. When all the balls are in the syrup, bring the syrup to boiling point, then remove from the heat. Cool and serve the gulab jamun at room temperature. Makes 24.

1 Roll the gulab jamun dough into smooth balls.

2 When they are golden brown, remove with a slotted spoon.

3 Serve at room temperature in the rose-flavoured syrup.

sago

Sago is a starch extracted from various Southeast Asian palms, processed into a flour or granulated into little balls called pearl sago. In Southeast Asia, sago is used both as a flour and in pearl form to make desserts.

Also known as — pearl sago

sago pudding with young coconut

170 ml (²/₃ cup) coconut milk
³/₄ teaspoon salt
110 g (4 oz) sago or tapioca
6 pandanus leaves
60 g (¹/₄ cup) caster (superfine) sugar
150 g (5¹/₂ oz) young coconut meat in syrup (tinned), drained

in a small saucepan, stir the coconut milk with ¹/₂ teaspoon salt until combined. Bring 1 litre (4 cups) water to a rolling boil in a saucepan. Add the sago and pandanus and stir occasionally with a wooden spoon for 15–20 minutes while simmering over medium heat. Stir until the grains are swollen, clear and shiny. Reduce the heat if necessary.

add the sugar and ¹/₄ teaspoon salt to the saucepan and stir until the sugar has dissolved. The sago should now be almost cooked. Add the coconut meat and gently mix. Remove the pandanus leaves. Leave to thicken for 5 minutes before dividing among individual bowls. Drizzle coconut milk on top. Serve warm. Serves 4.

semolina

A grain of wheat consists of an outer coating (bran), the embryo (wheat germ) and the endosperm, the floury part. During milling, the endosperm is ground into particles to produce flour and semolina, which may be milled into fine, medium or coarse grains. As semolina is granular, it swells when cooked to give a creamy, textured effect. It has little flavour of its own, which makes it suited to both sweet and savoury dishes. Although used in parts of Southeast Asia, semolina is most often seen in the Indian kitchen, where it is used in puddings, in breads and cakes, as a batter for fish and vegetable patties, and in the southern Indian savoury dish, upama.

upama

2 tablespoons gram lentils
(channa dal)
4 tablespoons ghee or oil
75 g (2½ oz) cashew nuts
1 teaspoon black mustard
seeds

15 curry leaves
½ onion, finely chopped
140 g (5 oz) coarse semolina
lime juice, to serve
cashew nuts, to serve

soak the lentils in plenty of water for 3 hours. Drain, then put in a saucepan with 500 ml (2 cups) water. Bring to the boil and cook for 2 minutes. Drain, then dry in a tea towel. Brush a little ghee onto the cashew nuts and toast them in a frying pan over low heat until golden.

heat the remaining ghee in a heavy-based frying pan and add the mustard seeds and cooked lentils. Cook until the seeds start to pop, then add the curry leaves and onion and cook until the onion softens. Add the semolina. Toss everything together, and when the semolina is hot and the grains are brown and coated in oil, sprinkle with 500 ml (2 cups) boiling water, 80 ml (⅓ cup) at a time, tossing and stirring after each addition until the water is absorbed. Season with salt, to taste. Sprinkle with lime juice and cashews. Serves 4.

sesame oil

Sesame oil is made from crushed sesame seeds and ranges in colour from amber-yellow to dark brown. The sesame oil sold in Indian stores may be labelled 'gingelly' or 'til oil'. This is paler and has a less intense flavour than the sesame oil used in Chinese, Japanese and Korean cooking, which is more aromatic and has a stronger flavour as it is made from toasted sesame seeds. Sesame oil is used in stir-fries, often added at the end of cooking, or in marinades. It can be used for frying as it has a high smoking point, although the roasted oil burns very quickly.

japanese-style steak salad

generously season the steak with salt and freshly cracked black pepper. Heat the oil in a large frying pan to very hot. Add the steak and cook for 2–3 minutes on each side, or until browned. Remove and leave to rest, covered, for 5 minutes.

put the wasabi paste, ginger, rice vinegar, pickled ginger, pickling liquid and ½ teaspoon salt in a large bowl and whisk together. Whisk in the oils, then add the spinach, mizuna, radish and cucumber to the bowl and toss to coat.

slice the steak across the grain into thin strips. Divide the salad among four serving plates, top with the beef slices and sprinkle with sesame seeds. Serve immediately. Serves 4.

750 g (1 lb 10 oz) rump
   steak
3 teaspoons oil
3 teaspoons wasabi paste
1 teaspoon grated ginger
2 tablespoons rice vinegar
3 tablespoons pickled ginger,
   plus 1 tablespoon pickling
   liquid
2 tablespoons roasted
   sesame oil
60 ml (¼ cup) oil, extra
100 g (3½ oz) baby English
   spinach leaves
100 g (3½ oz) mizuna or
   watercress, trimmed
4 radishes, thinly sliced
1 Lebanese (short) cucumber,
   peeled and cut into ribbons
   with a vegetable peeler
40 g (¼ cup) sesame seeds,
   toasted

Made from rice, millet, yeast and Shaoxing's local water, this Chinese rice wine is aged for at least 3 years, then bottled either in glass or decorative earthenware bottles (pictured left). Several varieties are available. Aged wines are served warm as a drink, and the younger wines are used for cooking. In China, it is sometimes referred to as 'daughter's wine' because of the tradition of putting some of the wine away at the birth of a daughter to be drunk at her wedding. If Shaoxing is unavailable, dry sherry is the best substitute.

drunken chicken

1.5 kg (3 lb 5 oz) chicken, rinsed and drained
150 ml (5 fl oz) Shaoxing rice wine
3 tablespoons Chinese spirit (Mou Tai) or brandy
3 slices ginger
3 spring onions (scallions), cut into short lengths
2 teaspoons salt
1/4 teaspoon freshly ground black pepper
coriander (cilantro) leaves, for garnish

remove any fat from the chicken cavity opening and around the neck. Cut off and discard the parson's nose. Blanch the chicken in a pan of boiling water for 2–3 minutes, then refresh in cold water.

put the chicken, breast-side down, in a bowl. Add the rice wine, Chinese spirit, ginger, spring onion and half the salt. Place the bowl in a steamer. Cover and steam over simmering water in a wok for 1 1/2 hours, replenishing with boiling water during cooking. Transfer the chicken to a dish, breast-side up, reserving the cooking liquid.

pour half the liquid into a wok or saucepan and add the remaining salt and the pepper. Bring to the boil, then pour the sauce over the chicken. Using a cleaver, cut the chicken through the bones into bite-size pieces. Garnish with the coriander. Serves 4.

shaoxing rice wine

Also known as — Chinese rice wine, Shao Hsing, Shao Xing

tangerine peel

Dried tangerine or orange peel is used as a seasoning. It looks like dark-brown strips of leather with a white underside, and is used mostly in Chinese braised dishes or 'master sauces' (page 88). It is not soaked first but is added straight to the liquid in the dish. Sold in Asian stores.

red-cooked chicken

red-cooking liquid

2 cinnamon or cassia sticks
1½ star anise
2 pieces dried tangerine or orange peel, about 5 cm (2 inches) long
½ teaspoon fennel seeds
375 ml (1½ cups) dark soy sauce

90 g (3¼ oz) sugar
125 ml (½ cup) Shaoxing rice wine

1.5 kg (3 lb 5 oz) chicken, rinsed and drained
1 tablespoon roasted sesame oil

to make the red-cooking liquid, put all the ingredients in a clay pot or casserole with 1.5 litres (6 cups) water, bring to the boil, then simmer for 30 minutes.

remove any fat from the chicken cavity opening and around the neck. Cut off and discard the parson's nose. Put the chicken, breast-side down, in the cooking liquid and cook for 1½ hours, turning two or three times. Turn off the heat and leave in the liquid for 30 minutes, then remove.

brush the chicken with the sesame oil, then, using a cleaver, cut the chicken through the bones into bite-size pieces. Spoon over a little liquid and serve hot or cold. Serves 6.

pastes and sauces

Clockwise from back left: brown bean sauce, yellow bean sauce, black bean sauce, and chilli bean paste.

bean pastes

Seasonings made from fermented and salted yellow or black soya beans, bean pastes have been used for thousands of years by the Chinese to flavour food. Bean pastes appear in many guises on the supermarket shelf and the labels vary enormously. Don't be discouraged by the pungent aroma when you open the jar as a spoonful or two of paste of any type will flavour a stir-fry perfectly. Following are only a few of the many pastes and sauces available.

bean pastes and sauces

black bean sauce Made from puréed, fermented black soya beans and flavoured with soy sauce, sugar, salt and spices. Some varieties also contain garlic, chilli or ginger. The salty flavour works well with fish, squid, crab or beef. Use in dipping sauces and marinades or toss with stir-fried chicken or beef.

brown bean sauce Sometimes called brown bean paste, ground bean sauce, bean sauce or yellow bean sauce. This sauce is made from ground or crushed yellow soya beans. It is usually sold as a smooth purée, although some brands include mashed beans to give it more texture. Despite sometimes being labelled as yellow bean sauce, it is different from the Southeast Asian yellow bean sauce—it is browner, thicker and richer.

yellow bean sauce Sometimes called fermented yellow soya bean paste. Not to be confused with the Chinese variety of the same name (see brown bean sauce, above), this version is made from salted and fermented soya beans, and has a runnier consistency and paler colour.

chilli bean paste Red or brown in colour and sometimes called hot bean paste, red bean chilli paste or chilli bean sauce. This is a thick bean sauce mixed with chilli and sometimes fermented black beans, garlic and spices. Some are extremely hot, so use with caution. Use with bland ingredients like bean curd (tofu), noodles and vegetables.

See also hoisin sauce, page 85.

chilli pastes and jams

chilli jam

3 tablespoons dried shrimp
500 ml (2 cups) vegetable oil
220 g (2 cups) sliced Asian
  shallots
110 g (1 cup) thinly sliced
  garlic

4–5 long, seeded and finely
  chopped red chillies
90 g (3¼ oz) grated light
  palm sugar
3 tablespoons tamarind purée
2 tablespoons fish sauce

soak the dried shrimp in hot water for 5 minutes, drain well, then dry and roughly chop.

heat the vegetable oil in a small saucepan over medium heat and add the Asian shallots and garlic and cook for 10 minutes, stirring constantly, until the shallots and garlic turn golden. Add the shrimp and chillies and cook for 5 minutes, stirring constantly. Remove from the heat. Drain, reserving the oil.

transfer the fried mixture to a food processor and blend gradually, adding 60 ml (¼ cup) of the reserved cooking oil to form a paste.

transfer the mixture to a saucepan over medium heat and, when it begins to simmer, add the palm sugar, tamarind purée and fish sauce. Cook the mixture for 5 minutes, stirring frequently, until it thickens. Allow to cool before serving. Store in a clean jar in the refrigerator for up to 6 months. Serve with Thai food or finger food such as spring rolls or money bags. Makes about 3 cups.

Chilli pastes and jams are used as condiments and as flavouring bases in Asian cooking. The flavours vary according to the country in which they are used, but they are generally made with ingredients such as chillies (some brands are hotter than others), tomatoes, onions, oil, tamarind, garlic, sugar, salt, spices and vinegar. Chilli jam, or sweet chilli jam, is used mainly in Thai cooking, either as a flavouring for stir-fries or as a dipping sauce for finger food such as spring rolls. Hot chilli paste, sambal oelek, is used as a relish in Malaysian and Indonesian cooking. It is made with chillies ground with salt and either vinegar or tamarind. For vegetarian cooking, check the label to ensure the brand you buy does not contain shrimp paste.

fish sauce

Popular throughout Southeast Asia, particularly in Thailand and Vietnam, fish sauce is a pungent, salty liquid used as a condiment and a flavouring. The liquid is amber to dark brown in colour, and is used like soy sauce. In Vietnam, fish sauce is served with most meals as a dipping sauce, where it may be flavoured with chillies, peanuts or sugar. Usually the more expensive sauces are used as dipping sauces as these tend to be less 'fishy'.

Fish sauce is made from salted dried fish or shrimp, which are layered into large wooden barrels and allowed to ferment. After about 3 months or so, the liquid is drained off to produce a sauce of high quality, normally reserved for table use. Subsequent drainings yield a fish sauce of lower quality, generally used for cooking. Some bottles of fish sauce, especially those from China and Hong Kong, may be labelled 'fish gravy'.

Also known as — nam pla, nuoc mam, nuoc nam, patis

mongolian lamb

2 garlic cloves, crushed
2 teaspoons finely grated
  ginger
60 ml (¼ cup) Shaoxing rice
  wine
60 ml (¼ cup) light soy sauce
2 tablespoons hoisin sauce
1 teaspoon roasted sesame
  oil

1 kg (2 lb 4 oz) lamb loin
  fillets, thinly sliced across
  the grain
80 ml (⅓ cup) peanut oil
6 spring onions (scallions), cut
  into 3 cm (1¼ inch) lengths
2 teaspoons chilli sauce
1½ tablespoons hoisin sauce,
  extra

combine the garlic, ginger, rice wine, soy sauce, hoisin sauce and sesame oil in a large non-metallic bowl. Add the lamb and toss until well coated. Cover with plastic wrap and marinate in the refrigerator overnight, tossing occasionally.

heat a wok over high heat, add 1 tablespoon of the peanut oil and swirl to coat the wok. Add the spring onion and stir-fry for 1 minute, or until lightly golden. Remove, reserving the oil in the wok.

lift the lamb out of the marinade with tongs, reserving the marinade. Add the meat in four batches and stir-fry for 1–2 minutes per batch, or until browned but not completely cooked through, adding more oil and making sure the wok is very hot before cooking each batch. Return all the meat and any juices to the wok with the spring onion and stir-fry for 1 minute, or until the meat is cooked through.

remove the meat and spring onion from the wok with a slotted spoon and put in a serving bowl, retaining the liquid in the wok. Add any reserved marinade to the wok along with the chilli sauce and extra hoisin sauce, then boil for 3–4 minutes, or until the sauce thickens and becomes slightly syrupy. Spoon the sauce over the lamb, toss together well, then serve with steamed rice. Serves 4–6.

hoisin sauce

A sweetly piquant reddish-brown sauce made from fermented soya beans, garlic, sugar and spices, hoisin sauce is used as both a condiment and a flavouring agent in Chinese cooking. It may be used as the sauce for Peking duck (though it is not the authentic sauce), in stir-fries or as a marinade for poultry or meat, especially char siu (barbecue pork) and shellfish. Store in the refrigerator after opening.

Also known as — Peking sauce

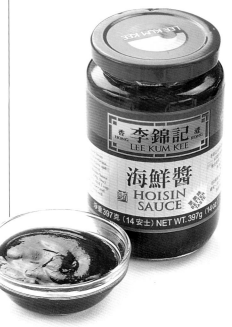

kecap manis

Kecap manis is a thick, dark, sweetened soy sauce made from black soya beans. It is used in Indonesia and Malaysia for rice and noodle dishes or to colour and flavour meat dishes. If it is not available, stir a little brown sugar into soy sauce until dissolved.

nasi goreng

150 g (5½ oz) finely chopped snake beans
3 garlic cloves, roughly chopped
1 onion, roughly chopped
1 red chilli, roughly chopped
2 tablespoons vegetable oil
200 g (7 oz) raw prawns (shrimp), peeled and deveined
250 g (9 oz) chicken breast fillet, thinly sliced
740 g (4 cups) cooked long-grain rice, cooled
4 spring onions (scallions), thinly chopped
1 tablespoon kecap manis
1–2 tablespoons light soy sauce

cook the snake beans in boiling water for 3 minutes. Drain, rinse and set aside.

blend the chopped garlic, onion and chilli in a mortar and pestle or in a food processor to form a rough paste. Heat the oil in a wok, swirl to coat the side of the wok, and cook the paste for 1 minute, or until fragrant.

add the prawns and chicken and stir-fry for 3 minutes, or until the prawns turn pink. Add the beans and 2 tablespoons water and season with salt and pepper.

stir in the rice, spring onions, kecap manis and soy sauce, stirring to break up any lumps until heated through. Serves 4.

note: Nasi goreng is usually served with shredded omelette and krupuk (prawn crackers) on the top.

maltose

peking duck

2.5 kg (5 lb 8 oz) duck
2 tablespoons maltose or
   honey, dissolved in
   2 tablespoons water
125 ml (½ cup) hoisin sauce
   or plum sauce

24 ready-made Mandarin
   (or duck) pancakes
6–8 spring onions (scallions),
   shredded
½ cucumber, shredded

cut the wing tips off the duck with a pair of poultry shears. Rinse the duck, drain, and remove any fat from the cavity opening and around the neck. Cut off and discard the parson's nose. Plunge the duck into a pot of boiling water for 2–3 minutes to tighten the skin. Remove and drain, then dry thoroughly.

while the skin is still warm, brush the duck all over with the maltose or honey and water, then hang it up to dry in a cool and airy place for at least 6 hours, or overnight, or leave it uncovered in the refrigerator.

preheat the oven to 200°C (400°F/Gas 6). Put the duck, breast-side up, on a rack in a roasting tin, and cook without basting or turning for 1½ hours. Check to make sure the duck is not getting too dark and, if it is, cover it loosely with foil.

to serve, remove the crispy duck skin in small slices by using a sharp carving knife, then carve the meat, or carve both together. Arrange on a serving plate.

to eat, spread about 1 teaspoon of the hoisin sauce or plum sauce in the centre of a pancake, add a few strips of spring onion, cucumber, duck skin and meat, roll up the pancake and turn up the bottom edge to prevent the contents from falling out. Serves 6.

A sweet syrup of malted grains, maltose is used to caramelize Peking duck and barbecued meats. Maltose is very thick and sticky, so use a strong spoon to spoon it out of its container—it may be easier if you heat the spoon in boiling water first. Buy from Chinese supermarkets but, if unavailable, honey can be used as a substitute. Maltose keeps for a long time and can be frozen.

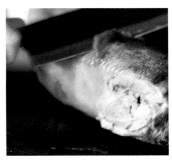

1 One method is to carve the duck so that each slice has a piece of both the crispy skin and the tender meat.

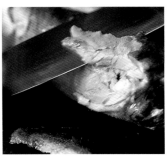

2 Another method is to serve the skin separately, wrapped in pancakes, and use the meat in a stir-fry.

Commercially made Mandarin pancakes are available in Asian shops, fresh or frozen, or from restaurants that sell take-away barbecued ducks and meat.

master sauce

Some of the ingredients used to make a 'master sauce'.

Master sauce is a basic stock used in Chinese cooking. It consists of soy sauce, rice wine, rock sugar, spring onions, ginger and star anise. Additional ingredients vary according to the tastes of the individual chef. Meat, poultry or fish is cooked in the stock, then the stock is reserved so it matures, taking on the flavours of everything that is cooked in it. The spices are replenished every few times the sauce is used. Master sauce spices can be bought as a mix, or a ready-made liquid version. Freeze between uses.

five-spice beef

750 g (1 lb 10 oz) shin of beef or stewing or braising beef, trimmed
2 spring onions (scallions), each tied in a knot
3 slices ginger, smashed with the flat side of a cleaver
4 tablespoons Chinese spirit (Mou Tai) or brandy
1.5 litres (6 cups) beef stock

1 teaspoon salt
4 tablespoons light soy sauce
3 tablespoons dark soy sauce
1 tablespoon five-spice powder
150 g (5½ oz) rock sugar
1 spring onion (scallion), extra, finely sliced
1 teaspoon roasted sesame oil

cut the beef into two or three long strips and put in a clay pot or casserole with the spring onions, ginger, Chinese spirit and stock. Bring to the boil and skim off any scum. Simmer, covered, for 15–20 minutes.

add the salt, soy sauces, five-spice powder and sugar to the beef, return to the boil, then simmer, covered, for 25–30 minutes.

leave the beef in the liquid to cool for 1 hour, then remove, drain and cool for 3–4 hours. Just before serving, slice thinly across the grain and sprinkle with the extra spring onion and sesame oil. The sauce can be reused as a 'master sauce'. Serves 8.

types of miso

hatcho-miso Very dark, strongly flavoured, salty miso used mainly in soups. Made only from soya beans. A similar miso is akadashi-miso.

inaka-miso Also called aka or red miso, this has barley mould added. Used in soups and stews and can be either sweet or salty.

shinshu-miso One of the most commonly found outside of Asia. It is smooth, yellow and salty and can be used in most recipes.

shiro-miso Also called white miso, this has a sweet, mild flavour that is good for dressings. Low in salt, it is often used in soups.

vegetable ramen noodle soup

250 g (9 oz) fresh ramen
  noodles
1 tablespoon vegetable oil
1 tablespoon chopped ginger
2 garlic cloves, crushed
150 g (5½ oz) oyster
  mushrooms, halved
1 small zucchini (courgette),
  thinly sliced
1 leek, halved lengthways
  and thinly sliced
100 g (3½ oz) snow peas
  (mangetout), halved

100 g (3½ oz) bean curd
  (tofu) puffs, julienned
80 g (⅓ cup) shiro-miso (white
  miso paste)
80 ml (⅓ cup) light soy sauce
60 ml (¼ cup) mirin
90 g (3¼ oz) soya bean
  sprouts, tailed
½ teaspoon roasted sesame oil
4 spring onions (scallions),
  thinly sliced
100 g (3½ oz) enoki
  mushrooms

bring a large saucepan of lightly salted water to the boil. Add the noodles and cook, stirring, for 2 minutes, or until just tender. Drain, rinse under cold running water, then drain again.

heat a wok over medium heat, add the vegetable oil and swirl to coat. Add the ginger and garlic and stir-fry for 30 seconds, then add the oyster mushrooms, zucchini, leek, snow peas and sliced bean curd puffs and stir-fry for 4 minutes. Pour in 1.5 litres (6 cups) water and bring to the boil, then reduce the heat and simmer. Stir in the miso paste, soy sauce and mirin until heated through, but don't let it boil. Just before serving, stir in the bean sprouts and sesame oil.

put the noodles in the bottom of six serving bowls, then pour the broth over the top of them. Sprinkle with the sliced spring onion and enoki mushrooms. Serves 6.

miso paste

One of the most important ingredients in Japanese cooking, miso is a paste of fermented soya beans with other flavourings. Miso is made by boiling soya beans, which are then ground to a paste with wheat and barley or rice. The mixture is injected with a yeast mould and left to mature. Miso is used as a condiment and a flavouring and there are over 50 different types, each with a distinctive flavour and colour, and each suited to a particular type of recipe. Colours range from light brown to a dark brown, but generally the lighter the colour the milder the flavour. Buy miso in tubs or plastic packs. It will keep in the refrigerator for several months.

From left to right: hatcho-miso, inaka-miso, shinshu-miso, shiro-miso.

oyster sauce

Widely used in Chinese cooking, oyster sauce is a thick, richly flavoured brown sauce made of dried oysters, brine and soy sauce. Oyster sauce imparts colour and a rich, salty flavour to stir-fries and braised dishes without ever overpowering their natural flavours. It is also used as a table condiment.

When buying oyster sauce, check the ingredients list to ensure it contains 'premium oyster extract' rather than an imitation. Vegetarian oyster sauce has a similar taste and is made using mushrooms as its flavour base instead of oysters. Oyster sauce is sold in bottles and once opened should be refrigerated.

beef with oyster sauce

**300 g (10½ oz) rump or
  sirloin steak, trimmed
1 teaspoon sugar
1 tablespoon dark soy sauce
2 teaspoons Shaoxing rice
  wine
2 teaspoons cornflour
  (cornstarch)
4 dried Chinese mushrooms
oil, for deep-frying**

**4 slices ginger
1 spring onion (scallion), cut
  into short lengths
70 g (2½ oz) snow peas
  (mangetout), ends trimmed
1 small carrot, thinly sliced
½ teaspoon salt
2–3 tablespoons beef stock
2 tablespoons oyster sauce**

cut the beef across the grain into thin bite-size slices. Combine with half the sugar, the soy sauce, rice wine, cornflour and 2 tablespoons water. Marinate in the refrigerator for several hours, or overnight.

soak the dried mushrooms in boiling water for 30 minutes, then drain and squeeze out any excess water. Remove and discard the stems. Cut the caps in half, or quarters if large.

fill a wok one-quarter full of oil. Heat to 180°C (350°F), or until a piece of bread fries golden brown in 15 seconds when dropped in the oil. Cook the beef for 45–50 seconds, stirring to separate the pieces, and remove as soon as the colour changes. Drain well in a colander. Pour the oil from the wok, leaving 2 tablespoons.

reheat the reserved oil over high heat until very hot, then add the ginger and spring onion and stir-fry for 1 minute. Add the snow peas, Chinese mushrooms and carrot and stir-fry for 1 minute, then add the salt, stock and remaining sugar and continue to stir for a minute or so. Toss with the beef and oyster sauce. Serves 4.

shrimp paste

Shrimp paste is made from partially fermented shrimp that are ground, salted and dried before being either bottled as they are or compressed into blocks and left to dry further in the sun. This block type is manufactured mostly in Malaysia and Indonesia; the Chinese version is softer and more sauce-like.

Shrimp paste has a strong, salty flavour and is used—sparingly—as a flavouring in Southeast Asian and Chinese foods such as soups, sauces and rice dishes. It may also be mixed with chillies and shallots before being used as a flavouring. Shrimp paste from Malaysia, called blachan, should be fried first in a little oil to bring out the flavour. Shrimp paste has a very pungent odour and, when opened, should be wrapped in plastic or stored in an airtight container. If stored in the refrigerator, it should keep indefinitely.

Also known as — bagoong, blacan, blachan, kapi, trassi

soy sauce

Soy sauce is an essential condiment and ingredient in the kitchens of Japan, China and Southeast Asia. Produced for thousands of years, soy (or soya) sauce is a naturally brewed salty liquid made from fermented soya beans mixed with wheat, water and salt (a good sauce will contain only these ingredients). The mixture is injected with yeasts and bacteria and left to ferment for 3 months, then is filtered to extract the sauce. Some soy sauces are made synthetically from hydrolyzed plant protein blended with caramel colouring and corn syrup—these are inferior in flavour. It is used to colour and flavour marinades, dips, sauces and many Asian dishes. See also kecap manis, page 86.

types of soy sauces

dark soy sauce Less salty, thicker and darker than light soy sauce because it has fermented for longer and may be mixed with caramel or molasses. Used in Chinese meat and chicken dishes to add richness of colour and flavour. Some are flavoured with mushrooms.

light soy sauce This has a light, delicate flavour, but is saltier than dark soy. Light soy is used in Chinese soups, with seafood and white meat dishes, as a dipping sauce, or in dishes where you don't want to darken the colour of the food. It may be labelled superior soy sauce or, simply, soy sauce.

shoyu Japanese soy sauce, naturally brewed and left to mature for up to 2 years. It is slightly sweeter, less salty and lighter in both colour and flavour than Chinese soy sauce.

tamari Naturally brewed slightly thick Japanese soy sauce made with soya beans and rice. Although thought to be wheat-free, some types may contain 5–20 per cent wheat.

From left: dark soy sauce, shoyu and tamari.

This Chinese dish uses both light and dark soy sauce as part of the marinade for the chicken.

soy chicken

1.5 kg (3 lb 5 oz) chicken
1 tablespoon ground Sichuan
  peppercorns
2 tablespoons grated ginger
2 tablespoons sugar
3 tablespoons Shaoxing
  rice wine

310 ml (1¼ cups) dark soy
  sauce
185 ml (¾ cup) light soy sauce
580 ml (2⅓ cups) oil
435 ml (1¾ cups) chicken stock
2 teaspoons roasted
  sesame oil

rinse the chicken, drain, and remove any fat from the cavity opening and around the neck. Cut off and discard the parson's nose. Rub the peppercorns and ginger all over the inside and outside of the chicken. Combine the sugar, rice wine and soy sauces, add the chicken and marinate in the refrigerator for at least 3 hours, turning occasionally.

heat a wok over high heat, add the oil and heat until very hot. Drain the chicken, reserving the marinade, and fry for 8 minutes until browned. Put in a clay pot or casserole dish with the marinade and stock. Bring to the boil, then simmer, covered, for 35–40 minutes. Leave off the heat for 2–3 hours, transferring to the refrigerator once cool. Drain the chicken, brush with oil and refrigerate for 1 hour.

using a cleaver, chop the chicken through the bones into bite-sized pieces, pour over a couple of tablespoons of sauce and serve. The sauce can be reused as a 'master sauce' (see page 88). Serves 4.

cooking

In Chinese cuisine, there is a distinction between light and dark soy sauce, as they have different flavours and uses. Where a recipe does not specify which soy sauce to use, it generally requires light soy sauce, as this is the type most commonly sold as generic soy sauce. If possible, use a Japanese brand of soy sauce when cooking Japanese recipes, and a Chinese brand for Chinese recipes.

1 Add the chicken to the marinade and put it in the refrigerator for 3 hours.

2 The marinade turns the chicken skin a rich dark brown when it is cooked.

**seasonings,
herbs and spices**

ajowan

Ajowan is the small seed of a native Indian plant and looks like a miniature cumin seed—it has a similar aroma but stronger flavour. It is used in Indian cooking, often to flavour root vegetables, green beans, lentil dishes and flour-based dishes such as breads. Use sparingly.

Also known as —
ajwain, bishop's weed,
omum

tandoori lobster

2 large or 4 small live
  lobsters
1 egg
4 cm (1½ inch) piece of
  ginger, grated
½ teaspoon paprika
2 teaspoons soft brown sugar
150 ml (5 fl oz) thick
  (double/heavy) cream
pinch of ajowan

4 garlic cloves, crushed
2 tablespoons lemon juice
2 tablespoons besan flour
2 teaspoons garam masala
½ teaspoon ground white
  pepper
20 g (¾ oz) unsalted butter,
  melted, for basting
coriander (cilantro) leaves, for
  garnish

to kill the lobsters humanely, put them in the freezer for 1 hour. Using a large, heavy-bladed knife or cleaver, cut the lobsters in half. Remove the flesh from the tail shells in one piece, then cut the flesh into large chunks. Clean out the head ends of the shells and wash the shells all over, scrubbing out any membrane.

break the egg into a bowl, add the ginger, paprika, sugar, cream, ajowan, garlic, lemon juice, besan flour, garam masala, white pepper and a pinch of salt and whisk together. Brush the lobster pieces with the mixture, then cover and marinate in the refrigerator for 2 hours.

preheat the oven to its highest setting. Fix the lobster pieces on long metal skewers, keeping the pieces 2 cm (¾ inch) apart. Put the skewers on a wire rack set over a baking tray.

roast the lobster for 6 minutes, turning once. Baste with the butter and roast again for 2–4 minutes, or until the lobster is cooked through. Roast the shells on a separate tray until they turn red. Take the lobster pieces off the skewers and put them back in the shells, garnish with coriander leaves and serve hot. Serves 4.

Amchur is a fine beige powder made from dried green mangoes. Popular in northern Indian dishes, it is one of the main ingredients in chaat masala (see page 104). It is used as a meat tenderizer or used like tamarind to sour curries, lentil and vegetable dishes, and to season fish.

Also known as — amchoor

alu chaat

1 kg (2 lb 4 oz) small salad potatoes, unpeeled
100 ml (3½ fl oz) tamarind purée
4 green chillies, seeded and finely chopped
4 tablespoons chopped coriander (cilantro) leaves
2 teaspoons chaat masala

boil the potatoes in their skins for 15 minutes, or until just tender. Peel the potatoes and slice them into small rounds. Place in a serving bowl.

mix the tamarind purée with 60 ml (¼ cup) water. Mix all the other ingredients with the tamarind, then season with salt.

gently toss the potato rounds with the tamarind mixture and serve as a snack or as a refreshing salad on a hot day. Serves 4.

anise

Both anise leaves (used in salads and to flavour fish and vegetables) and seeds have a sweet liquorice-like flavour. The seeds are used in both sweet and savoury cooking—in cakes, breads and confectionery, as well as with seafood and meat. In India, the seeds are used in some curries, often those with seafood, in chutneys and pickles, or they may be chewed after a meal as a digestive and to sweeten the breath. Buy the seeds whole as the powder quickly loses its flavour.

Also known as — aniseed

Annatto is a bright-orange food colouring, which is extracted from the dark red, triangular seeds of a small tree native to South America, which now grows throughout Southeast Asia. Although the seed is edible, it has little flavour and its culinary value lies more in its colouring properties. Annatto is widely used in Filipino cooking as a colouring agent. Usually the seeds are fried in oil or lard and then discarded, and the remaining yellow lard is used to fry vegetables or meat to give them a golden yellow coating. The seeds can also be added directly to the dish but are too hard to eat. When ground into a powder or paste, annatto is used to colour butter, margarine and smoked fish, or to darken the rind of some washed-rind cheeses. In the recipe below, annatto is used to make adobo, a vinegar-marinated chicken stew, considered to be the national dish of the Philippines.

Also known as — *achuete, anatto, anchiote*

annatto

chicken adobo

combine the garlic, vinegar, chicken stock, bay leaf, coriander seeds, black peppercorns, annatto seeds and soy sauce in a large bowl. Add the chicken, cover and leave to marinate in the refrigerator for 2 hours.

transfer the chicken mixture to a large, heavy-based pan and bring to the boil. Reduce the heat, cover and simmer for 30 minutes. Remove the lid and cook for 10 minutes, or until the chicken is tender. Remove the chicken and set aside. Bring the liquid to the boil again and cook over high heat for 10 minutes, or until the liquid has reduced by half.

heat the oil in a wok or large frying pan, add the chicken in batches and cook over medium heat for 5 minutes, or until crisp and brown. Pour over the reduced vinegar mixture and serve with rice. Serves 6.

note: If annatto seeds are unavailable, substitute 1/4 teaspoon paprika combined with a generous pinch of turmeric.

6 garlic cloves, crushed
250 ml (1 cup) cider vinegar
375 ml (1 1/2 cups) chicken
   stock
1 bay leaf
1 teaspoon coriander seeds
1 teaspoon black
   peppercorns
1 teaspoon annatto (see note)
3 tablespoons soy sauce
1.5 kg (3 lb 5 oz) chicken
   pieces
2 tablespoons oil

asafoetida

This yellowish powder or lump of resin is made from the dried latex of a type of fennel. Asafoetida has an extremely pungent smell, which has earned it the name 'devil's dung'. It is used in small quantities as a flavour enhancer in Indian cooking, in curries, fish and vegetable dishes, in pickles, and to make pulses and legumes more digestible. Hindu Brahmins and Jains use it instead of garlic and onions, which are forbidden to them. Asafoetida is always fried to calm its strong sulphurous aroma. It comes in small airtight containers and is available from Indian food shops.

Also known as — giant fennel, hing, stinking gum

urad dal

250 g (9 oz) split, unskinned black lentils (chilke urad)
¼ teaspoon ground turmeric
4 ripe tomatoes, chopped
1 small onion, roughly chopped
2 tablespoons oil
½ teaspoon cumin seeds
1 teaspoon fennel seeds
5 cm (2 inch) piece of ginger, grated
2 dried chillies, broken into pieces
pinch of asafoetida
coriander (cilantro) leaves, for garnish

put the lentils in a heavy-based saucepan and add 1 litre (4 cups) water, the turmeric, tomato and onion. Bring to the boil, then reduce the heat, cover and simmer for 40 minutes, or until the lentils are cooked and feel soft when pressed between the thumb and index finger.

heat the oil in a small saucepan, add the cumin and fennel seeds and allow them to pop. Add the ginger, chilli and asafoetida and fry over low heat for 30 seconds. Pour into the hot lentils and simmer for another 5 minutes. Season with salt, to taste. Garnish with coriander leaves before serving. Serves 4.

There are several types of basil, all with a different flavour. Basil is used extensively in Thai and Vietnamese cooking, in curries, soups and stir-fries. Thai sweet basil (above) is similar to that used in the West. It has purplish stems, green leaves and a sweet aniseed aroma and flavour. Holy basil has green to reddish purple leaves and a hot sharp flavour. Lemon basil, also called mint basil, is less common and has a citrus flavour and delicate leaves. Basil should be torn, not chopped, and added to hot food at the last moment.

basil

beef with thai sweet basil leaves

1 tablespoon fish sauce
3 tablespoons oyster sauce
4 tablespoons vegetable or
   chicken stock, or water
1/2 teaspoon sugar
2 tablespoons vegetable oil
4 garlic cloves, finely chopped

3 bird's eye chillies
500 g (1 lb 2 oz) tender rump
   or fillet steak, finely sliced
1 medium onion, cut into thin
   wedges
2 handfuls of Thai sweet basil
   leaves

mix the fish sauce, oyster sauce, stock and sugar in a small bowl.

heat the oil in the wok or frying pan and stir-fry half the garlic over medium heat until light brown. Lightly crush the chillies with the flat side of a cleaver, and add half the crushed chillies and half the meat and stir-fry over a high heat for 2–3 minutes, or until the meat is cooked. Remove from the wok and repeat with the remaining garlic, chillies and meat. Return all the meat to the wok.

add the onion and fish sauce mixture and stir-fry for 1 minute, then add the basil and stir-fry until the basil begins to wilt. Taste, then adjust the seasoning if necessary. Spoon onto a serving plate. Serves 4.

cardamom

Of the many varieties, the green cardamom from South India and Sri Lanka is superior. The tiny brown or black seeds inside the pod have a sweet, mild flavour. Use the whole pod or the seeds whole or ground to flavour both sweet and savoury Indian food, from curries, rice dishes, pickles and chutneys to sweet milk desserts. It is also used to flavour India tea and coffee.

masala coffee

500 ml (2 cups) milk
2 tablespoons sugar
2 cm (3/4 inch) piece of ginger
2 tablespoons freshly ground Keralan or other coffee
5 cardamom seeds, pounded
1 cinnamon stick
cocoa powder, to sprinkle

put the milk and sugar in a heavy-based saucepan, bring to the boil over low heat and keep at a low simmer.

dry-roast the ginger under a grill (broiler) for 1 minute on each side, then pound it a little in a mortar and pestle to crush it and release the juices. Add to the simmering milk with the coffee, cardamom and cinnamon. Cover and allow the flavourings to steep in the heat for 3 minutes.

strain off the dregs (the easiest way is to put the whole lot through a coffee plunger or very fine strainer), then pour the coffee from one jug to another in a steady stream. You need to hold the jugs far apart and repeat the process until the coffee begins to froth. Serve while still hot, garnished with a sprinkling of cocoa. Serves 4.

cassia

Cassia is a dried bark used in cooking as small pieces or in ground form. It has a taste similar to cinnamon, which can be used instead, but has less flavour and is harder and coarser. Cassia is used in Indian curries, and vegetable and rice dishes. The Chinese use it as an ingredient of Chinese five-spice powder.

The leaves of the cassia tree are used in Indian cooking and may be referred to as Indian bay leaves. They are usually sold dried. Cassia buds, sold dried with the stalk attached, are used in Indian cooking as a flavouring and in paan, a betel leaf parcel filled with nuts, seeds and spices.

Also known as —
Chinese cinnamon

beef and noodle hotpot

1 teaspoon oil
10 spring onions (scallions), cut into 4 cm (1 1/2 inch) lengths, lightly smashed with the flat side of a cleaver
10 garlic cloves, thinly sliced
6 slices ginger, smashed with the flat side of a cleaver
1 1/2 teaspoons chilli bean paste (toban jiang)
2 cassia or cinnamon sticks
2 star anise
125 ml (1/2 cup) light soy sauce
1 kg (2 lb 4 oz) chuck steak, trimmed and cut into 4 cm (1 1/2 inch) cubes
250 g (9 oz) rice stick noodles
250 g (9 oz) baby English spinach leaves
3 tablespoons finely chopped spring onion (scallion)

heat a wok over medium heat, add the oil and heat until hot. Stir-fry the spring onion, garlic, ginger, chilli paste, cassia and star anise for 10 seconds, or until fragrant. Transfer to a clay pot, casserole or saucepan. Add the soy sauce and 2.25 litres (9 cups) water. Bring to the boil, add the beef, then return to the boil. Reduce the heat and simmer, covered, for 1 1/2 hours, or until the beef is very tender. Skim the surface occasionally to remove any impurities and fat. Remove and discard the ginger and cassia.

soak the noodles in hot water for 10 minutes, then drain and divide among six bowls. Add the spinach to the beef and bring to the boil. Spoon the beef mixture over the noodles and sprinkle with the spring onion. Serves 6.

chaat masala

Chaat masala is a salty, tangy seasoning made up of cumin, salt, fennel seed, amchur, garam masala, asafoetida and chilli. Used in Indian dishes to season potato and vegetables, it can also be tossed through dry snack mixes or sprinkled onto fruit and vegetables as a seasoning.

chaat masala

4 tablespoons coriander seeds
2 tablespoons cumin seeds
1 teaspoon ajowan
3 tablespoons black salt (see note)
1 tablespoon amchur
2 dried chillies
1 teaspoon black peppercorns
1 teaspoon dried pomegranate seeds

place a small frying pan over low heat and dry-roast the coriander seeds until aromatic. Remove from the pan and dry-roast the cumin seeds, then, separately, the ajowan.

grind the roasted mixture to a fine powder with the other ingredients, using a spice grinder or mortar and pestle. Store in an airtight container. Makes 10 tablespoons.

note: Black salt is a rock salt mined in India and sold as black or dark brown lumps, or ground to a pinkish powder. Unlike white salt, it has a tangy, smoky flavour. Buy from Indian food shops.

To make the chaat masala, dry-roast the coriander and cumin seeds separately in a frying pan until they are aromatic.

Chillies belong to the Capsicum (pepper) family (the sweeter capsicums are not included here) and are native to South and Central America. They were taken by the Spanish and Portuguese to India and Southeast Asia, where they became integrated into local diets. Chilli is used in many forms—fresh, dried, powdered or made into sauces, oils and pastes for seasoning dishes such as soups, curries and stir-fries. Buy chillies that are uniform in colour and unbroken or the essential oils will be lost. Fresh chillies will be slightly flexible.

chillies

heat scale

Various methods can be used for measuring the heat in chillies including the Scoville scale, which ranges from grade 0 (sweet capsicum/pepper) to 300,000 (habanero), or a simple 1–10 (1 being the mildest) used by many supermarkets. No method is completely accurate, as chillies vary quite considerably, even those on the same bush.

Chillies are not merely hot: each has its own flavour and varies in its degree of 'hotness'. Although chillies are widely used throughout Asia, each country tends to use specific types of chillies for specific reasons. In Thailand, chillies are called phrik, and up to a dozen types appear in Thai cuisine despite the fact that the plant is not indigenous to the area. In Kashmir, in India's north, large red chillies are used in cooking more for their colour than for their heat, while southern Indian and Sri Lankan dishes are intensely hot. In Indonesia and Malaysia, larger, hotter chillies are preferred. In Indonesia, fresh chillies are mixed with vinegar and salt to make sambal oelek. Chillies are also used fresh and dried in Chinese cooking, but it is chilli oils, dried chilli flakes, and chilli pastes and sauces that are used extensively.

From left to right: red chillies; green and red 'bird's eye' or 'mouse dropping' chillies, the hottest chilli available in Thailand; orange chillies, rare outside Thailand, have a hot and sour flavour.

capsaicin

Chillies are hot because they contain an irritant alkaloid, a potent chemical that acts directly on the pain receptors in the throat and mouth to produce a burning sensation. The body reacts by secreting endorphins—these are natural painkillers that cause a physical 'high', thought to account for the addictiveness of eating chillies. Capsaicin is primarily found in the ribs (septa) and seeds of the chilli and is released when cut. Capsaicin is not very soluble in water (water does little to extinguish the heat) but is soluble in oil and alcohol (this is why milk, yoghurt and beer are good relief from the heat of curries).

cooking

When cutting chillies either wear rubber gloves or be very careful—don't put your hands near your face and wash your hands after handling them. Chilli oil remains on your skin for some time. If you do get chilli burn, run your hands under cold water and rub them against a stainless steel surface (the sink) or soak in milk. If you burn your mouth, eat dairy products or starchy foods.

Chilli will have different effects and flavours if used raw, roasted or dried. Roasting also gives a smoky flavour to the flesh. Drying chillies intensifies the flavour.

Cooking a whole chilli in a dish rather than chopping it will contain the heat somewhat. If in doubt about how hot your chilli is, use less than the recipe specifies: you can always add more. If the dish is too hot, add yoghurt, cream or coconut milk.

cutting and deseeding chillies

1 Wearing rubber gloves, cut the chillies in half and scrape out any seeds.

2 Cut away any septa (the fleshy membrane), then chop or slice the chillies.

In India, chillies are used to give food heat, colour and flavour. The most common chillies are the red and green finger-like chillies (left), which are also used dried, and have a medium heat. Mundu chillies (centre) are quite hot, but the tiny bird's eye chillies, also used in Thai cooking, are the hottest.

chilli oil

This oil, which is made by steeping red chillies in oil so they release their colour and flavour, has a hot and spicy taste. Chilli oil is used for brushing on or garnishing seafood and meat dishes. It can also be used in salad dressings, or drizzled onto soups and broths.

chilli oil

50 g (1¾ oz) dried chilli flakes
125 ml (½ cup) oil
60 ml (¼ cup) roasted sesame oil

put the chilli in a heatproof bowl. Put the oils in a saucepan and heat until they are very hot but not smoking. Pour onto the chilli and leave to cool. Try not to breathe in the fumes. When cool, transfer to a jar.

store the oil in the refrigerator for up to 6 months. The oil can be used as a flavouring, and the chilli at the bottom of the jar can be used instead of fresh chilli. Makes 200 ml (7 fl oz).

chilli powder

A wide variety of chillies are dried and crushed to make chilli powders. Some, for example, Kashmiri chilli powder and paprika, are used for colour, whereas others like cayenne are used for heat. Don't use chilli powder indiscriminately. The amount used can be varied, to taste, so start with a small amount and determine how hot it is.

chilli lamb cutlets

8 lamb cutlets
¼ teaspoon chilli powder
½ teaspoon ground turmeric
1 teaspoon garam masala
2 cm (¾ inch) piece of
   ginger, grated

1 garlic clove, crushed
1 tablespoon thick natural
   yoghurt
3 tablespoons lemon juice

trim the lamb of any fat and scrape the bone ends clean. Mix together the remaining ingredients to form a paste, adding a little of the lemon juice if necessary. Rub the paste over the cutlets, then cover and refrigerate for 2 hours, or overnight.

preheat the grill (broiler) to its highest setting or heat a chargrill pan (griddle) until very hot. Sprinkle the cutlets with salt on both sides and cook on each side for 2–3 minutes, or until browned and sizzling. Squeeze over the remaining lemon juice before serving. Makes 8.

chilli sauce

There are numerous kinds of chilli sauce used in Asian cooking. These range from thin dipping sauces to the thicker versions used in cooking. Chilli sauce is made from fresh chillies and a variety of other ingredients, such as garlic and vinegar.

After cooking, the chillies are mixed with salt, vinegar and sugar, then pushed through a sieve to make a chilli sauce (above).

singapore chilli crab

4 x 250 g (9 oz) live crabs
3 tablespoons oil
1 tablespoon Guilin chilli sauce, or any thick chilli sauce
2 tablespoons light soy sauce
3 teaspoons clear rice vinegar
4 tablespoons Shaoxing rice wine
1/2 teaspoon salt
2 tablespoons sugar
2 tablespoons chicken stock
1 tablespoon grated ginger
2 garlic cloves, crushed
2 spring onions (scallions), finely chopped

to kill the crabs humanely, put them in the freezer for 1 hour. Bring a large saucepan of water to the boil. Plunge the crabs into boiling water for about 1 minute, then rinse in cold water. Twist off and discard the upper shell, and remove and discard the spongy grey gill tissue from inside the crab. Rinse the bodies and drain well. Cut away the last two hairy joints of the legs. Cut each crab into four to six pieces, cutting so that a portion of the body is attached to one or two legs. Crack the claws using crab crackers or the back edge of a cleaver—this will help the flavouring penetrate the crab meat.

heat a wok over high heat, add 1 tablespoon of the oil and heat until very hot. Add half the crab and fry for several minutes to cook the meat right through. Remove and drain. Repeat with another tablespoon of the oil and the remaining crab.

combine the chilli sauce, soy sauce, rice vinegar, rice wine, salt, sugar and stock.

reheat the wok over high heat, add the remaining oil and heat until very hot. Stir-fry the ginger, garlic and spring onion for 10 seconds. Add the sauce mixture to the wok and cook briefly. Add the crab pieces and toss lightly to coat with the sauce. Cook, covered, for 5 minutes, then serve immediately. Serves 4.

note: Crab is best eaten with your hands, so supply finger bowls as well as special picks to help remove the meat from the crab claws.

chinese keys

steamed clams and mussels with chinese keys

450 g (1 lb) mixed clams and mussels in the shell
75 g (2½ oz) Chinese keys, finely sliced
2.5 cm (1 inch) piece of galangal, cut into 7–8 slices
1 long red chilli, seeded and finely chopped
2 teaspoons fish sauce
½ teaspoon sugar
basil leaves, for garnish

scrub the mussels and clams and remove any hairy beards from the mussels. Discard any open mussels or clams and any that don't close when tapped on the work surface. Wash them all in several changes of cold water until the water is clear, then put them in a large bowl, cover with cold water and soak for 30 minutes. This helps remove the sand from the clams.

put the clams and mussels, Chinese keys, galangal and chopped chilli in a large saucepan or wok. Cover loosely and cook over medium heat for 5 minutes, shaking the pan frequently.

add the fish sauce and sugar to the wok and toss together. Discard any unopened shells. Serve the steamed clams and mussels in a large bowl and garnish with basil leaves. Serves 2.

A member of the ginger family, Chinese keys is a root vegetable with thick, tapering beige roots that grow in a cluster, resembling a bunch of keys. Its spicy flavouring is used mainly with seafood, and also in curries and pickles in Thai and Indonesian cooking. It may also be ground and used as a powder. As well as being sold fresh, Chinese keys is sold preserved in brine in jars in Asian supermarkets.

Also known as — kachai, krachai

cinnamon

Black tea (chai) is drunk every day in India. Here, the chai is made with milk, sugar and a blend of spices, known as masala.

The cinnamon tree is native to Sri Lanka and it is the inner bark that is used, dried and sold as cinnamon quills or sticks. Cinnamon adds sweetness and warmth to dishes, often added whole to milk puddings, curries, pulao rice and pickles. Ground or powdered cinnamon is used in baking and desserts. Cassia bark is sometimes sold under the name of cinnamon, but true cinnamon is much paler and made up of very fine paper-like layers within the quill. Buy ground cinnamon in small quantities as it quickly loses its flavour once the jar is opened, or buy whole cinnamon quills and grate it as needed.

masala chai

2 cm (³/4 inch) piece of ginger
5 cm (2 inch) piece of
  cinnamon stick
4 peppercorns
3 cloves
3 cardamom pods
1 tablespoon black Indian tea
250 ml (1 cup) milk
3 tablespoons sugar

dry-roast the ginger under a grill (broiler) for 1 minute each side. Put the spices and ginger in a mortar and pestle and roughly crush them. Put the spices, tea and milk in a saucepan with 1 litre (4 cups) water and bring to the boil. Leave for 3 minutes, then add the sugar, to taste.

strain off the dregs (the easiest way is to put the whole lot through a coffee plunger or very fine strainer), then pour the tea from one jug to another. You need to hold the jugs far apart and repeat the process until the tea begins to froth. Serve while still hot, in glasses. Serves 6.

indonesian rendang

1.5 kg (3 lb 5 oz) chuck steak
2 onions, roughly chopped
4 teaspoons crushed garlic
410 ml (1²/₃ cups) coconut
   milk
2 teaspoons ground coriander
½ teaspoon ground fennel
2 teaspoons ground cumin

¼ teaspoon ground cloves
4 red chillies, chopped
1 stem lemon grass (white
   part only)
1 tablespoon lemon juice
2 teaspoons grated palm
   sugar

trim the meat of any fat and sinew, and cut it evenly into small 3 cm (1¼ inch) cubes.

put the onion and garlic in a food processor and process until smooth, adding water if necessary.

put the coconut milk in a large pan and bring it to the boil, then reduce the heat to moderate and cook, stirring occasionally, until the milk has reduced by half and the oil has separated out. Do not allow the milk to brown.

add the ground coriander, fennel, cumin and cloves and stir for 1 minute. Add the meat and cook for 2 minutes until it changes colour. Add the onion mixture, chilli, lemon grass, lemon juice and sugar. Cook over medium heat for about 2 hours, or until the liquid is reduced and the mixture is quite thick. Stir frequently to prevent it catching on the bottom of the pan.

continue cooking until the oil from the coconut milk begins to emerge again, letting the curry develop colour and flavour. The dish needs constant attention at this stage to prevent it from burning. The curry is cooked when it is brown and dry. Serves 6.

note: Like most curries, this one benefits from being made ahead of time to allow the flavours to mature. Prepare 2–3 days in advance and store, covered, in the refrigerator. Reheat over low heat. The curry can also be completely cooled in the refrigerator and then frozen for 1 month.

cloves

Cloves are the dried aromatic unopened flower buds of an evergreen myrtle tree, which is native to the Moluccas (the Indonesian 'Spice Islands'). Cloves have a very distinctive and powerful flavour and aroma, so should be used carefully as they can overpower the other flavours in the dish. In India, they are used in curries, rice dishes, pickles and in some sweet dishes. They are also added to blended spice mixtures. Cloves are available whole and ground.

coriander

coriander leaves

Coriander is used extensively in Southeast Asian cookery (except in Japan), most notably in Thailand. Coriander is an aromatic herb with a fresh, distinctive flavour and its bright green leaves give both colour and flavour to salads, are used as a garnish, and are added to both Indian and Thai curries.

Also known as — cilantro

coriander seeds

These small round seeds have a spicy aroma and a mild lemon flavour. They are used in Malaysian, Indonesian and Indian cooking, especially in curries or spice mixes such as garam masala. To intensify the flavour, lightly dry-roast the whole seeds until they are aromatic, then crush them.

spicy vietnamese beef and pork noodle soup

put the beef in the freezer for 20–30 minutes, or until partially frozen, then cut into paper-thin slices across the grain. Set aside.

heat a wok until hot, add 1 tablespoon of the oil and swirl to coat the side of the wok. Stir-fry the pork in batches for 2–3 minutes, or until browned. Remove from the wok. Add another tablespoon of oil and stir-fry the onion for 2–3 minutes, or until softened. Pour in the stock and 500 ml (2 cups) water. Bruise one of the lemon grass stems and add it to the wok.

return the pork to the wok and bring the liquid to the boil, then reduce the heat and simmer for 15 minutes, or until the pork is tender, skimming off any scum that rises to the surface. Meanwhile, thinly slice the white part of the remaining lemon grass stem.

remove the whole lemon grass stem from the broth and stir in the fish sauce, dried shrimp and sugar and keep at a simmer.

heat the remaining oil in a small frying pan over medium heat and cook the sliced lemon grass and chilli for 2–3 minutes, or until fragrant. Stir into the broth. Just before serving, bring the broth to the boil over medium–high heat.

put the rice noodles in a large heatproof bowl, cover with boiling water and gently separate the noodles. Drain immediately and rinse. Divide the noodles among four warm serving bowls. Top with the bean sprouts and cover with the boiling broth. Add the beef to the soup—the heat of the soup will cook it. Sprinkle with the mint and coriander, and fresh chilli, if desired. Serve immediately with some wedges of lemon. Serves 4.

300 g (10½ oz) beef fillet
  steak
60 ml (¼ cup) vegetable oil
300 g (10½ oz) pork leg
  fillet, cut into 3 cm
  (1¼ inch) cubes
1 large onion, cut into thin
  wedges
2 litres (8 cups) good-quality
  beef stock
2 stems lemon grass
2 tablespoons fish sauce
1 teaspoon ground dried
  shrimp
1 teaspoon sugar
2 large red chillies, sliced
400 g (14 oz) fresh round
  rice noodles
175 g (6 oz) soya bean
  sprouts, tailed
10 g (½ cup) mint leaves
15 g (½ cup) coriander
  (cilantro) leaves
thinly sliced chilli, to serve
  (optional)
lemon wedges, to serve

coriander roots

Coriander (cilantro) roots are an essential ingredient in much of Thai cooking, particularly where the flavour is wanted but not the bright green colour of the leaves. The roots are pounded and used as an ingredient in curry pastes (coriander stems are used when a strong flavour is needed).

thai hot and sour soup with mixed seafood

600 g (1 lb 5 oz) mixed fresh seafood such as raw prawns (shrimp), squid tubes, mussels, white fish fillets and scallops
1 litre (4 cups) vegetable stock
3 x 4 cm (1½ inch) lemon grass stalks, white part only, bruised
6 coriander (cilantro) roots, bruised
2–2½ tablespoons fish sauce
1½–2 tablespoons ready-made Chiang Mai curry paste, or 2 dried red chillies, soaked, drained and finely chopped
2–3 bird's eye chillies, bruised
2 Asian shallots, smashed with the flat side of a cleaver
110 g (4 oz) straw or mixed mushrooms, left whole if small, or quartered if large
150 g (5½ oz) baby tomatoes (about 12) or medium tomatoes, each cut into 6 pieces
8 makrut (kaffir) lime leaves, torn
3 tablespoons lime juice

peel and devein the prawns and cut each prawn along the back so it opens like a butterfly (leave each prawn joined along the base and at the tail).

peel off any skin from the squid tubes, rinse the insides and cut the tubes into 5 mm (¼ inch) rings. If the squid are very big, cut them in half, open the tubes and slightly score the inside of each squid with diagonal cuts to make a diamond pattern. Cut the tubes into pieces about 2 cm (¾ inch) square. Remove any dark veins from the scallops.

scrub the mussels and remove their hairy beards. Discard any open mussels and any that don't close when tapped on the work surface. Cut the fish into 2 cm (¾ inch) cubes.

put the stock, lemon grass, coriander roots, fish sauce, curry paste and chillies in a large saucepan and bring to a boil.

reduce the heat to medium, add the seafood and continue to cook for 2–3 minutes. (If using cooked mussels, add them after the tomatoes.) Add the shallots, mushrooms, baby tomatoes, makrut lime leaves and cook for another 2–3 minutes, taking care not to let the tomatoes lose their shape. Taste, add the lime juice, then adjust the seasoning if necessary. Spoon into a serving bowl. Serves 4.

cumin

punjabi cabbage

½ onion, roughly chopped
1 garlic clove, roughly
  chopped
2.5 cm (1 inch) piece of
  ginger, chopped
2 green chillies, seeded and
  chopped
4 tablespoons oil
1 teaspoon cumin seeds
1 teaspoon ground turmeric

500 g (1 lb 2 oz) green
  cabbage, finely shredded
1 teaspoon salt
½ teaspoon ground black
  pepper
2 teaspoons ground cumin
1 teaspoon ground coriander
¼ teaspoon chilli powder
20 g (¾ oz) unsalted butter

put the onion, garlic, ginger and chilli in a food processor and whiz until finely chopped but not a paste, or chop together with a knife.

heat the oil in a heavy-based frying pan over low heat and fry the onion mixture until softened but not browned. Add the cumin seeds and turmeric to the pan and stir for 1 minute. Mix in the cabbage, stirring thoroughly until all the leaves are coated in the yellow paste.

add the salt, pepper, ground cumin, coriander and chilli powder. Stir to coat the cabbage, then cook for 10 minutes with the pan partially covered, stirring occasionally until the cabbage is soft. If the cabbage becomes too dry and starts sticking to the pan, add 1–2 tablespoons water. Stir in the butter and season with salt, to taste. Serves 4.

These small, pale brown aromatic seeds (below, left) have a warm and earthy but slightly bitter flavour. Black cumin (below, right) is smaller than the common cumin and is sweeter in taste. Cumin is used whole and ground in many cuisines, but particularly in Indian cooking in rice dishes, curries, yoghurt and in some spice mixes. Light dry-roasting of the seeds releases their aroma. Cumin is best freshly ground for each dish.

Dark, shiny green leaves that look a little like bay leaves but have a distinctive curry flavour, curry leaves are used in southern Indian and Malaysian cooking. The leaves are added to dishes during cooking or used as a garnish. Unless the number of leaves are specified in a recipe, the whole stalk can be added to the dish (be careful if frying the fresh leaves in hot oil, as they have a tendency to spatter). Available fresh or dried from Indian food shops.

molee

1 tablespoon oil	**6 curry leaves**
1 large onion, thinly sliced	**400 ml (14 fl oz) coconut milk**
3 garlic cloves, crushed	**1/2 teaspoon salt**
2 small green chillies, finely chopped	**600 g (1 lb 5 oz) pomfret, sole or leatherjacket fillets, skinned**
2 teaspoons ground turmeric	
1 teaspoon ground coriander	**1 tablespoon chopped coriander (cilantro) leaves**
1 teaspoon ground cumin	
4 cloves	**curry leaves, extra, for garnish**

heat the oil in a deep, heavy-based frying pan, add the onion and cook for 5 minutes. Add the garlic and chilli and cook for another 5 minutes, or until the onion has softened and looks translucent. Add the turmeric, coriander, cumin and cloves and stir-fry with the onion for 2 minutes. Stir in the curry leaves, coconut milk and salt and bring to just below boiling point. Reduce the heat and simmer for 20 minutes.

cut each fish fillet into two or three large pieces and add them to the sauce. Bring the sauce back to a simmer and cook for 5 minutes, or until the fish is cooked through and flakes easily. Check the seasoning, add more salt if necessary, then stir in the coriander leaves. Garnish with the curry leaves. Serves 6.

curry leaf

Molee is a rich creamy dish popular in Kerala on India's west coast where it is made with local fish.

Dang gui is a slightly bitter Chinese herb used in Chinese soups or added to braises. It is also valued for its medicinal properties—it is thought to restore vitality. Dang gui is the root of the angelica plant. It can be found in Chinese shops and herbalists and looks like small bleached pieces of wood.

dang gui

yunnan pot chicken

25 jujubes
1.5 kg (3 lb 5 oz) chicken
6 wafer-thin slices dang gui
6 slices ginger, smashed with the flat side of a cleaver
6 spring onions (scallions), ends trimmed, smashed with the flat side of a cleaver
60 ml (¼ cup) Shaoxing rice wine
½ teaspoon salt

soak the jujubes in hot water for 20 minutes, then drain and remove the stones.

rinse the chicken, drain, and remove any fat from the cavity opening and around the neck. Cut off and discard the parson's nose. Using a cleaver, cut the chicken through the bones into square 4 cm (1½ inch) pieces. Blanch the chicken pieces in a pan of boiling water for 1 minute, then refresh in cold water and drain thoroughly.

arrange the chicken pieces, jujubes, dang gui, ginger and spring onions in a clay pot or casserole about 24 cm (9½ inches) in diameter. Pour the rice wine and 1 litre (4 cups) boiling water over the top and add the salt. Cover the pot tightly, adding a layer of wet muslin between the pot and lid to form a good seal, and put it in a steamer.

steam over simmering water in a covered wok for about 2 hours, replenishing with boiling water during cooking. Remove the pot from the steamer and skim any fat from the surface of the liquid. Discard the dang gui, ginger and spring onions. Taste and season if necessary. Serve directly from the pot. Serves 6.

dill

Dill is a herb with delicate feathery leaves that have an aniseed flavour and aroma. The leaves are used both fresh and dried, often to flavour vegetables such as potatoes, meat, fish and lentil dishes. Dill seeds are used in Indian curries, particularly those with fish. Fresh dill is used in some Indonesian, Laotian, Thai and Vietnamese dishes.

shebu bhaji

200 g (7 oz) potatoes
200 g (7 oz) dill
2 tablespoons oil
2 garlic cloves, chopped
1/4 teaspoon ground turmeric
1 teaspoon black mustard seeds
pinch of asafoetida
1 dried chilli

cut the potatoes into 2.5 cm (1 inch) cubes and cook in a saucepan of simmering water for 15 minutes, or until just tender. Drain well.

wash the dill in several changes of water and trim off the tough stalks. Roughly chop the dill.

heat the oil in a heavy-based saucepan, add the garlic and fry for 30 seconds over low heat. Add the turmeric, mustard seeds, asafoetida and the whole chilli, cover and briefly allow the seeds to pop. Stir in the potato until well mixed. Add the dill, cover and cook over low heat for 5 minutes. The dill contains sufficient moisture to cook without the addition of any water. Season with salt, to taste. Serves 2.

Dill can be used in abundance, as it is in this Indian dish (right), without being too overpowering. Indian dill (above) is similar to European dill, and they are interchangeable in this recipe.

lamb madras

**1 kg (2 lb 4 oz) boneless leg or shoulder of lamb,
    cut into 2.5 cm (1 inch) cubes**
1½ teaspoons ground turmeric
2 tablespoons coriander seeds
2 teaspoons cumin seeds
10 dried chillies
12 curry leaves, plus extra, for garnish
10 garlic cloves, roughly chopped
5 cm (2 inch) piece of ginger, roughly chopped
1 teaspoon fennel seeds
1 tablespoon tamarind purée
4 tablespoons oil or ghee
3 large onions, sliced
625 ml (2½ cups) coconut milk
8 cm (3 inch) piece of cinnamon stick
6 cardamom pods

rub the cubed lamb with the turmeric. Place a small frying pan over low heat and dry-roast the coriander seeds until aromatic. Remove and dry-roast the cumin seeds, then repeat with the chillies. Grind them all to a powder using a mortar and pestle or spice grinder. Add six of the curry leaves, the garlic and ginger and grind to a paste. Dry-roast the fennel seeds in the pan until they are brown and start to pop. Dissolve the tamarind in 125 ml (½ cup) hot water.

heat the oil or ghee in a casserole dish over low heat and fry the onion for 5–10 minutes until soft. Add the chilli paste and cook for a few minutes, or until aromatic. Add the meat and toss to mix with the paste. Add 500 ml (2 cups) of the coconut milk and 60 ml (¼ cup) water. Bring to the boil and simmer over medium heat for 10 minutes, or until the liquid has reduced.

add the remaining coconut milk, cinnamon stick, cardamom pods and whole fennel seeds. Season. Cook, partially covered, over medium heat for 1 hour, or until the meat is tender, stirring occasionally. Add the tamarind and check the seasoning. Stir until the oil separates out from the meat, then spoon it off or blot with paper towels before removing the pan from the heat.

stir well and add the remaining six curry leaves. Garnish with more curry leaves. Serves 6.

fennel seeds

Originally from southern Europe but now grown worldwide, fennel seeds have a slight liquorice or aniseed taste. To intensify the flavour, dry-roast the seeds before crushing them. Use in stuffings, salads, fish and seafood dishes. A popular spice in the Indian kitchen, the seeds are also added to curries, pickles and chutneys, or are offered after an Indian meal as a palate cleanser, sometimes coated in sugar or edible silver leaf. Fennel is also available ground.

fenugreek seeds

Fenugreek is not a true seed, but a dried legume. Ochre in colour, fenugreek has a curry aroma (it is a major ingredient in commercial curry powders) and a slightly bitter flavour. Fenugreek is a popular flavouring in Indian curries, and is also used in breads, chutneys and lentil dishes. The seeds are sold whole or ground into a powder. Fenugreek leaves, called *methi* in India, may be used fresh, or dried and ground.

goan beef curry

8 cardamom pods
1 teaspoon fennel seeds
8 cloves
10 cm (4 inch) piece of
   cinnamon stick
½ teaspoon fenugreek seeds
½ teaspoon ground black
   pepper
3 teaspoons coriander seeds
3 teaspoons cumin seeds
125 ml (½ cup) oil
2 onions, finely chopped
6 garlic cloves, finely chopped

10 cm (4 inch) piece of ginger,
   grated
1 kg (2 lb 4 oz) braising or
   stewing steak, cut into
   2.5 cm (1 inch) cubes
½ teaspoon ground turmeric
2 teaspoons chilli powder
100 g (3½ oz) creamed
   coconut, dissolved in
   300 ml (10½ fl oz) water,
   or 300 ml (10½ fl oz)
   coconut milk

remove the seeds from the cardamom pods and grind them in a spice grinder or mortar and pestle with the fennel seeds, cloves, cinnamon stick, fenugreek seeds, black pepper and the coriander and cumin seeds, until they form a fine powder.

heat the oil in a heavy-based frying pan or casserole dish over medium heat and fry the onion, garlic and ginger until lightly browned. Add the meat and fry until brown all over. Add all the spices and fry for 1 minute. Add the creamed coconut and bring slowly to the boil. Cover, reduce the heat and simmer for about 1 hour, or until the meat is tender.

if the liquid evaporates during cooking, add about 200 ml (7 fl oz) boiling water and stir to make a thick sauce. If the sauce is too liquid at the end of the cooking time, simmer with the lid off until it evaporates. Season with salt, to taste. Serves 6.

spicy salt and pepper spareribs

1 kg (2 lb 4 oz) Chinese-style pork spareribs
1 egg, beaten
2–3 tablespoons plain (all-purpose) flour
oil, for deep-frying
2 spring onions (scallions), finely chopped
2 small red chillies, finely chopped

marinade
½ teaspoon ground Sichuan peppercorns
½ teaspoon five-spice powder
½ teaspoon salt
1 tablespoon light soy sauce
1 tablespoon Shaoxing rice wine
¼ teaspoon roasted sesame oil

ask the butcher to cut the slab of spareribs crosswise into thirds that measure 4–5 cm (1½–2 inches) in length, or use a cleaver to do so yourself. Cut the ribs between the bones to separate them.

to make the marinade, combine the ingredients in a bowl. Add the ribs and toss lightly. Marinate in the refrigerator for at least 3 hours, or overnight.

mix the egg, flour and a little water to form a smooth batter the consistency of thick (double/heavy) cream. Fill a wok one-quarter full of oil. Heat the oil to 180°C (350°F), or until a piece of bread fries golden brown in 15 seconds. Dip the ribs in the batter and fry in batches for 5 minutes until they are crisp and golden, stirring to separate them, then remove and drain. Reheat the oil and fry the ribs for 1 minute to darken their colour. Remove and drain on paper towels.

soak the spring onion and chilli in the hot oil (with the heat off) for 2 minutes. Remove with a wire strainer or slotted spoon and sprinkle over the ribs. Serves 4.

five-spice powder

Of Chinese origin, five-spice powder consists of equal parts of Sichuan pepper, cinnamon or cassia, fennel seeds, star anise and cloves, to give a balance of sweet, hot and aromatic flavours. Use it either ground together as a powder or as whole spices tied in muslin. Five-spice powder is used in Chinese cooking in stir-fries, pork and beef dishes.

galangal

Galangal root is similar in appearance to its close relative ginger, but it is a pinkish colour and has a distinctive peppery flavour. Galangal is used in Southeast Asian cooking, especially in Thailand, Indonesia and Malaysia. When handling, take care not to get the juice on your clothes or hands as it stains. Dried galangal, sold in slices, must be soaked in hot water before it can be used. Galangal can also be bought sliced and bottled in brine, but is best used fresh whenever possible.

chicken, coconut and galangal soup

750 ml (3 cups) coconut milk
2 stems lemon grass, white part only, bruised
5 cm (2 inch) piece of galangal, cut into several pieces
4 Asian shallots, smashed with the flat side of a cleaver
400 g (14 oz) skinless chicken breast fillets, cut into slices
2 tablespoons fish sauce
1 tablespoon palm sugar
200 g (7 oz) baby tomatoes

150 g (5 1/2 oz) straw mushrooms or button mushrooms
3 tablespoons lime juice
6 makrut (kaffir) lime leaves, torn in half
3–5 bird's eye chillies, stems removed, bruised, or 2 long red chillies, seeded and finely sliced
a few coriander (cilantro) leaves, for garnish

put the coconut milk, lemon grass, galangal and shallots in a saucepan or wok over medium heat and bring to the boil. Add the chicken, fish sauce and palm sugar and simmer, stirring constantly, for 5 minutes, or until the chicken is cooked through.

add the tomatoes and mushrooms and simmer for 2–3 minutes, taking care not to let the tomatoes lose their shape. Add the lime juice, makrut lime leaves and chillies in the last few seconds. Taste, then adjust the seasoning if necessary. This dish is meant not to be overwhelmingly hot, but to have a sweet, salty, sour taste. Serve garnished with coriander leaves. Serves 4.

garam masala

Garam masala is a northern Indian mix of spices and the name means 'warming spice mixture'. There are many versions, which may include coriander seeds, chilli, black pepper, cinnamon, and fennel, cumin and cardamom seeds. Garam masala is usually added to meat dishes at the end of cooking as a final seasoning. Grind the spices yourself or buy a ready-made mix.

garam masala

remove the seeds from the cardamom pods. Break the cassia leaves into small pieces. Put them in a spice grinder or mortar and pestle with the remaining spices and grind to a fine powder. Store in a small airtight container until needed. Makes 3 tablespoons.

8 cardamom pods
2 cassia leaves (Indian bay leaves)
1 teaspoon black peppercorns
2 teaspoons cumin seeds
2 teaspoons coriander seeds
5 cm (2 inch) piece of cinnamon stick
1 teaspoon cloves

garlic

cooking

Raw garlic is more potent than cooked. When garlic is cooked, some of the starch converts to sugar, which makes the garlic less pungent.

Be careful not to overbrown or burn garlic as it can become very bitter.

Chopping or crushing garlic releases the flavours.

Flavour oil for stir-frying by frying slices of garlic in oil, then discard the slices.

Garlic is a strongly flavoured bulbous herb from the same family as the onion and the leek. Each 'head' of garlic is made up of a cluster of 10 to 16 cloves, and both head and individual bulbs are covered with a paper-like skin. There are many varieties, differing in size, pungency and colour. Garlic is a popular seasoning in many Asian countries, with the exception of Japan, where it is not often used. The Chinese use garlic in almost every dish; the Thais use it in curry pastes; the Indians, in curries; the Koreans are fond of garlic, and use it in such dishes as kim chi, pickled cabbage heavily flavoured with chilli and garlic.

Garlic is freshest in the summer when the bulbs are firm and the cloves are harder to peel. Later in the season, the garlic begins to dry out—it is easier to peel but the flavour is quite intense. Choose fresh, plump-looking garlic with a white skin and fat neck as these have a more delicate flavour; discoloured garlic or bulbs that are sprouting will have a rancid flavour. When cooking with garlic, don't be tempted to use more than the specified amount, as garlic will overpower the other flavours in the dish.

Whole garlic bulbs, garlic oil and young garlic (centre).

garlic and ginger prawns

2 tablespoons oil
1 kg (2 lb 4 oz) raw king prawns (shrimp), peeled, deveined, tails intact
3–4 garlic cloves, chopped
5 cm (2 inch) piece of ginger, cut into matchsticks
2–3 small red chillies, seeded and finely chopped
6 coriander (cilantro) roots, finely chopped
8 spring onions (scallions), cut diagonally into short lengths

½ red capsicum (pepper), thinly sliced
2 tablespoons lemon juice
125 ml (½ cup) white wine
2 teaspoons crushed palm sugar
2 teaspoons fish sauce
10 g (⅓ cup) coriander (cilantro) leaves, for garnish

heat the wok until very hot, add the oil and swirl it around to coat the side. Stir-fry half of the prawns, garlic, ginger, chilli and coriander root for 1–2 minutes over high heat, or until the prawns have just turned pink. Repeat with the remaining prawns, garlic, ginger, chilli and coriander root. Remove all of the prawns from the wok and set aside.

add the spring onion and capsicum to the wok. Cook over high heat for 2–3 minutes. Add the combined lemon juice, wine and palm sugar. Cook until the liquid has reduced by two-thirds.

return the prawns to the wok and sprinkle with the fish sauce, to taste. Toss until the prawns are heated through. Remove from the heat and serve sprinkled with coriander leaves. Serves 4.

ginger

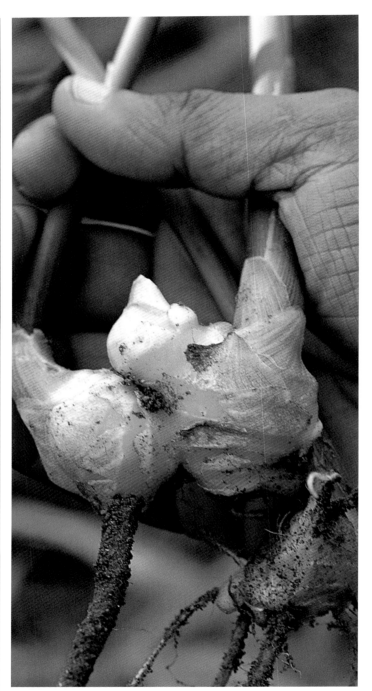

ginger juice

To make ginger juice, grate a 5 cm (2 inch) piece of ginger into a bowl. Wrap the ginger in a piece of muslin, twist it up tightly and squeeze out all the juice. Makes 2 tablespoons.

The knobbly, beige-coloured rhizome of a tropical plant, ginger is indigenous to Southeast Asia, but is now grown all over the world in tropical climates. It was originally used in Europe in powdered, dried, crystallized or preserved form, but as the popularity of Chinese, Indian, Middle Eastern and Caribbean cooking spread, ginger became increasingly available and it can now be bought fresh year-round. Store fresh ginger in the refrigerator tightly wrapped in plastic. Unless very fresh, ginger is usually first peeled, then grated or sliced. If it's fibrous, it is easier to grate it, preferably with a bamboo or ceramic grater.

types of ginger

fresh Best when young and juicy—the root is covered in a tender skin and has a sweet, peppery flavour. As it gets older, the flavour strengthens but the flesh becomes fibrous. Add to curries or Asian dishes.

ground (powdered) Not often used in Asian cooking, although sometimes seen in some Indian sweet and sour dishes.

preserved (candied) These are pieces of ginger that have been boiled in sugar syrup to preserve them.

pickled Sliced pieces of young ginger, pickled and often dyed pink. They are eaten as a palate cleanser between pieces of sushi.

mioga A relative of ginger used for its fragrant buds and stems. Sliced thinly and used as a garnish, or to flavour soups, tempura and sashimi.

cantonese-style steamed fish

750 g–1 kg (1 lb 10 oz–2 lb 4 oz) whole fish, such as carp, bream or sea bass, scaled and cleaned
2 tablespoons Shaoxing rice wine
1½ tablespoons light soy sauce
1 tablespoon finely chopped ginger
1 teaspoon roasted sesame oil
2 tablespoons oil
2 spring onions (scallions), finely shredded
3 tablespoons finely shredded ginger
¼ teaspoon freshly ground black pepper

rinse the fish under cold running water, pat dry with paper towels, then place it in a large bowl. Add the rice wine, soy sauce, chopped ginger and sesame oil, and toss lightly to coat. Cover with plastic wrap and leave to marinate in the refrigerator for 10 minutes.

arrange the fish on a heatproof plate, with the marinade, and put in a steamer. Steam over simmering water in a covered wok for 5–8 minutes, or until the fish flakes when the skin is pressed firmly or the dorsal fin pulls out easily. Remove the fish from the steamer and place on a heatproof platter.

heat a wok over high heat, add the oil and heat until smoking. Sprinkle the fish with the spring onion, shredded ginger and pepper, and slowly pour the hot oil over the fish. This will cause the skin to crisp, and cook the garnish. Serves 4.

From top: fresh ginger, ground (powdered) ginger, preserved ginger, pickled ginger, mioga.

kokum

Kokum is the dried purple fruit of the gamboge tree. It is used in Indian cuisine to impart an acid fruity flavour, and is often used in Indian curries made with coconut milk. Kokum looks like dried pieces of purplish-black rind and is quite sticky. It can be bought from Indian food shops. Soak briefly before use.

**Also known as —
kokam**

fish with kokum

3 x 5 cm (2 inch) pieces kokum or 2 tablespoons
  tamarind purée
4 ripe tomatoes
2 tablespoons oil
1 teaspoon black mustard seeds
1/2 teaspoon fenugreek seeds
3 cm (1 1/4 inch) piece of ginger, grated
4 green chillies, slit in half
1 garlic clove, crushed
2 onions, sliced
1 teaspoon ground turmeric
1 tablespoon ground coriander
250 ml (1 cup) coconut milk
800 g (1 lb 12 oz) skinless pomfret, sole or leatherjacket
  fillets, cut into large chunks
1 stalk of curry leaves

rinse the kokum, remove any stones and put the kokum in a bowl with cold water for a few minutes to soften. Meanwhile, score a cross in the top of each tomato. Plunge them into boiling water for 20 seconds, then drain and peel away the skin from the cross. Roughly chop the tomatoes, discarding the cores and seeds and reserving any juices.

remove the kokum from the water and slice it into pieces.

heat the oil over low heat in a deep, heavy-based frying pan, add the mustard seeds and cook until they start to pop. Add the fenugreek, ginger, chilli, garlic and onion and fry until the onion is soft. Add the turmeric and coriander and fry for 2 minutes. Add the coconut milk, tomato and kokum, bring to the boil and simmer for 5 minutes.

add the fish to the liquid and simmer for 2–3 minutes or until the fish flakes easily and is cooked through. Season with salt, to taste, and add the curry leaves. Serves 6.

lemon grass

lemon grass chicken skewers

4 chicken thigh fillets
1¹⁄₂ tablespoons soft brown sugar
1¹⁄₂ tablespoons lime juice
2 teaspoons ready-made green curry paste
18 makrut (kaffir) lime leaves
2 stems lemon grass

mango salsa

1 small mango, finely diced
1 teaspoon grated lime zest
2 teaspoons lime juice
1 teaspoon soft brown sugar
¹⁄₂ teaspoon fish sauce

discard any excess fat from the chicken fillets and cut them in half lengthways. Combine the brown sugar, lime juice, curry paste and 2 of the lime leaves, shredded, in a bowl. Add the chicken and mix well. Cover and refrigerate for several hours, or overnight.

trim the lemon grass to measure about 20 cm (8 inches), leaving the root end intact. Cut each lengthways into four pieces. Cut a slit in each of the remaining lime leaves and thread one onto each skewer. Cut two slits in the chicken and thread onto the lemon grass, followed by another lime leaf. Repeat with the remaining lime leaves, chicken and lemon grass. Pan-fry or barbecue until cooked through.

to make the mango salsa, put all the ingredients in a bowl and stir gently to combine. Serve with the chicken skewers. Serves 4.

With its subtle lemon flavour and fragrance, lemon grass adds a refreshing taste to many Thai and other Southeast Asian dishes. Strip off the tough outer layers until you reach the purple ring, then use whole in soups by lightly bruising the stems (remove before serving); finely chop the white part and use in curry pastes; or use whole as skewers for cooking meat, prawns (shrimp) and chicken.

Wrap in plastic and store in the refrigerator for 1–2 weeks. Lemon grass can also be bought dried in sticks or in powdered form, when it is called sereh powder. If lemon grass is unavailable, use grated lemon zest instead.

makrut lime leaves

These glossy, fragrant leaves are uniquely shaped in a figure of eight, and are widely used in Thai and Southeast Asian cooking. Finely shredded, the leaves are added to soups, curries and chilli dishes to give them a wonderful tangy flavour and aroma. To chop the leaves, stack two or three fresh leaves in a pile. Roll the leaves from tip to stem into a tight bundle, then slice finely. Discard the tough central stem. Whole leaves can be simmered in dishes but remove before serving as they are tough. They are sold fresh or dried from Asian supermarkets. If they are unavailable, use young lime leaves. See also makrut (kaffir) lime, page 180.

spicy ground duck

1 tablespoon jasmine rice
280 g (10 oz) minced (ground) duck
3 tablespoons lime juice
1 tablespoon fish sauce
2 stems lemon grass, white part only, finely sliced
50 g (1¾ oz) Asian shallots, finely sliced
5 makrut (kaffir) lime leaves, finely sliced
5 spring onions (scallions), finely chopped
¼–½ teaspoon roasted chilli powder, according to taste
a few lettuce leaves
a few mint leaves, for garnish
raw vegetables such as snake beans, cut into lengths, cucumber slices, thin wedges of cabbage, halved baby tomatoes, to serve

dry-fry the rice in a small pan over medium heat. Shake the pan to move the rice around for 6–8 minutes, or until the rice is brown. Using a mortar and pestle or a small blender, pound or blend the rice until it almost forms a powder.

in a saucepan or wok, cook the duck with the lime juice and fish sauce over a high heat. With the back of a spoon, crumble and break up the duck until the meat has separated into small pieces. Cook until light brown. Dry, then remove from the heat.

add the rice powder, lemon grass, shallots, makrut lime leaves, spring onions and chilli powder to the duck and stir together. Taste, then adjust the seasoning if necessary.

line a serving plate with lettuce leaves. Spoon the duck over the leaves, then garnish with mint leaves. Arrange the vegetables on a separate dish. Serves 4.

Also known as — kaffir lime leaves

mint

This dark green herb has a strong, fresh flavour. Of the many mint varieties, peppermint and spearmint are the most widely used. The leaves are often used as a garnish, or as an ingredient in Asian salads, drinks, ice creams or iced teas. In India, fresh mint is often accompanied with yoghurt as a fresh chutney for curries, or adds aroma and flavour to rice dishes such as pulaos.

mint and coriander chutney

wash the mint and coriander leaves. Discard any tough stalks but keep the young soft ones for flavour.

blend all the ingredients together in a blender or food processor, or chop everything finely and pound it together using a mortar and pestle. Taste the chutney and add more salt if necessary. If you want a creamier, milder chutney, stir in the yoghurt. Serves 4.

30 g (1 1/2 cups) mint leaves
30 g (1 cup) coriander
 (cilantro) leaves
1 green chilli
1 tablespoon tamarind purée
1/2 teaspoon salt
1 1/2 teaspoons sugar
3 tablespoons thick natural
 yoghurt (optional)

mustard seeds

Yellow, brown and black mustard seeds are a common ingredient in Indian curries, pickles and vegetable dishes. The brown and black mustard seeds are interchangeable. Mustard seeds are either added to hot oil to pop, which makes them taste nutty rather than hot, or are ground to a paste before use, in which case they are still hot. Black and brown mustard seeds are the smallest and hottest, whereas yellow mustard seeds are larger and have a milder flavour. Split mustard seeds are called mustard dal. See also mustard oil and powder, page 48.

cauliflower with mustard

2 teaspoons yellow mustard seeds
2 teaspoons black mustard seeds
1 teaspoon ground turmeric
1 teaspoon tamarind purée
2–3 tablespoons mustard oil
2 garlic cloves, finely chopped
1/2 onion, finely chopped
600 g (1 lb 5 oz) cauliflower, broken into small florets
3 mild green chillies, seeded and finely chopped
2 teaspoons nigella seeds

grind the mustard seeds together to a fine powder using a spice grinder or mortar and pestle. Mix with the turmeric, tamarind purée and 100 ml (3 1/2 fl oz) water to form a smooth, quite liquid paste.

heat 2 tablespoons of the oil in a large, heavy-based saucepan over medium heat until almost smoking. Reduce the heat to low, add the garlic and onion and fry until golden. Cook the cauliflower in batches, adding more oil if necessary, and fry until lightly browned. Add the chilli and fry for 1 minute, or until tinged with brown around the edges.

return all the cauliflower to the pan, sprinkle it with the mustard mixture and nigella and stir well. Increase the heat to medium and bring to the boil, even though there's not much sauce. Reduce the heat to low, cover and cook until the cauliflower is nearly tender and the seasoning is dry. Sprinkle a little more water on the cauliflower as it cooks to stop it sticking to the pan. If there is excess liquid when the cauliflower is cooked, simmer with the lid off until it dries out. Season with salt, to taste, and remove from the heat. Serves 4.

nigella seeds

spicy eggplant

800 g (1 lb 12 oz) eggplant (aubergine)
400 g (14 oz) tin chopped tomatoes
2.5 cm (1 inch) piece of ginger, grated
6 garlic cloves, crushed
300 ml (10½ fl oz) oil

1 teaspoon fennel seeds
½ teaspoon nigella seeds
1 tablespoon ground coriander
¼ teaspoon ground turmeric
½ teaspoon cayenne pepper
1 teaspoon salt

cut the eggplant into 4–5 cm (1½–2 inch) long wedges, put them in a colander, sprinkle with salt and leave for 30 minutes. Rinse, squeeze out any water, then pat dry with paper towels. Chop the tomatoes, discard the cores and seeds and reserve any juice. Purée the ginger and garlic with one-third of the tomato in a blender or food processor.

heat 125 ml (½ cup) of the oil in a large, deep, heavy-based frying pan. Add as many eggplant pieces as you can fit in a single layer. Cook over medium heat until brown on both sides, then transfer to a sieve over a bowl to drain. Add the remaining oil to the pan as needed and cook the rest of the eggplant in batches.

reheat the oil left in the pan and add the fennel seeds and nigella. Cover and allow to pop for a few seconds. Add the tomato and ginger mixture and the remaining ingredients, except the eggplant. Cook, stirring regularly, for 5–6 minutes, or until the mixture becomes thick and fairly smooth (be careful as it may spit). Carefully add the eggplant so the pieces stay whole, cover the pan and cook gently for 10 minutes. Store the eggplant in the sauce in the refrigerator. Pour off any excess oil before serving. Serve cold or gently warmed through. Serves 6.

These small black seeds, shaped like a tear-drop, have an onion flavour and a slightly peppery taste. They are used in Indian cooking, especially in fish and vegetable dishes, such as this spicy eggplant (aubergine) dish (left). Nigella seeds are also sprinkled on salads and on breads such as naan. The aromatic flavour is enhanced if the seeds are heated before use. Nigella is sometimes incorrectly referred to as black cumin.

Also known as — kalonji

nutmeg/ mace

Nutmeg is the seed of the yellow nutmeg fruit. When the fruit is ripe, it splits open to reveal the nutmeg seed (or nut), which is covered by a red aril, a lacy-like sheath, which will later become mace. The seed and aril are separated and dried. As the aril dries, it loses its colour and becomes the spice known as mace. The seed is dried and cracked open to obtain the kernel, which is nutmeg.

Nutmeg and mace are both obtained from the fruit of the nutmeg tree, an evergreen tree native to the Moluccas ('Spice Islands') in Indonesia. Nutmeg that is freshly grated just prior to use will give the best flavour—warm and spicy. It is used to enhance the flavour of savoury dishes such as mussaman beef curry, in Indian spice blends, and is particularly good with milk-based desserts and sauces. Buy whole if possible and store in an airtight container. Powdered nutmeg loses its flavour and fragrance quite quickly, so buy it in small amounts.

Mace is the outer, lace-like covering of the nutmeg. It has a similar but more delicate flavour, and is sold as fragments known as blades. It may also be ground into a powder. Use mace to flavour delicate dishes such as soups, sauces and milk puddings.

panch phoron

Panch phoron may be used whole or ground. Here the spices are shown whole.

Meaning 'five spices', this aromatic mix is used in Bengali and Bangladeshi cuisine. It contains fennel, brown mustard, nigella seeds, fenugreek and cumin seeds in equal amounts. It may be used whole or ground. The mix is fried at the beginning of the dish, or fried and added as a final seasoning.

Also known as — *panch phora*

ground panch phoron

grind all the spices to a fine powder using a spice grinder or a mortar and pestle. Store in a small airtight container until you need it. Makes 1 tablespoon.

1 teaspoon cumin seeds
1 teaspoon fennel seeds
1 teaspoon fenugreek seeds
1 teaspoon brown mustard seeds
1 teaspoon nigella seeds

pandanus

The long and flat, emerald-green pandanus leaves are used both for their appealing colour and fragrance in Southeast Asian cooking, particularly in Thailand, Indonesia and Malaysia. The leaves are crushed or tied in a knot so they fit easily into the pot, and added to rice dishes or curries during cooking, and removed before the dish is served. The fresh leaves are sold in bundles, but are also available dried or frozen. Dried leaves lack the intensity of flavour and the frozen leaf is much less fragrant.

Pandanus leaf essence is a fragrant flavouring extracted from the leaf and used in cakes and sweet dishes, mainly in Indian and Sri Lankan cooking. Vanilla extract can be substituted in sweet dishes.

Also known as — kewra, pandan, screwpine

pepper

rasam

3 tablespoons tamarind purée
1¹/₂ tablespoons coriander seeds
2 tablespoons cumin seeds
1 tablespoon black peppercorns
1 tablespoon oil
5 garlic cloves, skins on, roughly pounded
1 red onion, thinly sliced
2–3 dried chillies, torn into pieces
2 stalks curry leaves
200 g (7 oz) skinless chicken thigh fillets, cut into small pieces

mix the tamarind purée with 750 ml (3 cups) water. Place a small frying pan over low heat and dry-roast the coriander seeds until aromatic. Remove, then dry-roast the cumin seeds, followed by the black peppercorns. Grind them together using a spice grinder or mortar and pestle.

heat the oil in a large, heavy-based saucepan over low heat, add the garlic and onion and fry until golden. Add the chilli and the curry leaves and fry for 2 minutes, or until they are aromatic. Add the tamarind water and the ground spices and season with salt. Bring to the boil, reduce the heat and simmer for 10 minutes.

add the chicken to the saucepan with 250 ml (1 cup) water and simmer for 20 minutes, gradually adding another 250 ml (1 cup) water as the soup reduces. Remove any garlic skin that floats to the top. Season with salt, to taste. Serve with rice. Serves 4.

Pepper, in its fresh form (above, top), is indigenous to India. Pepper, the fruit of the pepper vine, is black, green or white. All three come from the same plant but are picked at various stages of ripeness. Black pepper (above) is made by drying and fermenting ripe peppercorns. Peppers such as red pepper, Sichuan and cayenne pepper are not botanically related to pepper. Sold whole, cracked, and coarsely or finely ground.

This Indian soup-like dish was originally known as *mulliga thanni*, meaning 'pepper water'. The British version is called mulligatawny.

poppy seeds

Poppy seeds come from the opium poppy, but once mature they lose their narcotic properties. The seeds vary in size, shape and colour. The blue-grey seed is the most common, and is sprinkled on top of breads and biscuits or used in cakes. The white-grey Indian poppy seed is used for thickening sauces and curries. They are often dry-fried before use in cooking. When roasted, the seeds take on a slight nutty flavour. The seeds are also used for their oil.

lamb korma

1 kg (2 lb 4 oz) boneless leg or shoulder of lamb, cut into 2.5 cm (1 inch) cubes

2 tablespoons thick natural yoghurt

1 tablespoon coriander seeds

2 teaspoons cumin seeds

5 cardamom pods

2 onions

2 tablespoons grated coconut or desiccated coconut

1 tablespoon white poppy seeds

3 green chillies, roughly chopped

4 garlic cloves, crushed

5 cm (2 inch) piece of ginger, grated

25 g (1 oz) cashew nuts

6 cloves

1/4 teaspoon ground cinnamon

2 tablespoons oil

put the meat in a bowl, add the yoghurt and mix to coat thoroughly.

place a small frying pan over low heat and dry-roast the coriander seeds until aromatic. Remove and dry-roast the cumin seeds. Grind the roasted mixture to a fine powder using a spice grinder or mortar and pestle. Remove the seeds from the cardamom pods and grind them.

roughly chop one onion and finely slice the other. Put only the roughly chopped onion with the ground spices, coconut, poppy seeds, chilli, garlic, ginger, cashew nuts, cloves and cinnamon in a blender, add 125 ml (1/2 cup) water and process to a smooth paste. If you don't have a blender, crush everything together using a mortar and pestle, or finely chop with a knife, before adding the water.

heat the oil in a casserole over medium heat. Add the finely sliced onion and fry until lightly browned. Pour the blended mixture into the pan, season with salt and cook over low heat for 1 minute, or until the liquid evaporates and the sauce thickens. Add the lamb with the yoghurt and slowly bring to the boil. Cover tightly and simmer for 1 1/2 hours, or until the meat is very tender. Stir the meat occasionally to prevent it from sticking to the pan. If the water evaporates during the cooking time, add another 125 ml (1/2 cup) water to make a sauce. The sauce should be quite thick. Serves 4.

pulao

500 g (2½ cups) basmati rice
1 teaspoon cumin seeds
4 tablespoons ghee or oil
2 tablespoons chopped almonds
2 tablespoons raisins or sultanas
2 onions, finely sliced
2 cinnamon sticks
5 cardamom pods
1 teaspoon sugar

1 tablespoon ginger juice (page 128)
15 saffron threads, soaked in 1 tablespoon warm milk
2 cassia leaves (Indian bay leaves)
250 ml (1 cup) coconut milk
2 tablespoons fresh or frozen peas
rosewater (optional)

wash the rice in a sieve under cold running water until the water from the rice runs clear. Drain the rice and put in a saucepan, cover with water and soak for 30 minutes. Drain. Place a small frying pan over low heat and dry-roast the cumin seeds until aromatic.

heat the ghee or oil in a heavy-based frying pan and fry the almonds and raisins until the almonds are browned. Remove from the pan. Fry the onion in the same ghee until dark golden brown, then remove.

add the rice, roasted cumin seeds, cinnamon, cardamom, sugar, ginger juice, saffron and a pinch of salt to the pan and fry for 2 minutes, or until aromatic. Add the cassia leaves and coconut milk, then add enough water to come about 5 cm (2 inches) above the rice. Bring to the boil, cover and cook over medium heat for 8 minutes, or until most of the water has evaporated.

add the peas to the pan and stir well. Reduce the heat to very low and cook until the rice is cooked through. Stir in the fried almonds, raisins and onion, reserving some for garnishing. Drizzle with a few drops of rosewater if you would like a more perfumed dish. Serves 6.

saffron

Saffron is the orange-red stigma of one species of the crocus plant, and the most expensive spice in the world. Each flower consists of three stigmas, which are hand-picked, then dried—a labour-intensive process. Saffron's flavour is pungent and aromatic, its colour intense, so use only a little. In India, saffron is grown in Kashmir (and is called zaffran) and is used in curries, pulaos and milk desserts. Sold as strands (which need to be soaked in water before use) and in powdered form. Beware—there is no such thing as cheap saffron.

shichimi togarashi

This is a Japanese mixture of seven ground spices, seeds and flavourings, which varies from city to city. It may consist of, for example, two hot and five aromatic flavours—red chilli flakes, sansho pepper, sesame seeds, flax seeds, poppy seeds, ground nori (seaweed) and dried tangerine or orange peel. Used mainly as a seasoning for noodles.

udon noodles in broth

2 teaspoons dashi powder
3 spring onions (scallions)
60 ml (¼ cup) mirin
60 ml (¼ cup) Japanese soy sauce
1 tablespoon sugar
400 g (14 oz) fresh udon noodles
shichimi togarashi, for garnish

pour 1.5 litres (6 cups) water into a large saucepan and bring to the boil. Reduce the heat to low, add the dashi powder and stir until the powder is dissolved.

trim 2 spring onions, then cut into 4 cm (1½ inch) pieces. Add to the dashi stock along with the mirin, soy sauce and sugar and stir to combine. Simmer, covered, over low heat for 5 minutes.

meanwhile, cook the noodles in a saucepan of boiling water for 1–2 minutes, or until tender. Drain, refresh under cold water, then divide among four serving bowls. Slice the remaining spring onion thinly on the diagonal and put on top of the noodles. Ladle the broth on top and sprinkle with shichimi togarashi. Serves 4.

sichuan pepper

Sichuan pepper is a Chinese spice made from the red berries of the prickly ash tree. It is sold whole or ground. Although not related to the peppercorn, the Sichuan berry is similar in appearance. It has a distinctive woody-spicy smell and a strong, hot, numbing aftertaste. Sichuan pepper is used widely in Chinese cooking (often in large amounts). The peppercorns may be crushed and dry-fried to bring out the flavour. Sichuan pepper is also used in Chinese five-spice powder. The Japanese pepper sansho, a close relation, is mostly bought ground and used with grilled eel and chicken, and in the spice mix, shichimi togarashi.

ma po tofu

750 g (1 lb 10 oz) soft or firm bean curd (tofu), drained
250 g (9 oz) minced (ground) beef or pork
2 tablespoons dark soy sauce
1½ tablespoons Shaoxing rice wine
½ teaspoon roasted sesame oil
2 teaspoons Sichuan peppercorns
1 tablespoon oil

2 spring onions (scallions), finely chopped
2 garlic cloves, finely chopped
2 teaspoons finely chopped ginger
1 tablespoon chilli bean paste
250 ml (1 cup) chicken or meat stock
1½ teaspoons cornflour (cornstarch)
1 spring onion (scallion), finely shredded

cut the bean curd into cubes. Put the meat in a bowl with 2 teaspoons of the soy sauce, 2 teaspoons of the rice wine and the sesame oil, and toss lightly. Dry-fry the Sichuan peppercorns in a wok or pan until brown and aromatic, then crush lightly.

heat a wok over high heat, add the oil and heat until very hot. Stir-fry the meat until browned, chopping to separate the pieces. Remove the meat with a wire sieve and heat the oil until any liquid from the meat has evaporated. Add the spring onion, garlic and ginger and stir-fry for 10 seconds. Add the chilli bean paste and stir-fry for 5 seconds.

combine the stock with the remaining soy sauce and rice wine. Add to the wok, bring to the boil, then add the bean curd and meat. Return to the boil, reduce the heat to medium and cook for 5 minutes, or until the sauce has reduced by a quarter. If using soft bean curd, do not stir or it will break up.

combine the cornflour with enough water to make a paste, add to the sauce and simmer until thickened. Season if necessary. Serve sprinkled with the spring onion and Sichuan peppercorns. Serves 6.

Also known as — anise pepper, Chinese aromatic pepper, Szechuan pepper, xanthoxylum

star anise

An aromatic ingredient in Chinese cooking, star anise is a star-shaped Chinese fruit made up of eight segments, with a flat seed found in each point. These seeds are sun-dried until hard and brown. Star anise has a similar flavour and aroma to fennel seed and aniseed. It is used whole in braises or soups and stocks, then removed before serving, or ground and used in five-spice powder.

five-spice duck and somen noodle soup

4 duck breasts, skin on
1 teaspoon five-spice powder
1 teaspoon peanut oil
200 g (7 oz) dried somen noodles

star anise broth
2 litres (8 cups) good-quality chicken stock
3 star anise
5 spring onions (scallions), chopped
3 tablespoons chopped coriander (cilantro) leaves

preheat the oven to 200°C (400°F/Gas 6). Trim the duck breast of excess fat, then lightly sprinkle both sides with the five-spice powder.

heat a wok over high heat, add the oil and swirl to coat the side of the wok. Add the duck breasts, skin-side down, and cook over medium heat for 2–3 minutes, or until browned and crisp. Turn and cook the other side for 3 minutes. Transfer to a baking tray and roast, skin-side up, for a further 8 minutes for medium–rare, or until cooked to your liking.

meanwhile, put the chicken stock and star anise in a clean non-stick wok. Bring to the boil, then reduce the heat and simmer, covered, for 5 minutes. Add the spring onion and coriander and simmer for a further 5 minutes.

cook the noodles in a saucepan of boiling water for 2 minutes, or until tender. Drain and divide among four large bowls. Ladle the broth on the noodles and top each bowl with one sliced duck breast. Serves 4.

tamarind

indian prawn curry with tamarind

**500 g (1 lb 2 oz) raw tiger
  prawns (shrimp)**
1/2 teaspoon fennel seeds
1 tablespoon oil
2 cinnamon sticks
3 cardamom pods
1 large onion, finely chopped
5 garlic cloves, crushed

**2 cm (3/4 inch) piece of ginger,
  grated**
1 stalk of curry leaves
1 teaspoon turmeric
1 teaspoon chilli powder
**1 1/2 tablespoons tamarind
  purée**

peel and devein the prawns, leaving the tails intact. Place a small frying pan over low heat and dry-roast the fennel seeds until aromatic.

heat the oil in a heavy-based frying pan and fry the fennel seeds, cinnamon, cardamom and onion until the onion is brown. Stir in the garlic, ginger and curry leaves, then add the prawns, turmeric, chilli powder and tamarind. Toss over high heat until the prawn tails turn pink and the prawns are cooked through. Remove from the heat and season with salt, to taste. Serves 4.

Also known as — Indian date

The tropical tamarind tree is prized for its pods, each containing a sticky, fleshy sweet-sour pulp wrapped around small hard seeds. The pulp is used in curries and chutneys, and in Thailand the pulp is sweetened with sugar and eaten as a sweetmeat. Tamarind is sold as a ready-made purée or as a thick concentrate, or in blocks or cakes that often contain the tamarind seeds. If buying a block, cut off a little, mix with hot water and press through a sieve to extract the pulp.

From left: tamarind pods, tamarind purée, and two blocks of compressed pulp, one with and one without seeds.

tiger lily buds

Despite their name, these buds aren't from tiger lilies but are the unopened flowers of day lilies. The buds are usually bought dried and then soaked, but are sometimes available fresh from Chinese markets. They have an earthy flavour and are used mainly in Chinese vegetarian dishes or in stir-fries.

Also known as — golden needles, lily buds

Tiger lily buds are bought dried and need to be soaked before use. When reconstituted, they resemble limp bean sprouts.

buddha's delight

25 g (1 oz) tiger lily buds
6–8 dried Chinese mushrooms
10 g (1/4 oz) dried black fungus (wood ears)
150 g (5 1/2 oz) ready-made braised gluten, drained
50 g (1 3/4 oz) bean curd (tofu) puffs
100 g (3 1/2 oz) soya bean sprouts
1 carrot
4 tablespoons oil
50 g (1 3/4 oz) snow peas (mangetout), ends trimmed
1 teaspoon salt
1/2 teaspoon sugar
4 tablespoons vegetable stock
2 tablespoons light soy sauce
1/2 teaspoon roasted sesame oil

soak the tiger lily buds in boiling water for 30 minutes. Rinse and drain them, and trim off any hard stem tips. Soak the dried Chinese mushrooms in boiling water for 30 minutes, then drain and squeeze out any excess water. Remove and discard the stems and cut the caps in half, or quarters if large. Soak the dried black fungus in cold water for 20 minutes, then drain and squeeze out any excess water. Cut any large pieces in half.

cut the gluten and bean curd into small pieces. Wash the bean sprouts, discarding any husks and straggly end pieces, and dry thoroughly. Diagonally cut the carrot into thin slices.

heat a wok over high heat, add the oil and heat until very hot. Stir-fry the carrot for 30 seconds, then add the snow peas and bean sprouts. Stir-fry for 1 minute, then add the gluten, bean curd, tiger lily buds, mushrooms, black fungus, salt, sugar, stock and soy sauce. Toss together, then cover and braise for 2 minutes at a gentle simmer.

add the sesame oil, toss it through the mixture and serve hot or cold. Serves 4.

turmeric/ zedoary

Turmeric is the vital ingredient in any Indian curry, both for its flavour and its deep yellow colour. Here, it is shown fresh.

A relative of ginger, turmeric is the underground root of a tropical plant. It has a musky, faintly peppery aroma and flavour and is used in curry powders, rice, lentil and potato dishes, and commercially to colour drinks, butter, cheese and mustards. It is sometimes called 'poor man's saffron'—its vivid yellow resembles that of the expensive spice—but the two are not interchangeable.

Zedoary, a rhizome found growing in India and Southeast Asia, bears a resemblance to turmeric (to which it is related) and ginger. The flesh is hard and orange and has a gingery mango flavour and musky aroma. Zedoary is sold fresh or dried and is commonly used in Indian pickles and, because of its high starch content, as a thickening agent.

Dried zedoary

This trailing herb with narrow, pointed and pungent-tasting leaves does not actually belong to the mint family. Its flavour resembles coriander, but is slightly sharper. The leaves are served as a garnish for laksa, Vietnamese soup (pho) and with spring rolls. It can be used in salads to give a spicy flavour.

Also known as — Cambodian mint, hot mint, laksa leaf

beef pho

200 g (7 oz) banh pho rice noodles
1.5 litres (6 cups) beef stock
2 tablespoons fish sauce
200 g (7 oz) beef fillet, very thinly sliced
90 g (1 cup) soya bean sprouts
1 red chilli, thinly sliced
Vietnamese mint, to serve
lemon wedges, to serve

cook the rice noodles in boiling water following the instructions on the packet. Drain and refresh under cold water.

put the stock in a saucepan and bring to the boil. Add the fish sauce and season. Divide the noodles among four bowls and top with the raw beef fillet. Pour over the hot broth (it is important that the broth is very hot as the heat will cook the beef).

serve the bean sprouts, chilli and mint separately for each person to scatter over their soup. Squeeze over some lemon juice. Serves 4.

vietnamese mint

From left: wasabi paste, fresh wasabi root, wasabi powder.

wasabi

Though often called Japanese horseradish because of its flavour, wasabi is, in fact, an unrelated herb. In Japan, it grows wild near freshwater streams, but it is also cultivated widely. Although all of the plant is used as food, it is the green root that is grated and eaten with sushi and sashimi, when it is sometimes mixed with soy sauce. Most of the so-called wasabi—in powder or paste form—available commercially is dyed horseradish with only a small portion of actual wasabi in it. Real wasabi is expensive and when buying it, look for hon (real) wasabi. Wasabi is very hot, so use it sparingly.

fresh produce

bananas

Floating market in Thailand (top). Banana leaves on sale in a market in Madras, India (above).

Bananas are thought to be one of the world's oldest cultivated fruit, and evidence of their cultivation dates back to the sixth century BC in India. Although the banana plant looks like a type of palm tree, it is actually classified as a giant herb. Bananas grow in bunches called 'hands' and each hand has 15 to 20 fingers (or fruit). They are harvested when green and ripen best after picking.

Bananas are used both as a fruit and a vegetable. The banana flower is also edible and the leaves are used as food 'containers' (see pages 154–5). Bananas for cooking should be firmer than the ones eaten raw. Cooking brings out their full flavour: fry in butter and brown sugar, or coat with batter and deep-fry. To prevent discolouration of the flesh, cut with a stainless steel knife and toss the slices in lemon juice.

Do not keep bananas in the refrigerator as the skin will turn black (although this doesn't actually affect the taste). If possible, store on a hook. Bananas produce ethylene, which will cause other fruit or vegetables sitting near them to ripen prematurely.

There are many varieties of banana used in Asian cooking (both raw and cooked), all with individual characteristics and flavours. Lady's finger bananas (bottom right) are known as egg bananas in Thailand. Nothing is wasted, as both the banana leaves and flowers (bottom left) are also used in cooking.

bananas in coconut milk

420 ml (1²/₃ cups) coconut milk
4 tablespoons sugar
5 just-ripe bananas
¹/₂ teaspoon salt

put the coconut milk, sugar and 125 ml (¹/₂ cup) water in a saucepan and bring to the boil. Reduce the heat and simmer until the sugar has dissolved.

peel the bananas and cut them into 5 cm (2 inch) lengths. If you are using very small bananas, leave them whole.

when the sugar in the coconut milk has dissolved, add the bananas and salt. Cook gently over a low to medium heat for 5 minutes, or until the bananas are soft.

divide the bananas and coconut milk among four bowls. Serve warm or at room temperature. Serves 4.

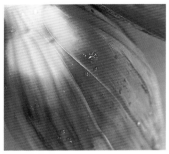

1 To prepare the banana flower, first peel off the outer leaves.

2 Then remove the immature stick-like bananas.

3 When you reach the core, chop off the top end.

banana flower

Banana flowers are the purple, tear-drop shaped part of the banana plant. The purple leaves and pale yellow buds are discarded, and only the inner pale core is eaten. This needs to be blanched in boiling water to remove any bitterness. Wear rubber gloves to prepare banana flower as it has a gummy substance that can stain your fingers. Slice thinly and use in salads or in a vegetable stir-fry. Buy from Asian markets.

spiced banana flower

1 banana flower	125 ml (½ cup) lime juice
½ lemon	1 red chilli, finely chopped
200 g (7 oz) raw prawns (shrimp)	2 tablespoons jaggery or soft brown sugar
1 tablespoon grated or desiccated coconut	1 tablespoon grated lime zest
1 tablespoon oil	mint leaves, for garnish

peel off one leaf at a time from the banana flower. Discard the stick-like immature bananas and the leaves until you reach the white inner core. Chop off the top end and discard it. Chop what is left into quarters and soak in a bowl of water with 1 teaspoon salt for 1 hour. Drain, transfer to a saucepan, cover with fresh water and add the juice from the half lemon. Bring to the boil and cook for 15–20 minutes, or until soft. The banana flower will darken in colour as it cooks. Drain and slice into julienne strips. Peel and devein the prawns and cut each one in half.

place a heavy-based frying pan over low heat and dry-roast the coconut, stirring constantly until the coconut is golden brown. Finely grind using a mortar and pestle or a spice grinder.

heat the oil in the frying pan and fry the prawns until pink and cooked through. Mix the prawns with the lime juice, chilli, jaggery and lime zest. Season with salt, to taste, then leave to cool. Just before serving, add the banana flower and coconut to the prawns and toss well. Serve cold, garnished with the mint leaves. Serves 4.

banana leaves

These large green leaves can be used as a wrapping for food such as rice, fish or chicken—the parcel is then steamed or grilled (broiled). The leaves add subtle flavour and protect the food inside from direct heat. Banana leaves can also be used as a 'plate' to eat off. Dip in boiling water to soften the leaves before use. Sold in Asian supermarkets.

grilled fish in banana leaves

1 Score the fish three or four times with a sharp knife.

2 Lay the prepared fish on the softened banana leaves.

4 red tilapa, grey/red mullet or mackerel (about 300 g/ 10 oz each)
8–10 garlic cloves, roughly chopped
6 coriander (cilantro) roots, chopped
1 teaspoon ground white pepper
1 teaspoon salt
1 tablespoon vegetable oil
8 pieces of banana leaf
a chilli sauce, to serve

clean and gut the fish, leaving the heads on. Dry the fish thoroughly. Score each fish three or four times on both sides with a sharp knife.

using a mortar and pestle or a small blender, pound or blend the garlic, coriander roots, ground pepper, salt and oil into a paste. Rub the garlic paste inside the cavity and all over the fish. Cover and marinate in the refrigerator for at least 30 minutes.

to soften the banana leaves and prevent them from splitting, blanch them briefly in boiling water. Using two pieces of banana leaf, each with the grain running at right angles to the other, wrap up each fish like a parcel. Pin the ends of the banana leaves together with toothpicks to hold the parcel together.

3 Wrap up each fish like a parcel, pinning the ends with toothpicks.

heat a grill (broiler) or barbecue to medium. Barbecue or grill (broil) the fish for about 15 minutes on each side, or until the fish is light brown and cooked. To make the fish easier to lift and turn during cooking, you can put the fish in a fish-shaped griddle that opens out like tongs. Transfer the fish to a serving plate. Serve with a chilli sauce. Serves 4.

Used in Chinese, Southeast Asian and Indian cooking, bitter melon really lives up to its name—it really is bitter and is something of an acquired taste. In most Asian countries, bitter melon is eaten because its taste is one of the five sought-after flavours: bitter, sweet, sour, salty and aromatic. The bitter melon looks like a pale-green cucumber covered in a warty skin. Blanch the flesh in boiling water or degorge before use to reduce its bitterness. It may be braised or stuffed with pork and served with black bean sauce, or cooked in curries. Pale or yellowy melons are less bitter but more fibrous.

Also known as — bitter gourd, warty melon

prawns with bitter melon

1 kg (2 lb 4 oz) bitter melons, sliced in half
2 tablespoons oil
1/2 tablespoon ground turmeric
1 tablespoon ground coriander
1 tablespoon ground cumin
1 teaspoon chilli powder
4–5 green chillies
300 g (10 1/2 oz) raw prawns (shrimp), peeled and deveined
pinch of sugar
4 curry leaves
1/4 teaspoon cumin seeds

scoop out the seeds and membrane from the bitter melons, then slice into half-moon shapes 5 mm (1/4 inch) thick. Sprinkle with salt and degorge in a colander for 30 minutes. Rinse, drain, then dry in a tea towel.

heat 1 tablespoon oil in a heavy-based frying pan, add the bitter melon, stir, then cover and cook for 3–4 minutes (the bitter melon will sweat out liquid). Mix the turmeric, coriander, cumin and chilli powder to a paste with a small amount of water. Add to the pan and cook over high heat until the liquid is reduced to almost dry. Add the chillies and prawns and cook, tossing until dry. Season with sugar and a little salt.

heat the remaining oil in a small pan, fry the curry leaves and cumin for 1 minute, then pour onto the bitter melon. Serves 4.

bitter melon

Use a spoon to scrape out the seeds and membrane of the bitter melon in one piece, then discard them (above). In this recipe (right), the bitter melon is prepared Indian style, mixed with chillies and spices.

cabbages

There are many vegetables that belong to the brassica family. Chinese broccoli, Chinese cabbage, Chinese flowering cabbage (also called choy sum, pictured below), Chinese mustard cabbage and Chinese white cabbage are commonly used in the Asian kitchen, and are featured on the following pages.

bok choy

This is a mild, open-leaved cabbage with a fat white or pale-green stem and dark-green leaves. Separate the leaves, wash well and use in stir-fries or steam and serve with oyster sauce. A smaller, more compact variety is called Shanghai or baby bok choy (pictured below, right). These may be cooked whole.

Also known as — Chinese chard, Chinese white cabbage, pak choi

stir-fried bok choy

400 g (14 oz) bok choy (pak choi)
2 tablespoons oil
2 garlic cloves
3 thin slices of ginger
60 ml (¼ cup) chicken stock
1 teaspoon sugar
salt or light soy sauce, to taste
1 teaspoon roasted sesame oil

cut the bok choy into 5–8 cm (2–3 inch) lengths. Trim off any roots that may hold the pieces together, then wash well and dry thoroughly.

heat a wok over high heat, add the oil and heat until very hot. Smash the garlic and ginger with the flat side of a cleaver, add to the wok and stir-fry for 30 seconds. Add the bok choy and stir-fry until it begins to wilt, then add the stock and sugar and season with the salt or soy sauce. Simmer, covered, for 2 minutes, or until the stems and leaves are tender but still green. Add the sesame oil and serve hot. Serves 4.

chinese broccoli

Chinese broccoli is similar to Western-style broccoli but is distinguished by its clumps of small white flowers. It has crisp, crinkly leaves that look a bit like broccoli leaves and the stems have a distinctive bittersweet flavour. Steam Chinese broccoli whole and serve with oyster sauce, or cut up the leaves and stems and add them to soups and stir-fries. The young stalks are crisp and mild; thicker stalks need to be peeled and halved. Widely available.

Also known as — gai lan, Chinese kale

Chinese broccoli differs from its Western relative in that the stems are long, the florets are tiny, and the flavour is slightly bitter. Chinese broccoli is available from Chinese grocers and some supermarkets in the green (the most common) and dark purple varieties.

chinese broccoli in oyster sauce

1 kg (2 lb 4 oz) Chinese broccoli
1 1/2 tablespoons oil
2 spring onions (scallions), finely chopped
1 1/2 tablespoons grated ginger
3 garlic cloves, finely chopped
3 tablespoons oyster sauce
2 tablespoons light soy sauce
1 tablespoon Shaoxing rice wine
1 teaspoon sugar
1 teaspoon roasted sesame oil
125 ml (1/2 cup) chicken stock
2 teaspoons cornflour (cornstarch)

wash the broccoli well. Discard any tough-looking stems and diagonally cut into 2 cm (3/4 inch) pieces through the stem and the leaf. Blanch in a pan of boiling water for 2 minutes, or until the stems and leaves are just tender, then refresh in cold water and dry thoroughly.

heat a wok over high heat, add the oil and heat until very hot. Stir-fry the spring onion, ginger and garlic for 10 seconds, or until fragrant. Add the broccoli and cook until it is heated through. Combine the remaining ingredients, add to the wok, stirring until the sauce has thickened, and toss to coat the broccoli. Serves 6.

chinese cabbage

This is a versatile vegetable with a mild, sweet flavour. Commonly used in stir-fries, braises, soups and hotpots, it can also be shredded and eaten raw in salads, or used to make cabbage rolls. Chinese cabbage is used to make the Korean accompaniment, kim chi, and in Japanese cooking to make sukiyaki. Choose firm cabbages with tightly packed, green-tipped leaves. To prepare, trim the root end, slice it in half lengthways, then cut out the central core and discard it.

Also known as — celery cabbage, Chinese leaves, napa cabbage, Peking cabbage, wom bok, wong bok

chinese flowering cabbage

This cabbage has smooth green leaves and pale green stems with clusters of tiny flowers on the tips of the inner shoots. The mild mustard-flavoured leaves cook quickly. Cut into shorter lengths and steam them, then serve with garlic or oyster sauce, or chop the leaves and add to stir-fries or soups.

Also known as — choy sum

chinese mustard cabbage

There are two varieties commonly available. Swatow mustard cabbage is a strong, bitter cabbage that is generally pickled as Sichuan pickled cabbage or used in pork-based soups. Another variety, bamboo mustard cabbage (chuk gai choy) has a very strong mustard flavour that lessens after blanching, so is often used in soups, or blanched and used in stir-fries.

Also known as — gai choy

tatsoi

Tatsoi is a type of bok choy. It looks like a giant flower with pretty, shiny dark-green leaves that grow out flat. The leaves need to be thoroughly washed before use as they hold a lot of dirt. They can then be steamed or stir-fried or used in soups. Baby tatsoi can be used raw in salads.

Also known as — flat cabbage, rosette bok choy, rosette cabbage

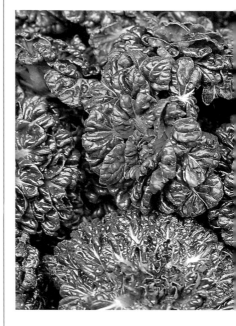

tatsoi with black pepper

separate the tatsoi leaves, wash well and dry thoroughly.

heat a wok over high heat, add the oil and heat until very hot. Stir-fry the garlic for a few seconds. Add the tatsoi leaves and stir-fry until they have just wilted. Add the pepper and rice wine and toss together. Season with the soy sauce and add the sesame oil. Serves 4.

1 tatsoi
1 tablespoon oil
2 garlic cloves, sliced
1/4 teaspoon freshly ground
   black pepper
2 teaspoons Shaoxing
   rice wine
light soy sauce, to taste
2 teaspoons roasted
   sesame oil

chinese celery

Chinese celery is similar to celery but has darker stems and a more pronounced flavour.

The stalks of the Chinese celery are thin and hollow and they have a stronger taste and smell than Western celery. It is used in stir-fries and soups, or blanched and used in salads. When buying, make sure the stems are firm.

chinese celery salad

2 tablespoons dried shrimp
2 tablespoons Shaoxing rice wine
8 Chinese celery stalks
1 tablespoon light soy sauce
1 tablespoon sugar
1 tablespoon clear rice vinegar
1 teaspoon roasted sesame oil
1 tablespoon finely chopped ginger

soak the dried shrimp in the rice wine for 1 hour.

cut the celery into thin slices and blanch in a pan of boiling water for 1–2 minutes, then refresh in cold water and dry thoroughly. Arrange the celery on a serving dish.

combine the soaked shrimp and rice wine with the soy sauce, sugar, rice vinegar, sesame oil and ginger. Blend well and pour over the celery just before serving. Serves 4.

fresh noodles with beef and chinese chives

250 g (9 oz) rump or sirloin steak, trimmed
2 large garlic cloves, crushed
3 tablespoons oyster sauce
2 teaspoons sugar
1 tablespoon dark soy sauce
3 teaspoons cornflour (cornstarch)
¼ teaspoon roasted sesame oil
3 tablespoons oil
1 red capsicum (pepper), thinly sliced
150 g (5½ oz) Chinese chives, cut into 5 cm (2 inch) lengths
1 kg (2 lb 4 oz) fresh rice noodle rolls, cut into 2 cm (¾ inch) thick slices and separated slightly
chilli sauce, to serve

cut the beef across the grain into thin bite-sized strips. Combine the beef with the garlic, 1 tablespoon of the oyster sauce, 1 teaspoon of the sugar, 2 teaspoons of the soy sauce, the cornflour and sesame oil. Marinate in the refrigerator for at least 30 minutes, or overnight.

heat a wok over high heat, add the oil and heat until very hot. Stir-fry the capsicum for 1–2 minutes, or until it begins to soften. Add the beef and toss until it changes colour. Add the Chinese chives and the noodles and toss for 1–2 minutes, or until they soften. Add the remaining oyster sauce, sugar and soy sauce and toss until combined.

serve with some chilli sauce on the side. Serves 6.

Chinese chives have thick, flat garlic-scented leaves and are stronger in flavour than the slender variety used in Western cooking.

chinese chives

Chinese chives have either a long, flat green leaf and are very garlicky, or are yellow with a milder taste. Flowering chives are round-stemmed with a flower at the top, which is edible. In Asian cooking, both Chinese chives and flowering chives are used more as a vegetable, usually in stir-fries, than as a herb.

Also known as —
Chinese garlic chives, garlic chives

chinese spinach

Although called a spinach, Chinese spinach is in fact a member of the amaranth family. There are at least two types available, one with small green leaves that are red in the middle, the other plain green. Chinese spinach can be eaten fresh or used in Chinese stir-fries; in India it may be cooked with lentils or vegetables, such as the dish saag bhaji (saag is the Indian term for 'leafy greens'). The leaves wilt quickly, like most leafy greens, so add them towards the end of cooking if using in a stir-fry. The leaves can also be used in soups.

Also known as —
amaranth, een choy

saag bhaji

200 g (7 oz) small turnips, finely chopped
1 kg (2 lb 4 oz) mixed English spinach leaves and Chinese
    spinach leaves, finely shredded
1/2 teaspoon chilli powder
1 tablespoon ghee or oil
2 cm (3/4 inch) piece of ginger, grated
1 onion, finely chopped
1 1/2 tablespoons lemon juice

bring 125 ml (1/2 cup) water to the boil in a large heavy-based saucepan over medium heat. Add the turnip, cook for 1–2 minutes, then add the mixed spinach leaves. Stir in the chilli powder and a pinch of salt and cook for 2–3 minutes, or until almost all the water has evaporated. Mash the mixture well and remove from the heat.

heat the ghee or oil in a heavy-based saucepan over low heat and fry the ginger and onion for 2–3 minutes. Add the mashed vegetables, mix well and keep tossing until everything is well mixed. Season with salt, to taste. Serve warm with a dash of lemon juice. Serves 4.

coconut

coconut milk and cream

**1 coconut (yields about
300 g/10½ oz flesh)**

drain the coconut by punching a hole in two of the 'eyes'. Drain out the liquid and use it as a refreshing drink. Holding the coconut in one hand, tap around the circumference with a hammer or pestle. This should cause the coconut to split open evenly. (If it doesn't, put it in a 150°C (300°F/Gas 2) oven for 15 minutes. This may cause it to crack as it cools. If it doesn't, it will crack easily when hit with a hammer.)

if using a specialized coconut grater, scrape out the coconut from each half, catching the grated flesh in a large bowl. Alternatively, prise the flesh out of the shell, trim off the hard brown, outer skin and grate either by hand on a box grater or chop in a food processor. Grated coconut can be frozen in small portions until needed.

mix the grated coconut with 125 ml (½ cup) hot water and steep for 5 minutes. Pour the mixture into a container through a sieve lined with muslin, then gather it into a ball to squeeze out any remaining liquid. This will make a thick coconut milk, usually called coconut cream.

repeat the process with another 250 ml (1 cup) water to make thinner coconut milk. Makes 125 ml (½ cup) coconut cream and 250 ml (1 cup) coconut milk.

note: Grated coconut is best when it is fresh. Dried or desiccated coconut can also be used to make coconut milk but it needs to be soaked, then chopped more finely or ground to a paste, otherwise the coconut milk will be fibrous.

Indigenous to India, coastal Southeast Asia and the Caribbean, the coconut is a versatile fruit. Its name is derived from the Spanish and Portuguese word 'coco' referring to a monkey face, because the three small depressions at the base are reminiscent of a grinning monkey face. Coconut flesh when immature is soft and jelly-like. It becomes white and hard when mature, and can be eaten fresh or dried. The juice contained within the nut is not the heavy, milky liquid used in cooking, but a thin, watery sweet liquid that makes a refreshing drink. Coconut milk is extracted from the flesh of the coconut.

If buying them fresh, choose coconuts that are dry, with no 'weeping' in the eyes. They should be heavy and sound full of liquid. The flesh is also sold desiccated or as shreds/flakes (sweeter and moister than desiccated). Although coconut cream and milk can be made at home, it is also readily available tinned or in powdered form (see page 18).

cucumber

In India, cucumbers are sold with both a yellow (above, left) and green skin. Peeled cucumbers may be sold on the roadside as a cool and refreshing snack (above, right). They are often dipped in salt for a little flavour.

The cucumber is one of the oldest cultivated vegetables and, many would say, the most refreshing. It exists in over 100 varieties—including at least one described as 'burpless'—and many shapes. It can be eaten raw in salads, cooked in a soup, or mixed with yoghurt to make raita, an accompaniment to Indian curries. In Cantonese cooking, cucumber is considered to be a strongly yin food (yin representing cool, water, female). To create balance in a meal, chefs will combine the yin of the cucumber with the yang (hot, fire, male) of another ingredient, such as chicken. Choose firm cucumbers with no signs of bruising and store them in the refrigerator wrapped in plastic to prevent their odour spreading to other foods. In cooking, cucumber varieties are mostly interchangeable.

raita

450 g (1 lb) Lebanese (short) cucumbers, grated
1 large, ripe tomato, finely chopped

250 g (1 cup) thick natural yoghurt
1/2 tablespoon oil
1 teaspoon black mustard seeds

put the cucumber and tomato in a sieve for 20 minutes to drain off any excess liquid. Mix them in a bowl with the yoghurt and season with salt, to taste.

heat the oil in a small saucepan over medium heat, add the mustard seeds, then cover and shake the pan until the seeds start to pop. Pour the seeds and oil over the yoghurt. Serves 4.

Daikon is a variety of white radish with firm, crisp flesh and a mild flavour, similar to a white turnip. Some varieties have a mild peppery taste, while others are slightly sweeter. Daikon is a popular vegetable in Asia, particularly in Japan (daikon is actually a Japanese word, meaning large root). Raw daikon can be diced and added to salads, or used like a potato or turnip and added to soups, stews or stir-fries. In Japan, grated raw daikon is formed into a small pile as the traditional accompaniment to sashimi or tempura. It is eaten as pickles, and is used to make a summer version of the pungent Korean condiment, kim chi. The daikon leaves are added to soups, stews and stir-fries.

Choose firm, smooth and slightly shiny daikon, as this is a good indication that it's fresh. Daikon don't store for long periods as they lose moisture quickly. Remove their green tops and store wrapped in plastic in the vegetable crisper of the refrigerator. Use the root end for eating raw or grating as it is sweeter, and cook the remainder. If eating raw, use within 3–4 days, or it will last up to 1 week if you intend to cook it.

daikon

**Also known as —
Chinese radish,
Japanese radish, mooli,
Oriental radish**

drumstick beans

Drumstick beans are long, dark-green, ridged fibrous pods. Drumsticks, so called because of their rigidity, need to be cut into lengths before being cooked. The inner pulp, the only part eaten, is scooped out with a spoon or scraped out with your teeth. Buy uniformly slim, green pods or buy in tins. Drumstick leaves may also be eaten.

sambhar

225 g (8 oz) yellow lentils (toor dal)
2 tablespoons coriander seeds
10 black peppercorns
1/2 teaspoon fenugreek seeds
2 tablespoons grated coconut
1 tablespoon gram lentils (channa dal)
6 dried chillies
2 drumstick beans, cut into 5 cm (2 inch) pieces
2 carrots, cubed

1 onion, roughly chopped
125 g (41/2 oz) eggplant (aubergine), cubed
60 g (21/4 oz) small okra, topped and tailed
1 tablespoon tamarind purée
2 tablespoons oil
1 teaspoon black mustard seeds
10 curry leaves
1/2 teaspoon ground turmeric
1/2 teaspoon asafoetida

soak the lentils in 500 ml (2 cups) water for 2 hours. Drain and put in a saucepan with 1 litre (4 cups) water. Bring to the boil, then skim off any scum from the surface. Cover and simmer for 2 hours, or until the lentils are cooked and tender.

place a small frying pan over low heat and dry-roast the coriander seeds, peppercorns, fenugreek, coconut, lentils and chillies, stirring constantly until the coconut is golden brown. Grind the roasted mixture to a fine powder using a mortar and pestle or a spice grinder.

bring 750 ml (3 cups) water to the boil in a pan. Add the drumsticks and carrot and bring back to the boil. Simmer for 10 minutes, then add the onion, eggplant and okra and more water if necessary. Simmer until the vegetables are almost cooked. Put the lentils and its liquid, the ground spices, the vegetables (with any vegetable water) and tamarind in a large saucepan and bring slowly to the boil. Reduce the heat and simmer for 30 minutes. Season with salt, to taste.

heat the oil in a small pan over medium heat and add the mustard seeds. Cover and shake the pan until they start to pop. Add the curry leaves, turmeric, asafoetida and a little salt. Pour onto the simmering lentils and stir until well mixed. Serve with dosas. Serves 6.

note: This Indian dish is often served with dosas (see page 36) or rice for breakfast or lunch.

durian

Native to Southeast Asia, the durian is a large fruit covered with an armour of close-set hard spines. Its name is derived from the Malay *duri*, meaning 'thorn'. The fruit has sticky, cream-coloured flesh and is especially noted for the contrast between its putrid odour (described by some as smelling like rotten onions) and its juicy, sweet flesh. Outside its native home, where it is highly prized and considered to be an aphrodisiac, durian is quite rare and is expensive when available. The fruit is divided into five or six segments, each containing several seeds. The flesh can be eaten with a spoon, or used in ice creams and cakes, or cooked with Indonesian rice dishes. Roasted or baked, the seeds can be eaten as nuts; in Indonesia, they are eaten with rice or mixed with sugar to make sweetmeats.

When buying durian, look for fruit with undamaged skin and a yellowish rind, which is a good indication that it's ripe. At home, insert a knife into the fruit—if the knife comes out sticky, it is ready to eat. Store in the refrigerator for 2–3 days and wrap the fruit well to prevent its odour contaminating other foods.

Preparing durians for sale in a Thai market.

eggplant

Clockwise from top left: the Chinese eggplant (aubergine), unlike its Western cousin, is long and thin, about the size of a zucchini (courgette); pea eggplants, commonly used in Thai curries; large eggplants; Thai eggplants.

Eggplants (aubergines) are often thought of as vegetables, but they are actually fruit and a member of the same family as the tomato and potato. The eggplant is a native of Southeast Asia, but its versatility has made it a widely used ingredient in cuisines around the world. Eggplants can be served hot or cold, puréed, fried, stuffed or battered.

Eggplants vary in size and shape from small, round pea shapes to large, fat pumpkin-shaped fruit. Their colour too can range from green, cream or yellow, to pale or dark purple. Look for firm, heavy eggplants that have shiny, smooth skins with no brown patches, and a distinct cleft in the wider end.

indian sambal with eggplant

2 medium eggplants (aubergines), about 500 g (1 lb 2 oz)
½ tablespoon oil
½ teaspoon ground turmeric
3 tablespoons lime juice
2 red chillies, seeded and finely diced
1 small red onion, finely diced
4 tablespoons thick natural yoghurt
coriander (cilantro) leaves, for garnish

preheat the oven to 200°C (400°F/Gas 6). Slice each eggplant in half and brush the cut halves with the oil and ground turmeric. Put the eggplant in a roasting tin and roast them for 30 minutes, or until they are browned all over and very soft.

scoop the eggplant pulp into a bowl. Mash the pulp with the lime juice, chilli and onion, reserving some chilli and onion for garnish. Season with salt, to taste, then fold in the yoghurt. Garnish with the coriander leaves and remaining onion and chilli. Serve as an accompaniment to Indian food or eat it as a dip with Indian bread. Serves 4.

Also known as — aubergine, brinjal, garden egg, guinea squash

hairy melon/ winter melon

The hairy melon looks like a cucumber covered in tiny hairs. It is used in Cantonese cookery. Remove the hairs by scrubbing or peeling it, then bake or boil the flesh; cut it into strips and stir-fry; cut into large chunks, core and fill with a meat stuffing; or use in braised dishes.

Hairy melon

A relative of the hairy melon, the winter melon is a very large gourd or squash that looks like a watermelon. The skin is dark green, often with a white waxy bloom, and the flesh is pale green. You can usually buy pieces of it in Chinese shops.

Hairy melon is also known as — fuzzy melon
Winter melon is also known as — wax gourd

The delicate flesh of the winter melon becomes almost translucent when cooked and tastes a little like marrow. At Chinese banquets, winter melon soup may be served in a hollowed-out melon shell.

winter melon and ham soup

1 tablespoon dried shrimp
250 g (9 oz) winter melon, rind and seeds removed
750 ml (3 cups) chicken stock
150 g (5½ oz) Chinese ham or prosciutto, chopped

soak the dried shrimp in boiling water for 1 hour, then drain. Cut the winter melon into small pieces.

bring the stock to a rolling boil in a large clay pot or saucepan. Add the shrimp, winter melon and ham. Return to the boil, then reduce the heat and simmer for 2 minutes. Season with salt and white pepper. Serve hot. Serves 4.

jackfruit

Native to Malaysia and India, the jackfruit is one of the world's largest fruit, some weighing up to 40 kg (90 lb). It's covered with green, knobbly skin, which turns yellow or brown as it ripens, and has a juicy, sweet flesh. When unripe, both seeds and the flesh are eaten as a vegetable, usually cooked in curries, or made into chutney. Ripe fruit may be eaten on its own or added to fruit salads. Its ripeness is easily detected by a strong and unpleasant odour (although the flesh inside smells sweet). Jackfruit is sold fresh and in tins.

sweet jackfruit rolls

1 jackfruit, cut into 1 x 4 cm (1/2 x 1 1/2 inch) pieces
1 banana, sliced
spring roll wrappers
caster (superfine) sugar, to sprinkle
lime wedges, to sprinkle
flavourless oil, for frying

lay a piece of jackfruit and a slice of banana (roughly the same size) on a spring roll wrapper. Sprinkle with caster sugar and a few drops of lime juice, then roll up like a spring roll. Heat the oil in a frying pan and fry the rolls on all sides until they are golden brown and cooked. Serve as a snack.

Jackfruit have a flavour like fruit salad and a slightly rubbery texture. The tough, spiky, outer skin is peeled away to reveal segments of flesh (bottom, right), which are then seeded.

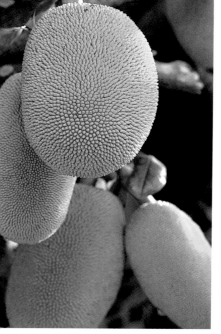

The jicama is a bulb-like root vegetable, similar in appearance to a very large turnip. It has thin, beige leathery skin and sweetish, crisp white flesh. A native of Mexico, the jicama is also used in Southeast Asian cuisine. To prepare it, peel the skin, including the fibrous flesh directly under it, then slice and use raw in salads, add to stews, or cut into cubes and use in stir-fries as a substitute for water chestnuts, which it resembles in flavour. They may also be used in the filling for spring rolls. Jicamas are a good source of starch and, like potatoes, if stored in the refrigerator for too long will convert their starch to sugar. Buy firm, heavy roots with smooth skins that are relatively free of blemishes.

Also known as — jicana, Mexican potato, Mexican turnip, yam bean

jicama

kohlrabi

The bulbous stalk and the leaves of this vegetable are both edible. The flesh is crisp and mild in flavour, somewhat turnip-like, and it can be eaten in the same way as a turnip, either grated or sliced raw, added to stews, mashed or cooked in chunks and tossed in butter. Kohlrabi may be used in Chinese stir-fries or soups.

Also known as — knol-khol

lettuce

Iceberg lettuce

There are many varieties of lettuce, used mainly fresh in salads in the West, but usually cooked or used to wrap parcels of food in Asian cooking. In Vietnamese and Chinese cuisine, lettuce is used as a 'cup' in dishes such as Chinese san choy bau, which is also called *saang choy bow*, from the Chinese word *saang*, meaning lettuce (see page 240 for recipe). In China, lettuce is generally lightly blanched and added to soups, stir-fries and casseroles, or it may be cooked on its own as a vegetable.

stir-fried lettuce

750 g (1 lb 10 oz) crisp lettuce
1 tablespoon vegetable oil
4 tablespoons oyster sauce
1 tablespoon roasted sesame oil

cut the lettuce in half and then into wide strips, trimming off any roots that may hold the pieces together. Wash well and dry thoroughly.

heat a wok over high heat, add the oil and heat until very hot. Toss the lettuce pieces around the wok until they start to wilt, then add the oyster sauce and toss everything together. Sprinkle with the sesame oil, season and serve. Serves 4.

preparation

Lettuce leaves need to be washed thoroughly and dried before use. Either dry them in tea towels or paper towels or use a salad spinner. If using lettuce in a salad or as a wrapper for food, any moisture left on the leaves will dilute the dressing. If using as an ingredient in a stir-fry, any moisture left clinging to the leaves will cause the lettuce to steam rather than fry.

limes

There are many varieties of limes, which are small green-skinned citrus fruit native to the tropics where they are widely used in cooking. Limes are only green because they are picked unripe—if left to ripen they turn yellow. Limes can be used like lemons but, as the juice is more acidic, usually less is needed. Both lime juice and zest add a piquant flavour to sweet dishes such as ice cream and sorbets, as well as to curries, stews and fish. In India, pickled limes are served with meat and fish dishes. In Thailand, limes are used not only for their sourness but also as a tenderizer. Warm limes in a microwave for 2–3 seconds before squeezing them to make the juice flow, or roll them back and forth on the bench. See also makrut (kaffir) limes, page 180.

steamed whole fish with chilli, garlic and lime

1–1.5 kg (2 lb 4 oz–3 lb 5 oz)
  whole snapper, cleaned
1 lime, sliced
finely chopped red chillies,
  for garnish
coriander (cilantro) leaves,
  for garnish
lime wedges, for garnish

sauce
2 teaspoons tamarind purée
5 long red chillies, seeded
  and chopped
6 large garlic cloves, roughly
  chopped
6 coriander (cilantro) roots
  and stalks
8 Asian shallots, chopped
1½ tablespoons vegetable oil
2½ tablespoons lime juice
130 g (4½ oz) shaved palm
  sugar
60 ml (¼ cup) fish sauce

rinse the fish and pat dry with paper towels. Cut two diagonal slashes through the thickest part of the fish on both sides. Put the lime slices in the fish cavity, cover with plastic wrap and refrigerate until ready to use.

to make the sauce, combine the tamarind with 60 ml (¼ cup) water. Blend the chilli, garlic, coriander and shallots in a food processor until finely puréed—add a little water, if necessary.

heat the oil in a saucepan. Add the paste and cook over medium heat for 5 minutes, or until fragrant. Stir in the tamarind mixture, lime juice and palm sugar. Reduce the heat and simmer for 10 minutes, or until thick. Stir in the fish sauce.

line a bamboo steamer with baking paper and place the fish on top. Cover and steam over a wok of simmering water for 6 minutes per 1 kg (2 lb 4 oz) fish, or until the flesh flakes easily when tested with a fork. Pour the sauce over the fish and garnish with the chilli, coriander and lime wedges. Serve with steamed rice. Serves 4–6.

longans

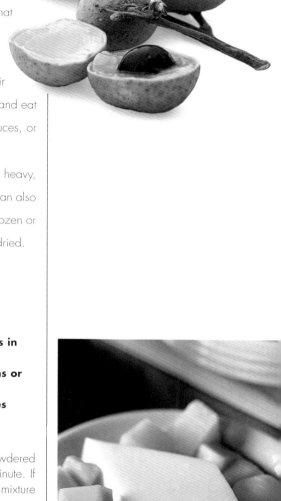

Native to China, but now grown in many parts of Southeast Asia, longan fruit range in size from as small as olives to as big as plums. Longans are covered with a smooth leathery skin that changes colour from orange to brown when ripe. Inside, the flesh is translucent, similar in both flavour and texture to its closest relative, the lychee. Longans are also noted for their fragrance, which is likened to that of a gardenia. Peel the fruit and eat fresh, add to fruit salads, use to garnish ice creams, use in sauces, or substitute them for grapes in any sweet recipe.

Longans are in season in summer, when you should look for heavy, uncracked fruit. They last for 2–3 weeks in the refrigerator, but can also be frozen in their skins (defrost just before use and use slightly frozen or the flesh will become flabby). Longans are also sold tinned or dried.

Also known as — dragon's eye, lungan

almond bean curd with fruit

2½ tablespoons powdered gelatine or 6 gelatine sheets
90 g (⅓ cup) caster (superfine) sugar
125 ml (½ cup) condensed milk
2 teaspoons almond extract

400 g (14 oz) tin lychees in syrup
400 g (14 oz) tin longans or loquats in syrup
½ papaya, cut into cubes
½ melon, cut into cubes

put 125 ml (½ cup) water in a saucepan. If you are using powdered gelatine, sprinkle it on the water and leave to sponge for 1 minute. If you are using sheets, soak in the water until floppy. Heat the mixture slightly, stirring constantly to dissolve the gelatine.

put the sugar, condensed milk and almond extract in a bowl and stir to combine. Slowly add 625 ml (2½ cups) water, stirring to dissolve the sugar. Stir in the dissolved gelatine. Pour into a chilled 23 cm (9 inch) square tin. Chill for at least 4 hours, or until set.

drain half the syrup from the lychees and the longans and place, with their remaining syrup, in a large bowl. Add the cubed papaya and melon. Cut the almond 'bean curd' into diamond-shaped pieces and arrange on plates, then spoon the fruit around it. Serves 6.

During hot weather in China, refreshing fruit salads are popular snacks. The milky square of almond jelly that goes with this fruit salad is said to resemble bean curd, hence the name of the recipe.

lotus roots

Lotus is a member of the waterlily family, with beautiful white and pink flowers. In cooking, nothing from the plant is wasted: the leaves, roots and seeds are all utilized in the cuisines of Japan, China and India. In India, the stamens from the flowers are used to make fragrant tea. In cooking, the root is commonly used.

lotus root When sliced horizontally, the lotus root displays a floral-like pattern of holes. This decorativeness along with its crisp, delicately flavoured flesh is much appreciated in Chinese and Japanese cuisine. First peel the root, then slice it before eating raw or cooked. Add to salads or stir-fries, or cut into chunks, stuff it, or serve as a vegetable. Store the cut slices of root in water with a squeeze of lemon juice to prevent them from turning brown. Lotus roots are available fresh as well as dried, frozen and in tins.

lotus leaves The dried leaves of the lotus need to be soaked before use and are used for wrapping up food, such as fish or glutinous rice. They are sold in packets in Chinese shops. In Thailand, young fresh leaves are eaten with a savoury sauce.

lotus seeds These seeds, sometimes called lotus nuts, are considered by the Chinese to be medicinal. They are used in eight-treasure dishes, as well as being roasted, salted or candied and eaten as a snack. Lotus seeds are also made into a sweet paste to fill buns and pancakes. Dried and fresh lotus seeds are both available, and dried seeds need to be soaked before use.

The lotus root has a crispy, crunchy texture that makes it ideal for use in stir-fries such as this.

The lychee has been cultivated in its native China for thousands of years, but it is now also grown in Southeast Asia and India. About the size of a small plum, the lychee fruit has a knobbly, rust-coloured leathery skin, which encases a sweet and fragrant creamy flesh around a hard stone.

Lychees are important in Chinese cuisine as they are said to promote fertility and good luck. They appear in dishes such as chicken cooked with lychees, as well as desserts and sweets. Eat fresh or add to fruit salads and ice creams, purée or poach in a light syrup. Because fruit with green skins won't ripen once picked, you must buy lychees at their peak—when their skin is red. As the fruit ages, its skin becomes more brittle and brown. Lychees are also available tinned and dried. When dried, the fruit acquire a nutty, raisin-like taste, perfect for snacking.

Also known as — litchi

lychee sorbet

peel and stone the lychees, then purée the flesh until smooth. Mix in the lime juice and caster sugar. Churn in an ice-cream maker or pour into a freezerproof container and freeze.

if using a freezerproof container to set the sorbet, stir the sorbet every hour to break up any ice crystals (do this 3 or 4 times, or until the sorbet reaches a smooth, thick consistency), then freeze overnight. Serves 6.

1 kg (2 lb 4 oz) fresh lychees
60 ml (1/4 cup) lime juice
160 g (2/3 cup) caster
(superfine) sugar

makrut limes

The makrut lime is a small, fragrant citrus fruit widely used in Thai and Southeast Asian cuisine. The fruit have a distinctive knobbly, dark-green skin and glossy leaves (see makrut lime leaves, page 132). The limes are used for their zest rather than for their juice, which is quite bitter. Finely shredded or grated, the zest is added to soups, curries, salads and chilli dishes to give them a wonderful fresh and tangy flavour. Makrut limes are available from Asian food stores or supermarkets. They freeze well. If makrut limes are unavailable, use Tahitian or West Indian lime zest.

Also known as — kaffir lime

mango

Mangoes are native to India but now grow in many tropical climates worldwide. The fruit ranges in colour from green to golden yellow and orange-red, and its flesh is a juicy, deep orange surrounding a large, flat, inedible stone. Mangoes are best eaten out of hand, but they also make excellent ice creams, sorbets and sauces; are good in drinks like smoothies; go well with seafood or in salads; make good pickles and chutneys; and act as tenderizers when added to curries. In Asian cooking, green mango is used in pickles, raw in salads or as a vegetable. Store unripe mangoes at room temperature, then put them in the refrigerator when ripened.

mango salad

300 g (10½ oz) grated fresh coconut (page 165) or desiccated coconut

2 dried chillies, seeded and chopped

1 tablespoon grated jaggery or soft brown sugar

300 g (10½ oz) ripe mango flesh, cubed

1 tablespoon oil

½ teaspoon coriander seeds

½ teaspoon black mustard seeds

6 curry leaves

put the coconut, chilli and jaggery in a blender and add enough water to make a thick, coarse paste. Alternatively, crush everything together using a mortar and pestle, adding a little water as you go.

transfer the paste to a bowl and toss the mango through. Season with salt, to taste, then refrigerate. Heat the oil in a small frying pan over low heat and add the coriander seeds, mustard seeds and curry leaves. Cover and shake the pan until the seeds start to pop. Pour the oil and seeds over the mango mixture and stir. Serves 4.

buying and preparation

You can determine if a mango is ripe, not by its colour, but by both its smell and feel—a ripe mango has a wonderful aroma and will yield when gently pressed. When it is ready to eat, the best way to prepare it is to cut it into a 'hedgehog'. Slice off the two cheeks of an unpeeled mango close to the stone and, without cutting the skin, score the flesh in a hatched pattern. Push the skin inside out so the cubes of flesh pop out, then slice them off.

Serve this spicy mango salad as a side dish with any Indian curry.

mangosteen

Contrary to its name, the mangosteen doesn't resemble or taste like the mango; rather, it is deep purple and round, similar in size to a mandarin. The mangosteen comes from a native Asian tree that takes 10–15 years to bear fruit. The highly prized fruit has a thick skin that is hard and inedible and which, when cut open, reveals a soft, white flesh divided into segments, some of which contain seeds. The taste is delicate, reminiscent of pineapple.

To open, cut it in half through the skin only and lightly twist the halves apart. Eat the white flesh in segments like an orange, add to fruit salads or use in sorbets. Look for mangosteens during spring and summer. Colour is a good indication of ripeness—pale-green fruit are immature and turn dark purple or red-purple when ripe. The fruit will keep for a few days without refrigeration but will keep for longer if wrapped and stored in the refrigerator.

The kokum (see page 130), a relative of the mangosteen, is used dried in southern Indian cooking as a souring agent like tamarind.

mizuna

ginger noodle salad

500 g (1 lb 2 oz) salmon
  fillet, skin removed
1 tablespoon oil
1 avocado, halved and stone
  removed
500 g (1 lb 2 oz) dried soba
  noodles

3 tablespoons pickled ginger,
  well drained and shredded
85 g (3 oz) mizuna, trimmed
80 ml (1/3 cup) ponzu sauce
  (see note, page 223)
1 tablespoon black sesame
  seeds

put the salmon in a bowl and rub the surface with the oil, salt and pepper. Slice each avocado half lengthways into quarters, then cut each quarter into 1 cm (1/2 inch) long pieces from the base to the stem end.

heat a large frying pan over medium-high heat, and just before the pan begins to smoke add the salmon—if your fillet is too large to fit, cut it in half. Cook for 3 minutes on each side, or until golden—this will depend on the size and thickness of your fillet. Remove from the pan and allow to cool.

bring a large saucepan of water to the boil over high heat. Add the noodles and stir to separate. Return to the boil, then add 250 ml (1 cup) cold water. Repeat this step three times as the water just comes to the boil. Test a piece of soba—it should be tender to the bite, cooked through but not mushy. If it's not quite done, repeat one more time. Drain and rinse under cold water until the noodles are cold.

combine the noodles, avocado, ginger and mizuna in a large bowl. Flake the salmon into small pieces and add to the noodles with any juices, then add the ponzu sauce. Gently toss until well combined. To serve, divide the noodle salad among the serving dishes and sprinkle with the sesame seeds. Serves 4.

A Japanese green, mizuna is a delicate, feathery green salad leaf available in spring and summer. The young leaves have a mild mustardy flavour and are used in salad mixes or as a garnish on Japanese food, while older leaves are used in stir-fries. Refrigerate in a container or plastic bag and wash and dry before use.

mung bean sprouts

The sprouts of small, olive-green mung beans are used in salads and Chinese stir-fries. In Southeast Asia, mung beans are ground to make a flour used for sweets and doughs. The starch is used for making fine noodles called bean thread noodles (mung bean vermicelli). See also soya bean sprouts, page 194.

mixed sprout salad

600 g (1 lb 5 oz) mixed sprouts (such as snow pea sprouts, mung bean sprouts, soya bean sprouts)
4 rashers streaky bacon, fried and chopped
2 skinless chicken breasts, cooked and chopped into cubes
4 spring onions (scallions), finely chopped
2 garlic cloves, crushed
100 ml (3¹/₂ fl oz) extra virgin olive oil
1¹/₂ tablespoons lemon juice
2 tablespoons chopped parsley

put the sprouts in a large bowl, add the cooked bacon pieces, chicken cubes and spring onion.

mix the garlic with the olive oil, lemon juice and parsley and toss through the sprouts. Season well. Serves 4.

mushrooms/ fungi

Some of the most exciting food known to humanity is found in dark, damp habitats, on forest floors, living off live, decaying and dead organic matter. There are countless varieties of edible mushrooms, some cultivated, others gathered from the wild. In many countries, hunting for mushrooms and fungi is a national pastime. There are thousands of types, but only a few are edible. Never take a risk on eating mushrooms and fungi you have gathered yourself without having them properly identified. Some are poisonous enough to make you ill, and some may be lethal—and cooking will not make them any less so. If in doubt, do not use them. Wild mushrooms are generally in season during autumn, with the exception of morels, which are picked in spring, and cultivated mushrooms are available year round.

Cultivated mushrooms may be found as the small button closed-cup mushroom, good for salads or stir-fries; as an open cup mushroom, ideal for stews; or as a flat (field) mushroom, which has a good earthy flavour and meaty texture.

Oyster mushrooms are fan- or oyster-shaped, pale creamy grey or brown in colour with a slight peppery flavour that becomes milder when cooked. Straw mushrooms are small, unopened button-shaped mushrooms. Usually bought it tins. Drain and rinse well before use. Shiitake mushrooms grow on rotting wood. Enoki mushrooms are tiny white Japanese mushrooms on long, thin stalks growing in clumps. Shimeji have a delicate flavour and are light grey or pale brown in colour. For dried fungi and mushrooms, see pages 38–9.

From front to back: enoki mushrooms, shiitake mushrooms, oyster mushrooms.

mixed mushrooms with noodles

trim and wipe the mushrooms with a damp cloth, slicing any larger ones. Melt the butter in a frying pan and add the oil. Add the chopped chilli, shallot and garlic clove and fry briefly.

add the mushrooms and toss over high heat until cooked through and beginning to brown (if using shimeji or enoki mushrooms, put them in at the end). Add the coriander and soy sauce, season well and drizzle with sesame oil.

serve tossed through noodles. Serves 6.

500 g (1 lb 2 oz) mixed mushrooms, such as enoki, oyster, swiss brown, shiitake and shimeji
25 g (1 oz) butter
1 tablespoon oil
1 chilli, finely chopped
1 Asian shallot, finely chopped
1 garlic clove, chopped
1 tablespoon chopped coriander (cilantro) leaves
1 tablespoon soy sauce
roasted sesame oil, to serve

okra

Okra is a slender, five-sided pod containing numerous white seeds. When young, okra is eaten as a vegetable; the older pods are usually dried, then powdered and used as a flavouring. When cooked, okra releases a sticky, gelatinous substance, which serves as a thickening agent. Okra is used extensively in Asian cooking, particularly in India (where it is called bhindi), where it may be stir-fried or used in spicy vegetable curries.

Buy pods that are healthy green in colour, they should snap rather than bend, and should be no more than 10 cm (4 inches) long. If too ripe, the pod will feel very sticky. To prepare, gently scrub with paper towels or a vegetable brush. Rinse and drain, then trim the ends. If using as a thickener, blanch whole first, then slice and add to the dish about 10 minutes before the end of cooking. In some recipes, the pod is used whole, thus preventing the release of the sticky substances within.

Also known as — bhindi, gumbo, ladies' fingers

spicy okra

450 g (1 lb) okra
2 tablespoons oil
1 small onion, finely chopped
½ teaspoon ground cumin
½ teaspoon ground coriander
½ teaspoon chilli powder
    (optional)
¼ teaspoon ground turmeric
150 g (5½ oz) tinned
    chopped tomatoes

wash the okra and pat dry with paper towels. Trim the tops and tails and cut into 2.5 cm (1 inch) pieces. Ignore any sticky, glutinous liquid that appears because this will disappear as the okra cooks.

heat the oil in a deep, heavy-based frying pan over medium heat and fry the onion until lightly browned. Add the spices and tomato and fry for 1 minute until well mixed, squashing the tomato to break it up.

add the okra and stir until well coated. Bring to the boil, cover and simmer for 5–8 minutes, or until the okra is cooked through and no longer slimy. If there is any excess liquid, simmer, uncovered, until the liquid evaporates. Season with salt, to taste. Serves 4.

papaya

Papaya is a large tropical fruit whose juicy ripe flesh can be creamy orange, red or yellow. In the centre is a mass of large peppery black seeds, which are edible and sometimes crushed and used as a spice. Unripe papayas are used as a vegetable in Thai salads or to make Indian pickles. An enzyme called papain is extracted from unripe papayas, which breaks down protein and is used to tenderize meat. Chopped papaya can also cause fruit in a fruit salad to soften if left for a while, so add it just before serving. Sprinkle papaya with a little lime juice to bring out the flavour.

thai chicken and papaya salad

250 ml (1 cup) coconut cream
200 g (7 oz) skinless chicken breast fillet, trimmed
200 g (1 cup) jasmine rice
330 ml (1⅓ cups) coconut milk
2 garlic cloves, chopped
3 Asian shallots, chopped
3 small red chillies
1 teaspoon small dried shrimp

2 tablespoons fish sauce
8 cherry tomatoes, cut in halves
150 g (5½ oz) green papaya, grated
2 tablespoons lime juice
30 g (1½ cups) mint leaves, chopped
20 g (⅔ cup) coriander (cilantro) leaves, chopped

bring the coconut cream to the boil in a small saucepan. Add the chicken and simmer over low heat for 5 minutes. Turn off the heat and cover the pan for 20 minutes, then remove the chicken and shred it.

wash the rice under cold water until the water runs clear. Put the rice and coconut milk in a small saucepan and bring to the boil. Reduce the heat to low, cover with a tight-fitting lid and simmer for 20 minutes. Remove from the heat and leave the lid on until ready to serve.

using a mortar and pestle or blender, pound or blend the garlic, shallots and chillies together. Add the shrimp and fish sauce and pound to break up the dried shrimp. Add the tomatoes and pound all the ingredients together to form a rough paste.

in a bowl, combine the shredded chicken and chilli paste mixture with the grated papaya, lime juice, mint and coriander. Serve with the hot coconut rice. Serves 4.

Also known as —
pawpaw

pea shoots

Pea shoots are the tender leaves of the garden pea that have been prevented from flowering or shooting to encourage the growth of the small leaves. Used in Chinese stir-fries, often with garlic or ginger, or in soups. Buy on the day that you want to use them as they don't stay fresh for more than 2 days.

flash-cooked pea shoots with garlic

350 g (12 oz) pea shoots
1 teaspoon oil
2 garlic cloves, finely chopped
1 1/2 tablespoons Shaoxing rice wine
1/4 teaspoon salt

trim the tough stems and wilted leaves from the pea shoots. Wash well and dry thoroughly.

heat a wok over high heat, add the oil and heat until very hot. Add the pea shoots and garlic and toss lightly for 20 seconds, then add the rice wine and salt, and stir-fry for 1 minute, or until the shoots are slightly wilted, but still bright green.

transfer to a platter, leaving behind most of the liquid. Serve hot, at room temperature, or cold. Serves 6.

pineapple

The pineapple's name is derived from the Spanish word *pina* meaning pine cone. Pineapple is a tropical fruit native to South America but now cultivated in most tropical and subtropical climates. The pineapple plant bears over 100 purple flowers in a spiral shape, and it is these unfertilized flowers that fuse together to form a single fruit. The pineapple is actually a composite of several individual fruits, called 'eyes'.

Pineapples are juicy and have a sweet—but sometimes slightly tart—fragrant flavour. They are best eaten fresh; simply slice down the side of the fruit to remove its hard skin, then cut into chunks or slices, use in fruit salads or grill (broil) and serve with meats. In Asia, they are also used in other ways—to make chutneys, and as an ingredient in curries and soups. Choose pineapples that are heavy for their size and slightly aromatic. A good test for ripeness is to pull out a leaf from the crown—if it comes away easily, it is ripe.

cooking

Pineapple contains bromelin, an enzyme that breaks down protein (similar to the papain in papaya). This means that meat that is marinated in fresh pineapple juice will fall apart if left for too long. Also, if pineapple is added to gelatine, such as in jellies, the bromelin will prevent the gelatine from setting. Bromelin is destroyed by heating, so cooked or tinned pineapple or pasteurized pineapple juice can be safely added to gelatine.

pomegranate

A round fruit the size of a large apple, the pomegranate has thick, tough, reddish skin enclosing hundreds of edible seeds, each encased in a juicy, translucent-red pulp. To use, cut the fruit in half with a very sharp knife and scoop out the tangy-sweet seeds. Separate them from the white pith and eat them fresh, add to salads or use as a garnish on sweet and savoury dishes. In India, dried pomegranate seeds and flesh are used whole or ground to add a sour, tangy flavour to dishes. In the recipe below, the dried seeds are used with besan flour to make a flavoursome batter for prawns (shrimp).

Choose pomegranates that are heavy for their size with smooth skin that gives slightly when pressed. They are usually available in autumn.

Also known as — Chinese apple

prawn pakoras

600 g (1 lb 5 oz) raw prawns
　(shrimp)
55 g (½ cup) besan flour
1 large red onion, finely
　chopped
1 teaspoon dried
　pomegranate seeds
4 green chillies, seeded and
　finely chopped
2 tablespoons finely chopped
　coriander (cilantro) leaves
pinch of bicarbonate of soda
ghee or oil, for deep-frying

peel and devein the prawns, then cut into small pieces. Put the besan flour in a bowl and add 2 tablespoons water, or enough to make a thick batter, mixing with a fork to beat out any lumps. Add the remaining ingredients, except the oil, to the batter, season with salt and mix well.

fill a heavy-based saucepan one-third full with ghee or oil and heat to 180°C (350°F), or until a cube of bread browns in 15 seconds. Drop 1 heaped teaspoon of batter at a time into the ghee and deep-fry in batches until they are brown all over. Remove and drain on paper towels. Serve hot. Makes 30.

rambutan

The most distinguishing feature of the rambutan, a native of Malaysia but grown widely in Southeast Asia, is its long, dense red tendrils. The fruit, about 5 cm (2 inches) in diameter, is named from the Malay for 'hair of the head'. Related to the lychee and the longan, it has a juicy whitish pulp, which is mildly sweet to refreshingly acidic, depending on the variety, surrounding a single inedible seed. Rambutans are mostly eaten fresh or added to fruit salads, but can also be served in a syrup or cooked and served with meat or vegetables. To prepare, cut in half, just through the skin, then twist apart. Choose brightly coloured fruit with fleshy tendrils. Store for only a short time in a plastic bag in the refrigerator—they are best eaten as soon as possible after buying as they perish easily.

Also known as — hairy lychee

A long, green stringless bean, some varieties of snake bean may be up to 40 cm (16 inches) in length. The darker green variety has a firmer texture than the paler green one, which is more fibrous. Use as soon as possible after purchase—snip off the ends and then cut into bite-sized pieces. If unavailable, stringless green beans can be used instead.

Also known as — long beans, yard-long beans

thai fish cakes

fish cakes
500 g (1 lb 2 oz) redfish fillets, skin removed
1½ tablespoons ready-made Thai red curry paste
60 g (¼ cup) sugar
60 ml (¼ cup) fish sauce
1 egg
200 g (7 oz) snake beans, sliced
10 makrut (kaffir) lime leaves, finely chopped
oil, for deep-frying

dipping sauce
125 g (½ cup) sugar
60 ml (¼ cup) white vinegar
1 tablespoon fish sauce
1 small red chilli, chopped
¼ small carrot, finely chopped
¼ cucumber, peeled, seeded and finely chopped
1 tablespoon roasted peanuts, chopped

to make the dipping sauce, put the sugar, vinegar, fish sauce, chilli and 125 ml (½ cup) water in a saucepan. Simmer for 5 minutes, or until the sauce has thickened slightly. Allow to cool. Stir in the remaining ingredients, then set aside until needed.

to make the fish cakes, put the fish in a food processor and blend until smooth. Add the curry paste, sugar, fish sauce and egg. Process for another 10 seconds, or until combined. Stir in the beans and lime leaves. Shape into golf-ball-size balls, then flatten into patties.

fill a wok one-third full of oil and heat to 180°C (350°F), or until a cube of bread browns in 15 seconds. Cook the fish cakes in batches for 3–5 minutes, turning occasionally. Drain on crumpled paper towels. Serve with the dipping sauce. Serves 6.

snake beans

snake gourds

Snake gourds are exceptionally long vegetables that grow hanging down from vines. The gourds are light green with dark green ridges and, as the name implies, they are long and thin, often twisted, somewhat like a snake. Growers sometimes tie a weight to the bottom of the vegetable to straighten it as it grows. Snake gourds have a mild flavour, so they are often mixed with spicy ingredients.

snake gourd with yoghurt

250 g (9 oz) snake gourd
1 teaspoon ground turmeric
1 tablespoon oil
1/2 teaspoon black mustard seeds
1/2 teaspoon whole black

lentils (sabat urad)
2 dried chillies, cut in half
4 stalks of curry leaves
1 1/2 red onions, finely chopped
250 ml (1 cup) thick natural yoghurt

In this Indian dish, the snake gourds are fried with spices and then mixed with yoghurt. You could also use bitter melon or eggplant (aubergine) instead of snake gourds.

peel the snake gourd, slice it in half horizontally, then slice diagonally into pieces about 1 cm (1/2 inch) thick. Put the gourd in a bowl, add the turmeric and a pinch of salt and rub into the pieces of gourd. Put the gourd in a sieve to allow any liquid to drain off.

heat the oil in a heavy-based frying pan over low heat. Add the mustard seeds and black lentils and, when the mustard seeds pop, add the chilli and curry leaf stalks and one-third of the onion. Cook until the onion is browned and softened. Add the snake gourd and toss over medium heat for about 10 minutes, or until the mixture looks dry and the gourd is tender. Remove from the heat.

combine the yoghurt and the remaining onion in a bowl and stir well. Fold the fried snake gourd into the yoghurt just before serving and season with salt, to taste. Serves 4.

soya bean sprouts

In China, soya bean sprouts are usually only lightly cooked to maintain their crispness. Here, they are lightly stir-fried with oil, chilli and soy sauce.

Soya bean sprouts are crisp, whitish-yellow sprouts, high in vitamin C, and used as a vegetable in stir-fries, eaten raw in salads, added to soups or used in dishes such as phad Thai. Bean sprouts are sold in tins, or fresh in containers or bags. They are often labelled simply as bean sprouts. Although they are best eaten on the day of purchase, keep fresh bean sprouts in cold water in the refrigerator and change the water daily.

phad thai

250 g (9 oz) dried rice stick noodles
1 small red chilli, chopped
2 garlic cloves, chopped
2 spring onions (scallions), sliced
1 tablespoon tamarind purée, mixed with 1 tablespoon water
1½ tablespoons sugar
2 tablespoons fish sauce
2 tablespoons lime juice
2 tablespoons vegetable oil
2 eggs, beaten
150 g (5 oz) pork fillet, thinly sliced
8 large raw prawns (shrimp), peeled and deveined, with tails intact
100 g (3½ oz) bean curd (tofu) puffs, julienned
90 g (3¼ oz) soya bean sprouts, tailed
40 g (¼ cup) chopped roasted peanuts
3 tablespoons coriander (cilantro) leaves
1 lime, cut into wedges

soak the noodles in warm water for 15–20 minutes, or until tender, then drain.

pound together the chilli, garlic and spring onion using a mortar and pestle. Gradually blend in the tamarind mixture, sugar, fish sauce and lime juice.

heat a wok over high heat, add 1 tablespoon of the oil and swirl to coat. Add the egg, swirl to coat and cook for 1–2 minutes, or until set and cooked. Remove and shred.

heat the remaining oil, stir in the chilli mixture and stir-fry for 30 seconds. Add the pork and stir-fry for 2 minutes, or until tender. Add the prawns and stir-fry for a further 1 minute. Stir in the noodles, egg, bean curd and half the bean sprouts, and toss to heat through.

serve immediately, topped with the peanuts, coriander, lime and remaining bean sprouts. Serves 4–6.

note: Use a non-stick or stainless steel wok to cook this dish as the tamarind will react with the metal in a regular wok and taint the dish.

spring onions

spring onion pancakes

**250 g (2 cups) plain
(all-purpose) flour
1 tablespoon oil
3 tablespoons roasted
sesame oil**

**2 spring onions (scallions),
green part only, chopped
oil, for frying**

combine the flour and ½ teaspoon salt in a mixing bowl. Add the oil and 220 ml (8 fl oz) boiling water and, using a wooden spoon, mix to a rough dough. Turn out onto a lightly floured surface and knead for 5 minutes, or until smooth and elastic. If the dough is very sticky, knead in a little more flour. Cover with a cloth and let it rest for 20 minutes.

on a lightly floured surface, roll the dough into a long roll. Divide into 24 pieces. Working with one portion at a time, place the dough, cut edge down, on the work surface. Using a small rolling pin, roll it out to a 10 cm (4 inch) circle. Brush the surface generously with sesame oil and sprinkle with some spring onion. Starting with the edge closest to you, roll up the dough and pinch the ends to seal. Lightly flatten the roll, then roll it up again from one end like a snail, pinching the end to seal. Repeat to make the remaining pancakes. Rest for 20 minutes.

put each roll flat on the work surface and press down. Roll out to a 10 cm (4 inch) circle and put on a floured tray. Stack the pancakes between lightly floured sheets of baking paper. Rest for 20 minutes.

heat a frying pan over medium heat, brush with oil, and add two or three pancakes at a time. Cook for 2–3 minutes on each side, turning once, until the pancakes are light golden brown and crisp. Remove and drain on paper towels. Serve immediately. Makes 24.

These are immature onions, which are pulled before the bulb has started to form, and sold in bunches with the roots intact. Discard the roots and base of the stem, and wash the stem leaves well before use. Both the white and green parts can be used. Spring onions add colour and a mild onion flavour and need little cooking. Chop them and use as a garnish, or add to dishes such as soups, stir-fries and fried rice, to name a few. In China, they are used to make spring onion pancakes, eaten as a snack straight from the hot oil. Spring onions are sometimes erroneously referred to as shallots.

***Also known as — green
onions, scallions***

1 Sprinkle the spring onion over the dough and then roll it up.

2 Roll the dough into a snail shape, pinching the end to seal.

3 Cook for 2–3 minutes each side until brown and crisp.

star fruit

The scientific name of this tropical fruit native to India, China and Indonesia, *averrhoa carambola*, gives the star fruit its alternative name of carambola. This unusually-shaped fruit has a waxy golden orange or green skin (depending on variety), crisp, slightly tart flesh, and five ridges that run down its length which, when sliced, resemble a five-pointed star. The flavour differs depending on the variety and when it is picked. Some are sweeter than others, but it is difficult to determine the fruit's sweetness by looking at it, though often the fatter fruit are sweetest. Choose shiny, plump yellow fruit without any damage to the ridges. As the fruit ripens, the ridges may turn slightly brown, but this is normal. The star fruit's decorative shape lends itself to fruit salads, or fry them in butter and sugar and add to hot desserts. The sour varieties are often used in pickles and chutneys.

**Also known as —
carambola, five-corner fruit**

taro

The general name for a family of tropical tubers, and a staple in Asia, the Pacific Islands and West Indies. Taros have either a brown or yellow skin and must be washed and peeled well, as the skin contains calcium oxalate crystals, which causes irritation to the mouth and tongue. These crystals are neutralized after cooking. Like potato, taro can be boiled, steamed or used in soups and stews, but add at the end as they fall apart easily. Taro starch, used in Asian cooking, is similar to arrowroot.

The taro also produces edible shoots (below). These should be washed well, peeled and sliced for use in soups and stir-fries. Thin slices may be deep-fried.

Taro shoots are also known as — pak ha

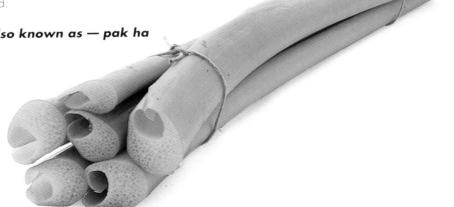

water spinach

This green vegetable thrives in swampy areas, hence its alternative name of swamp spinach. There are several varieties, but two are commonly used—one has long, dark-green pointed leaves and long hollow stems; the other has light green leaves and thicker stems. In Thailand (where it is called *pak boong*) it is eaten raw in salads or used as a vegetable, while in Malaysia and China (where it is called *ong choy*), it is often stir-fried with fish sauce.

Also known as — kangkong, morning glory, ong choy, pak boong, swamp spinach, water convolvulus

stir-fried water spinach

1 1/2 tablespoons oyster sauce
1 teaspoon fish sauce
1 tablespoon yellow bean sauce
1/4 teaspoon sugar
1 1/2 tablespoons vegetable oil
2–3 garlic cloves, finely chopped
350 g (12 oz) water spinach, cut into 5 cm (2 inch) lengths, keeping stalks and leaves separate
1 red bird's eye chilli, slightly crushed (optional)

mix the oyster sauce, fish sauce, yellow bean sauce and sugar in a small bowl.

heat the oil in a wok or a frying pan and stir-fry the garlic over medium heat until light brown. Increase the heat to very high, add the stalks of the water spinach and stir-fry for 1–2 minutes. Add the leaves of the water spinach, the sauce mixture and the crushed chilli and stir-fry for another minute. Serves 4.

This unusual bean is the seed pod of a climbing vine native to tropical areas of southeast Asia. All parts of the plant are edible but it is the wing bean that is most commonly eaten. It grows to about 10 cm (4 inches) and has four distinctive sides, earning it the names angle bean or frilly bean. The pods are green, with a central core containing tiny black, edible seeds. Wing beans are cultivated as garden vegetables and in cooking are used in stir-fried dishes or Thai salads. Lightly cooked, they retain their striking appearance and crisp texture.

wing bean salad

oil, for frying
75 g (3 oz) Asian shallots, finely sliced
175 g (6 oz) wing beans
55 g (2 oz) cooked chicken, shredded
1 lemon grass stalk, white part only, finely sliced
2 tablespoons dried shrimp, ground

1 1/2 tablespoons fish sauce
3–4 tablespoons lime juice
1/2 long red chilli or 1 small red chilli, finely chopped
55 g (2 oz) whole salted roasted peanuts
125 ml (1/2 cup) coconut milk, for garnish

heat 2.5 cm (1 inch) oil in a wok or deep frying pan over a medium heat. Deep-fry the shallots for 3–4 minutes, or until they are light brown (without burning them). Lift out with a slotted spoon and drain on paper towels.

slice the wing beans diagonally into thin pieces. Blanch the wing beans in boiling water for 30 seconds, then drain and put them in cold water for 1–2 minutes. Drain and transfer to a bowl. Add the cooked chicken, lemon grass, dried shrimp, fish sauce, lime juice, chilli and half the peanuts. Mix with a spoon. Taste, then adjust the seasoning if necessary.

put the wing bean salad in a serving bowl, drizzle with coconut milk and sprinkle with the crispy shallots and the rest of the peanuts. Serves 4.

wing bean

yams

Yams are edible tubers of a tropical and subtropical climbing plant, and the staple food of many countries. Strictly speaking, yams are the tubers of the genus *Dioscorea*, but the word is often used loosely to encompass a range of other tropical roots such as sweet potato, taro and cassava. In the United States, sweet potatoes are called yams.

There are many varieties of yams and these vary in size, colour and shape. Some have a coarse skin, others smooth, while some may be pale, brown or purple in colour. The flesh colour also varies, from white to cream, yellow, pink or purple. Some commonly available varieties are used in Chinese cuisine, in Japan it is used a vegetable for tempura, or it is mixed with coconut milk in Malaysia and Indonesia as a dessert.

Yams resemble potatoes in flavour, although they are more starchy and mealy. They must be cooked before eating to destroy the bitter toxic substance (dioscorine) that they contain. They may be boiled, puréed, baked, added to soups and stews and deep-fried. Store in a cool, dark and well-ventilated place.

yoghurt

Yoghurt is a fermented and coagulated milk, which results when milk sugar (lactose) is converted to a lactic acid, producing a bacterial change. Yoghurt can occur naturally or it can be made commercially by adding active bacteria such as *Lactobacillus bulgaricus* and *Streptococcus thermophilus* to milk. Yoghurt is usually made from cow's milk but milk from the goat, sheep, mare, yak, buffalo or camel is also used.

Yoghurt is used in Central Asia and is a vital ingredient in many Indian and Sri Lankan dishes. It is used as a medium for marinating and cooking meat (it also acts as a tenderizer); is treated as a sauce in many meat and vegetable dishes; mixed with cucumber to make raita, served as an accompaniment to spicy Indian dishes; or is used in the Indian drink, lassi. Yoghurt in India is made with whole milk and is a thick, set yoghurt. If you use commercial yoghurt when making an Indian dish, you may need to drain it in muslin first to remove excess liquid.

cooking

Yoghurt is more easily digested than milk and lower in fat than cream, for which it can be substituted in some recipes. However, yoghurt is unstable with heat so, to stop it separating, add a little cornflour before adding it to hot ingredients. Add the yoghurt at the last minute and do not allow it to boil.

tandoori chicken

1.5 kg (3 lb 5 oz) chicken or
skinless chicken thighs and
drumsticks

yoghurt marinade
2 teaspoons coriander seeds
1 teaspoon cumin seeds
1 onion, roughly chopped
3 garlic cloves, roughly
chopped
5 cm (2 inch) piece of ginger,
roughly chopped
250 ml (1 cup) thick natural
yoghurt
grated zest of 1 lemon
3 tablespoons lemon juice
2 tablespoons clear vinegar
1 teaspoon paprika
2 teaspoons garam masala
1/2 teaspoon tandoori food
colouring (optional)

2 tablespoons ghee
onion rings
lemon wedges

remove the skin from the chicken and cut the chicken in half. Using a sharp knife, make 2.5 cm (1 inch) long diagonal incisions on each limb and breast, taking care not to cut through to the bone. If using thighs and drumsticks, trim away any fat and make an incision in each piece.

to make the marinade, put a frying pan over low heat and dry-roast the coriander seeds until aromatic. Remove and dry-roast the cumin seeds. Grind the roasted seeds to a fine powder using a spice grinder or in a pestle with a mortar. In a food processor, blend all the marinade ingredients to form a smooth paste. Season with salt, to taste. If you don't have a food processor, chop the onion, garlic and ginger more finely and mix with the rest of the ingredients in a bowl.

marinate the chicken in the yoghurt marinade for at least 8 hours, or overnight. Turn the chicken occasionally in the marinade to ensure that all sides are soaked.

heat the oven to 200°C (400°F/Gas 6). Put the chicken on a wire rack on a baking tray. Cover with foil and roast on the top shelf for 45–50 minutes, or until cooked through (test by inserting a skewer into a thigh—the juices should run clear). Baste the chicken with the marinade once during cooking. Remove the foil 15 minutes before the end of cooking, to brown the tandoori mixture. Preheat the grill (broiler) to its highest setting.

prior to serving, while the chicken is still on the rack, heat the ghee, pour it over the chicken halves and cook under the grill for 5 minutes to blacken the edges of the chicken like a tandoor.

serve the chicken garnished with onion rings and lemon wedges. The chicken pieces can also be barbecued or spit-roasted. Serves 4.

Newly made yoghurt is left to set in porous earthenware bowls, which help to drain and thicken it.

mango lassi

chop the mango to a pulp with a knife or in a blender, add a pinch of salt and push through a nylon sieve with the back of a spoon. Discard any fibres. The remaining syrup should be thick but should not contain any stringy bits of pulp. Refrigerate until cold.

blend the mango with the milk and yoghurt, either by hand or in a blender. If you would like the lassi a little colder, add about 8 ice cubes to the blender, or stir them into the blended lassi.

if you want to use green unripe mangoes, cook them with 250 g (9 oz) sugar and a little water and add 500 ml (2 cups) milk to the lassi, instead of yoghurt and milk. Serves 4.

500 g (1 lb 2 oz) ripe mango
250 ml (1 cup) chilled milk
250 ml (1 cup) thick natural yoghurt

salt lassi

1 teaspoon cumin seeds
600 ml (20½ fl oz) thick natural yoghurt
½ teaspoon salt

put a small frying pan over low heat and dry-roast the cumin seeds until browned and aromatic.

blend the roasted cumin seeds (reserve a few for garnish) with the yoghurt, salt and 310 ml (1¼ cups) water, either by hand or in a blender, and serve in tall glasses. If you would like the lassi a little colder, add about 8 ice cubes to the blender, or stir them into the blended lassi. Garnish with the reserved cumin seeds. Serves 4.

speciality shopping

abalone

This single-shelled mollusc is a delicacy in China and Japan. Sometimes available fresh from specialist fish shops, but more often used dried or tinned. Dried abalone, bought from Chinese dried goods shops, needs to be soaked for 6 hours, and then simmered for 4 hours. The tinned version can be used as it is.

abalone with snow peas and oyster mushrooms

1.3 kg (3 lb) fresh abalone (450 g/1 lb prepared weight) or
    450 g (1 lb) tinned abalone
300 g (10½ oz) snow peas (mangetout),
    ends trimmed
150 g (5½ oz) oyster mushrooms
2 tablespoons oil
2 garlic cloves, finely chopped
2 teaspoons finely chopped ginger
2 tablespoons oyster sauce
2 teaspoons light soy sauce
1 teaspoon sugar
3 teaspoons cornflour (cornstarch)

prepare the fresh abalone by removing the meat from the shell using a sharp knife. Wash the meat under cold running water, rubbing well to remove any dark-coloured slime. Trim off any hard outer edges and the mouth as well as any hard patches on the bottom of the foot. Pound the meat with a mallet for 1 minute to tenderize it, but be careful not to break the flesh.

put the fresh abalone in a saucepan of simmering water and cook, covered, for about 2 hours, or until the meat is tender (test it by seeing if a fork will pierce the meat easily). Drain the abalone and, when it is cool enough to handle, cut it into thin slices.

if you are using tinned abalone, simply drain, reserving the juice, and cut into thin slices. Cut any large snow peas in half diagonally. Halve any large oyster mushrooms.

heat a wok over medium heat, add the oil and heat until hot. Stir-fry the snow peas and mushrooms for 1 minute. Add the garlic and ginger and stir for 1 minute, or until aromatic.

reduce the heat slightly and add the oyster sauce, soy sauce, sugar and the sliced abalone. Stir well to combine. Combine the cornflour with enough water (or the reserved abalone juice if using tinned abalone) to make a paste, add to the sauce and simmer until thickened. Serves 4.

Remove the meat from the abalone by cutting the muscle that holds it to the shell.

bamboo shoots

Fresh bamboo shoots (left). Tinned bamboo
shoots and Chinese mushrooms make a quick and
easy stir-fry (above).

Bamboo is a giant grass and its shoots are used in Asian cooking,
particularly in China and Japan. Bamboo leaves are used to wrap food
prior to cooking. Bamboo shoots have a crunchy texture and a mild
flavour, and are often added to stir-fries and soups. Fresh shoots (these
are seasonal and expensive) are cone-shaped and can contain a toxin
called hydrocyanic acid, which is removed by boiling for 5 minutes.
The readily available tinned ones are usually already cut into strips and
only need to be rinsed. Dried or preserved bamboo shoots may also
be available. Dried ones should be soaked. Winter shoots are more
highly prized than spring shoots as they are more
tender—bamboo may be referred
to as 'winter' in some recipes.

Tinned bamboo shoots (right) and a fresh
bamboo shoot (far right).

red curry fish with bamboo shoots

60 ml (¼ cup) coconut cream
2 tablespoons ready-made
  Thai red curry paste
440 ml (1¾ cups) coconut
  milk
1½–2 tablespoons palm sugar
3 tablespoons fish sauce
350 g (12 oz) skinless firm
  white fish fillets, cut into
  3 cm (1¼ inch) cubes

275 g (10 oz) tin bamboo
  shoots in water, drained,
  cut into matchsticks
50 g (2 oz) galangal, finely
  sliced
5 makrut (kaffir) lime leaves,
  torn in half
a handful of Thai sweet basil
  leaves, for garnish
1 long red chilli, seeded and
  finely sliced, for garnish

put the coconut cream in a wok or saucepan and simmer over medium heat for about 5 minutes, or until the cream separates and a layer of oil forms on the surface. Stir the cream if it starts to brown around the edges. Add the red curry paste, stir well to combine and cook until lightly fragrant.

stir in the coconut milk, then add the sugar and fish sauce and cook for 2–3 minutes. Add the fish and bamboo shoots and simmer for about 5 minutes, stirring occasionally, until the fish is cooked.

add the galangal and makrut lime leaves. Taste, then adjust the seasoning if necessary. Spoon onto a serving plate and sprinkle with the basil leaves and sliced chilli. Serves 4.

The fish should be cut into bite-sized pieces and the bamboo shoots into matchsticks.

barbecue pork

Barbecue pork is a Cantonese speciality that can be seen hanging in Chinese roast meat restaurants. These pork pieces are coated in maltose or honey and roasted until they have a red, lacquered appearance. Char siu means 'suspended over fire'.

Also known as — char siu

rice noodle rolls with pork filling

350 g (12 oz) barbecue pork (char siu), chopped
3 spring onions (scallions), finely chopped
2 tablespoons chopped coriander (cilantro) leaves
4 fresh rice noodle rolls (see note)
oyster sauce, to serve

to make the filling, combine the pork, spring onion and coriander.

carefully unroll the rice noodle rolls (don't worry if they crack or tear a little at the sides). Trim each one into a neat rectangle 15 x 18 cm (6 x 7 inches), or you may be able to get two out of one roll if they are very large. Divide the filling among the rolls, then re-roll the noodles. Put the rolls on a plate in a large steamer, cover and steam over simmering water in a wok for 5 minutes. Serve cut into pieces and drizzled with the oyster sauce. Makes 4.

note: Don't refrigerate rice noodle rolls. They are sold as a long sheet folded into a roll and must be used at room temperature or will break.

The char siu is hung to roast over a tray of water. This creates a steamy atmosphere, which helps keep the meat moist.

bean curd

Fresh soft bean curd (left) and firm bean curd (right).

A white cheese-like curd made by coagulating soya bean milk, bean curd was invented by the Chinese about 2000 years ago. The Chinese call it *doufu*, meaning 'rotten beans', and the Japanese name is *tofu*. Bean curd is commonly marketed throughout the world under the name of tofu.

A food rich in protein, easy to digest, and sold in a range of shapes and forms, bean curd plays an essential role in the Asian kitchen. Although it is bland in taste, its soft, silken texture absorbs the flavour of the ingredients it is cooked with. Bean curd is widely available and is sold in blocks, soft, firm or pressed, depending on the water content. Keep the blocks in water in the refrigerator, changing the water frequently, for 2–3 days. Japanese tofu can be used, but the silken variety is softer than Chinese soft bean curd.

Also known as — tofu

making bean curd

To make bean curd, dried soya beans are first soaked, then crushed with water to make soy 'milk', which is boiled, then coagulated. The curd is left to set and drain like fresh cheese. Soft bean curd is allowed to retain a lot of moisture. The silky curds may be scooped into a bowl and served with sweet syrup or spiced oil. Firm bean curd is better drained, and pressed bean curd has had almost all of its moisture removed. Both firm and pressed bean curd are robust enough to be added to stir-fries and braised dishes.

bean curd products

Bean curd can also be processed or cooked in many ways.

fermented bean curd A marinated bean curd that is either red, coloured with red rice, or white, and may also be flavoured with chilli. It is sometimes called preserved bean curd or bean curd cheese and is used as a condiment or flavouring. Buy in jars from Chinese shops.

mouldy bean curd This has been allowed to ferment like cheese and grow a furry white mould. It is used as a pungent ingredient in Chinese cooking.

bean curd skins Also called bean curd sheets or wrappers, these are made by lifting off the skin that forms on top of boiling soy milk before coagulation and drying it. The brittle sheets and rolled sticks need to be reconstituted in water before use. The skins or sheets are used as wrappers for food, which may be then deep-fried, steamed or braised, and the sticks are added to soups or braises.

bean curd puffs Crispy, porous deep-fried pieces of bean curd. Sold as large cubes, usually in plastic bags, and used in stir-fries and soups. If using in soups such as laksa, prick the skin a few times to help them absorb the flavours. Add them at the last minute or they will soak up all the soup.

See also Bean pastes and sauces, page 82.

From top: fermented bean curd, bean curd skins, bean curd puffs.

fragrant bean curd and tomato soup

paste

½ teaspoon dried shrimp paste
1 teaspoon small dried prawns (shrimp)
4 Asian shallots, roughly chopped
½ teaspoon white peppercorns
2 coriander (cilantro) roots
1 garlic clove, chopped
2 teaspoons grated ginger

1 tablespoon vegetable oil
750 ml (3 cups) chicken stock or water
3 tablespoons tamarind purée
1 tablespoon palm sugar
2 tablespoons fish sauce
3 cm (1¼ inch) piece of ginger, julienned
3 Asian shallots, smashed with the flat side of a cleaver
300 g (10 oz) silken bean curd (tofu), cut into 2 cm (¾ inch) cubes
2 tomatoes, each cut into 8 wedges
1 tablespoon lime juice
2 tablespoons coriander (cilantro) leaves, to garnish

to make the paste, use a pestle and mortar or food processor to pound or blend the shrimp paste, dried prawns, shallots, peppercorns, coriander roots, garlic and ginger together.

heat the oil in a saucepan over a low heat, add the paste and cook for 10–15 seconds, stirring constantly. Add the chicken stock or water, tamarind purée, palm sugar, fish sauce and ginger. Gently simmer for 5 minutes to soften the ginger.

add the shallots, bean curd, tomatoes and lime juice to the pan and cook for 3 minutes to heat. Garnish with coriander leaves. Serves 4.

northern chinese-style bean curd

holding a cleaver parallel to the cutting surface, slice each bean curd cake in half horizontally. Cut each piece into 3 cm (1¼ inch) squares.

fill a wok one-quarter full of oil. Heat the oil to 190°C (375°F), or until a piece of bread fries golden brown in 10 seconds. Coat each piece of bean curd in the cornflour, then dip in the beaten egg. Cook in batches for 3–4 minutes on each side, or until golden. Remove with a slotted spoon and drain. Pour the oil from the wok, leaving 1 teaspoon.

reheat the reserved oil over high heat until very hot and stir-fry the ginger for 5 seconds, or until fragrant. Add the stock, rice wine, salt and sugar and bring to the boil. Add the fried bean curd and pierce the pieces with a fork so they will absorb the cooking liquid. Cook over medium heat for 20 minutes, or until all the liquid is absorbed. Drizzle the sesame oil over the bean curd, toss carefully to coat, sprinkle with the spring onion and serve. Serves 6.

1 kg (2 lb 4 oz) firm bean
 curd (tofu), drained
oil, for deep-frying
125 g (1 cup) cornflour
 (cornstarch)
2 eggs, lightly beaten
1 tablespoon finely chopped
 ginger
330 ml (1⅓ cups) chicken
 stock
2 tablespoons Shaoxing rice
 wine
1 teaspoon salt, or to taste
½ teaspoon sugar
1½ teaspoons roasted sesame
 oil
2 spring onions (scallions),
 green part only, finely
 chopped

easy prawn laksa

1 tablespoon oil
2–3 tablespoons ready-made
 laksa paste
560 ml (2¼ cups) coconut
 milk
750 ml (3 cups) chicken stock
600 g (1 lb 5 oz) raw prawns
 (shrimp), peeled and
 deveined, tails intact
250 g (9 oz) rice vermicelli

100 g (3½ oz) bean curd
 (tofu) puffs, cut into thin
 strips
100 g (3½ oz) soya bean
 sprouts
15 g (½ cup) coriander
 (cilantro) leaves
3 tablespoons roughly
 chopped Vietnamese mint
lime wedges, to serve

heat the oil in a wok, add the laksa paste and cook over medium heat, stirring, for 2–3 minutes. Stir in the coconut milk and chicken stock, bring to the boil and simmer for 5 minutes. Add the prawns, bring to the boil, then reduce the heat and simmer for 5 minutes, or until the prawns are cooked.

cook the rice vermicelli for 5 minutes in boiling water until soft. Drain and divide among four deep serving bowls, along with the bean curd puffs and the bean sprouts and ladle in the hot soup. Garnish with coriander and mint. Serve with lime wedges. Serves 4.

mushrooms with bean curd

350 g (12 oz) firm bean curd (tofu)

1 teaspoon sesame oil

2 teaspoons light soy sauce

¼ teaspoon ground black pepper, plus some to sprinkle

1 tablespoon finely shredded ginger

5 tablespoons vegetable stock or water

2 tablespoons light soy sauce

2 teaspoons cornflour (cornstarch)

½ teaspoon sugar

1½ tablespoons vegetable oil

2 garlic cloves, finely chopped

200 g (7 oz) oyster mushrooms, hard stalks removed, cut in half if large

200 g (7 oz) shiitake mushrooms, hard stalks removed

2 spring onions (scallions), sliced diagonally, for garnish

1 long red chilli, seeded and finely sliced, for garnish

drain each block of bean curd and cut into 2.5 cm (1 inch) pieces. Put them in a shallow dish and sprinkle with the sesame oil, light soy sauce, ground pepper and ginger. Leave to marinate for 30 minutes.

mix the stock with the light soy sauce, cornflour and sugar in a small bowl until smooth.

heat the oil in a wok or frying pan and stir-fry the garlic over medium heat until light brown. Add all the mushrooms and stir-fry for about 4 minutes, or until the mushrooms are cooked. Add the cornflour liquid, then carefully add the pieces of bean curd and mix for 1–2 minutes. Taste, then adjust the seasoning if necessary.

spoon onto a serving plate and sprinkle with spring onions, chilli slices and ground pepper. Serves 2.

1 Stir-fry the mushrooms, tossing to ensure an even cooking.

2 Add the bean curd and cornflour liquid, then gently stir to mix.

The betel leaf is a thick, dark green leaf, broad at one end and with a point at the other. The leaves are used as wrappers for paan, which is a roll of spices, areca nuts (also called betel nuts) and sometimes other ingredients such as tobacco or shredded coconut. This roll is chewed slowly, often after a meal, as a digestive and breath-freshener, particularly in India. A related leaf, often called betel leaf as well (or *cha plu* in Thailand), but much finer and more delicately flavoured, is used in Vietnamese and Thai cooking as a wrapper or 'plate' for snacks.

betel leaves with savoury topping

**betel
leaf**

2 tablespoons peanut oil
4 Asian shallots, finely sliced
2 garlic cloves, smashed with the side of a cleaver
150 g (5½ oz) minced (ground) chicken or pork
2 tablespoons fish sauce
1 tablespoon tamarind purée
1 tablespoon dried shrimp, chopped
2 tablespoons palm sugar
1 cm (½ inch) piece of ginger, grated
2 bird's eye chillies, finely chopped
1 tablespoon roasted peanuts, chopped
1 tablespoon chopped coriander (cilantro) leaves
16 betel leaves
lime wedges, for squeezing

heat the oil in a wok and fry the shallots and garlic for 1–2 minutes until brown. Add the chicken and fry it until the meat turns opaque, breaking up any lumps with a spoon. Add the fish sauce, tamarind, shrimp and palm sugar and cook until the mixture is brown and sticky. Stir in the ginger, chillies, peanuts and coriander leaves.

lay the betel leaves out on a large plate and top each with some of the mixture. Serve with the lime wedges to squeeze over the mixture. Makes 16.

bird's nest

An exotic and expensive delicacy with a delicate flavour and texture, bird's nest is an ingredient used mainly in Chinese cooking, usually reserved for festive occasions. It is typically served in a clear soup—bird's nest soup—named after its highly prized main ingredient.

The nest is made from the saliva excreted by a species of swifts and is hand-picked off the walls of the caves where they live. This is dangerous and difficult work, hence the nests come with a high price tag. Black nests are cheaper as they need to have the debris picked out of them by hand before they are clean enough to eat; white nests are cleaner and therefore more expensive. The Chinese believe them to be good for the blood and the complexion.

dried scallops

noodles with seafood and dried scallops

4 dried scallops
12 raw prawns (shrimp)
200 g (7 oz) squid tubes
400 g (14 oz) thin rice stick
    noodles
1 tablespoon oil
2 tablespoons shredded ginger
2 spring onions (scallions),
    thinly sliced

150 g (5½ oz) Chinese
    cabbage, finely shredded
250 ml (1 cup) chicken stock
2 tablespoons light soy sauce
2 tablespoons Shaoxing rice
    wine
1 teaspoon roasted sesame oil

put the dried scallops in a heatproof bowl with 1 tablespoon water and put them in a steamer. Cover and steam over simmering water in a wok for 30 minutes, or until they are completely tender. Remove the scallops and shred the meat.

peel the prawns and cut them in half through the back, removing the vein.

open up the squid tubes by cutting down one side, scrub off any soft jelly-like substance, then score the inside of the flesh with a fine crisscross pattern, making sure you do not cut all the way through. Cut the squid into 3 x 5 cm (1¼ x 2 inch) pieces.

soak the noodles in hot water for 10 minutes, then drain.

heat a wok over high heat, add the oil and heat until very hot. Stir-fry the ginger and spring onion for 1 minute, then add the prawns and squid and stir-fry until just opaque. Add the scallops and Chinese cabbage and toss together. Pour in the stock, soy sauce and rice wine and boil for 1 minute. Add the noodles and sesame oil, toss together and serve. Serves 4.

Scallops dried to thick amber discs, these are regarded as a delicacy in China. They have a strong flavour so you don't need many, and because they are expensive they are mostly eaten in banquet dishes. Dried scallops need to be soaked or steamed until soft and are often shredded before use.

Also known as — conpoy

Because the scallops have a strong flavour, they are best shredded into small pieces.

gluten

Gluten is a wheat flour dough that has had the starch washed away, so, it is spongy and porous, rather like bean curd but much firmer. It is used in vegetarian Chinese recipes, such as mock duck, to take the place of meat as it can be cooked in the same way. Dried gluten (called *fu*) is used in Japanese cooking in soups and stews to add bulk and texture. Ready-made gluten is sold in Asian supermarkets.

1 Rinse the gluten under cold water to get rid of the starch.

2 Slice the gluten, then cut it into smaller, bite-sized pieces.

mock duck

1 kg (8 cups) plain (all-purpose) flour
1 teaspoon salt
1½ tablespoons cornflour (cornstarch)
2 tablespoons oil
1 green capsicum (pepper), diced
80 ml (⅓ cup) vegetable stock
2 tablespoons light soy sauce
2 teaspoons Shaoxing rice wine
1 teaspoon sugar
1 teaspoon roasted sesame oil

sift the flour into a bowl with the salt and slowly add 560 ml (2¼ cups) warm water to make a dough. Knead until smooth, then cover with a damp cloth and leave in a warm place for 55–60 minutes. (Alternatively, buy 300 g (10½ oz) ready-made gluten.)

rinse the dough under cold water and wash off the starch by pulling, stretching and squeezing the dough with your hands. You should have about 300 g (10½ oz) gluten after 10–15 minutes of washing and squeezing. Squeeze the dough hard to extract as much water as possible, then cut it into bite-sized pieces. Dry thoroughly.

toss the gluten in 1 tablespoon of the cornflour. Heat a wok over high heat, add the oil and heat until very hot. Quickly stir-fry the gluten until browned all over, then remove from the wok. Stir-fry the capsicum until browning around the edges, then remove. Pour off any excess oil. Add the stock, soy sauce, rice wine and sugar to the wok and bring to the boil. Return the gluten and capsicum and simmer for 1 minute.

combine the remaining cornflour with enough water to make a paste, add to the sauce and simmer until thickened. Sprinkle with the sesame oil and serve. Serves 4.

kamaboko

Kamaboko fish cakes are sausage-like compounds made from spongy fish paste. They can be sliced and eaten as is or added to stir-fries and hotpots. Kamaboko are available from Japanese supermarkets.

Also known as —
Japanese fish cakes

nabeyaki udon

- 250 g (9 oz) fresh udon noodles
- 2 teaspoons dashi granules
- 80 ml (1/3 cup) Japanese soy sauce
- 1 tablespoon sugar
- 2 tablespoons mirin
- 4 large fresh shiitake mushrooms, stems removed and caps cut into 1 cm (1/2 inch) slices
- 1 chicken breast fillet, cut into 1 cm (1/2 inch) slices
- 8 medium raw prawns (shrimp), peeled, deveined, tails intact
- 1 kamaboko fish cake, thinly sliced
- 4 eggs, lightly beaten
- 2 spring onions (scallions), thinly sliced

cook the noodles in a saucepan of boiling water for 1–2 minutes, or until tender. Drain and rinse well.

mix the dashi granules with 1 litre (4 cups) water in a large saucepan. Bring to the boil over high heat and stir to dissolve. Add the soy sauce, sugar, mirin and 2 teaspoons salt, then reduce the heat and simmer.

place the noodles, mushrooms, chicken, prawns and fish cake in a 1.5 litre (6 cup) flameproof casserole dish. Pour the hot broth on top and simmer, covered, over medium heat for 3–5 minutes, or until the prawns and chicken are cooked through. Gently pour the egg into the centre of the mixture and continue to cook for 2 minutes, or until the egg has just set. Sprinkle with spring onions and serve. Serves 4.

one-thousand-year-old eggs

These eggs have been preserved by coating them in a layer of wood ash, slaked lime and then rice husks. The eggs are left to mature for 40 days (not quite as long as their name suggests) to give them a blackish-green yolk and amber white. To eat, the coating is scraped off and the shell peeled. The eggs have a smooth, creamy texture and a pungent, cheese-like flavour. They are popular in Chinese cuisine, eaten as an hors d'oeuvre or used to garnish congee. Available from speciality Chinese markets.

Also known as — century eggs, one-hundred-year-old eggs

plain congee with accompaniments

220 g (1 cup) short-grain rice
2.25 litres (9 cups) chicken stock or water
light soy sauce, to taste
roasted sesame oil, to taste
white pepper, to taste

toppings
3 spring onions (scallions), chopped
4 tablespoons chopped coriander (cilantro) leaves
30 g (1 oz) sliced pickled ginger
4 tablespoons finely chopped preserved turnip
4 tablespoons roasted peanuts
2 one-thousand-year-old eggs, cut into slivers
2 tablespoons toasted sesame seeds
2 fried dough sticks, diagonally sliced

Congee is eaten in China for breakfast or as a snack at any time of the day. It is served with lots of different accompaniments to sprinkle over it, and with a fresh fried dough stick, available at Chinese shops.

put the rice in a bowl and, using your fingers as a rake, rinse under cold running water. Drain the rice in a colander. Place in a clay pot, casserole or saucepan and stir in the stock or water. Bring to the boil, then reduce the heat and simmer very gently, stirring occasionally, for 1¾–2 hours, or until it has a porridge-like texture and the rice is breaking up.

add a sprinkling of soy sauce, sesame oil and white pepper to season the congee. The congee can be served plain, or choose a selection from the toppings listed and serve in bowls alongside the congee for guests to help themselves. Serves 4.

paneer

Paneer is a fresh cheese used in Indian cooking, made by coagulating milk with lemon juice and leaving it to drain. When sugar and maida flour are added to the paneer, it is then known as chenna. Paneer is used in Indian vegetarian cooking, usually cut into cubes and added to dishes such as saag paneer, where it is cooked with spinach, tomatoes and spices. It's easy to make your own paneer, or you can buy it, usually pressed into a block, in the refrigerated section of Indian food shops.

paneer

to make the paneer, pour the milk into a large, heavy-based saucepan. Bring to the boil, stirring with a wooden spoon so that the milk doesn't stick to the base of the pan. Reduce the heat and stir in the lemon juice, then heat over low heat for a few more seconds before turning the heat off as large bits of curd start to form. Shake the pan slowly to allow the curds to form and release the yellow whey.

if the curds are slow to form, put the pan over low heat again for a few seconds. This helps with the coagulation.

line a colander with muslin or cheesecloth so that it overlaps the sides. Pour off the whey, collecting the curds gently in the colander. Gently pull up the corners of the cheesecloth so that it hangs like a bag, twist the cloth so that the whey is released, then hold the 'bag' under running water to wash off the remaining whey, twisting some more to remove the excess liquid.

leave the bag to hang from your tap for several hours so the weight of the curds releases more liquid and the cheese compacts. To remove more liquid, press the bag under a heavy weight, such as a tray with some tinned food piled on top, for about 1 hour. This will form a firm block of paneer. When the block is firm enough to cut into cubes, the paneer is ready for use.

3 litres (12 cups) milk
6 tablespoons strained lemon juice, or vinegar

Paneer can also be bought ready-made pressed into blocks.

matar paneer

225 g (8 oz) paneer
2 tablespoons ghee
50 g (⅓ cup) chopped onion
200 g (7 oz) fresh or frozen peas
½ teaspoon sugar
5 cm (2 inch) piece of ginger, grated
2–3 green chillies, finely chopped
1 spring onion (scallion), finely chopped
½ teaspoon garam masala
1 tablespoon chopped coriander (cilantro) leaves

Fry the cubes of paneer until they are golden brown. Make sure the oil is hot enough, otherwise they may stick to the pan.

cut the paneer into 2.5 cm (1 inch) cubes. Heat the ghee in a heavy-based frying pan over medium heat and carefully fry the paneer until golden on all sides. Remove from the pan.

fry the onion lightly in the same ghee, until softened and lightly golden. Remove the onion from the pan. Add 5 tablespoons hot water and a pinch of salt to the ghee and gently simmer for 1 minute. Add the peas and sugar, cover the pan and cook for 5–6 minutes, or until the peas are nearly cooked.

add the onion, paneer, ginger, chilli and spring onion to the pan and cook for 2–3 minutes. Add the garam masala and coriander leaves. Season with salt, to taste. Serves 4.

panko

Used in Japanese cooking, and derived from the word *pan*, meaning bread, panko is a mixture of flour and breadcrumbs. The breadcrumbs give a very light and crispy coating to dishes such as tonkatsu, crumbed fried pork, or to seafood such as prawns. Two varieties of breadcrumbs are available: fine and coarse.

**Also known as —
Japanese breadcrumbs**

japanese crumbed prawns with ponzu

18 large raw prawns (shrimp)
2 tablespoons cornflour (cornstarch)
3 eggs
120 g (2 cups) panko
peanut oil, for deep-frying
80 ml (1/3 cup) ponzu sauce (see note)

peel and devein the prawns, leaving the tails intact. Cut down the back of each prawn to form a butterfly, then place between two layers of plastic wrap and beat gently to form a cutlet.

put the cornflour, eggs and breadcrumbs in separate bowls. Lightly beat the eggs. Dip each prawn first into the cornflour, then into the egg and finally into the breadcrumbs, ensuring that each cutlet is well covered in crumbs.

fill a wok one-third full of oil and heat it to 180°C (350°F), or until a cube of bread browns in 15 seconds. Cook six prawn cutlets at a time for about 1 minute each side, or until the crumbs are golden—be careful they don't burn. Serve immediately with ponzu sauce. Makes 18.

note: If ponzu sauce isn't available, mix 60 ml (1/4 cup) soy sauce with 1 tablespoon lemon juice.

preserved plums

Plums have been cultivated in China since ancient times, where they symbolize good fortune. In Japan, too, plums are greatly valued and the start of the plum season in February is heralded by plum trees decorating the streets with their pretty blossoms. In order to enjoy plums out of season, plums are preserved in brine, and have a salty, sour-sweet taste. It is common to serve them in China with cups of green tea. In Hawaii, 'plum crackseed' is eaten—preserved plum seeds seasoned with licorice, salt and sugar. The preserved plum seeds were brought to Hawaii with Chinese immigrants in the early nineteenth century. Plums are also preserved in a powder form and served as a dip for guava fruit.

steamed fish with preserved plums

1 tablespoon light soy sauce
1/2 teaspoon sugar
1 large or 2 smaller pomfret, flounder, or turbot (total weight about 1 kg/2 lb 4 oz)
50 g (2 oz) mushrooms, roughly sliced
2 small preserved plums, bruised
5 cm (2 inch) piece of ginger, julienned
4 spring onions (scallions), sliced diagonally
2 long red or green chillies, seeded and finely sliced
a few coriander (cilantro) leaves, for garnish
a sprinkle of ground white pepper

put in a small bowl the light soy sauce and sugar and mix together.

clean and gut the fish, leaving the heads on. Dry the fish thoroughly. Score the fish 3 or 4 times on both sides with a sharp knife. Put the fish on a deep plate slightly larger than the fish itself. Use a plate that will fit on the rack of a traditional bamboo steamer basket or on a steamer rack inside the wok. Sprinkle the mushrooms, preserved plums and ginger over the fish. Pour the light soy sauce mixture all over the fish.

fill a wok or a steamer pan with water, cover and bring to a rolling boil over a high heat. Taking care not to burn your hands, set the rack or basket over the boiling water and put the plate with the fish on the rack. Reduce the heat to a simmer. Cover and steam for 25–30 minutes (depending on the variety and size of the fish), or until the skewer will slide easily into the fish. Check and replenish the water about every 10 minutes. Remove the fish from the steamer. Serve on the same plate. Sprinkle with the spring onions, chillies, coriander leaves and ground white pepper. Serves 4.

roe

Roe are the eggs (or spawn) of a female fish, and are also called hard roe. Soft roe are the sperm (or milt) of a male fish. Caviar, the most sought after roe, is from the sturgeon. Lesser but still delicious roe come from salmon, trout, herring, flying fish and lumpfish.

In Japan, roe are used for sushi. The roe used in sushi are generally soft and are often made into *gunkan maki* (battleship sushi, pictured above), where the sides of the seaweed are higher than the rice so as to form a little wall to hold in the roe. The most common roe are the large orange salmon roe (ikura) and the smaller, red flying fish roe (tobiko), often served as part of sushi rolls (maki zushi). Salted cod roe (tarako) is also a popular choice.

Golden tobiko or flying fish roe (yellow roe), orange tobiko or flying fish roe (small orange roe) and ikura or salmon roe (large orange roe).

sea cucumber

A slug-like sea creature related to the starfish, sea cucumbers are sold dried or ready-prepared (reconstituted). The dried ones need to be soaked before use. It has little flavour of its own and is more prized for its texture, which, like bean curd, absorbs the flavours of the ingredients it is cooked with. Used mainly in Chinese and Japanese cooking.

Also known as — bêche de mer, sea slug

sea cucumber with mushrooms

3 dried or ready-prepared sea cucumbers
24 dried Chinese mushrooms
4 tablespoons oil
1 skinless chicken breast fillet, cut into 2 cm (3/4 inch) cubes
1 egg white

3–4 tablespoons cornflour (cornstarch)
1 tablespoon light soy sauce
3 tablespoons oyster sauce
3 teaspoons sugar
2 spring onions (scallions), cut into 2 cm (3/4 inch) lengths

to prepare the dried sea cucumbers, allow up to 4 days for them to rehydrate. On the first day, soak them in water overnight. Drain and cook in a saucepan of simmering water for 1 hour, then drain again. Soak overnight and repeat the cooking and soaking process at least three times to allow the sea cucumbers to soften. Then, cut in half lengthways, scrape out and discard the insides and cut into chunks. If using ready-prepared sea cucumbers, they only need to be rinsed, drained and have the insides discarded before cutting into chunks.

put the dried mushrooms in a saucepan and add 500 ml (2 cups) water and half the oil. Cover, bring to the boil, then reduce the heat and simmer for 1 hour. Drain the mushrooms, reserving 250 ml (1 cup) of the liquid. Remove and discard the stems.

combine the chicken with the egg white and 1 tablespoon of the cornflour until it is completely coated. Heat a wok over high heat, add the remaining oil and heat until very hot. Stir-fry the chicken in batches for 3 minutes, or until browned. Return all the chicken to the wok and add the sea cucumber, mushrooms, reserved liquid, soy sauce, oyster sauce, sugar and spring onion. Stir, then cook for 2 minutes.

combine the remaining cornflour with enough water to make a paste, add to the sauce and simmer until thickened. Serves 4.

1 Slice the cucumber in half and scrape out the insides.

2 Use a cleaver to cut the sea cucumber into chunks.

seaweed

Seaweed describes any edible sea plant belonging to the algae family. The many varieties can be divided into four main groups: brown (arame, hijiki, kombu, wakame); green (sea lettuce, sea grapes); red (nori, dulse, carrageen, agar-agar); and blue-green (spirulina). Rich in iodine, seaweeds are widely used in Asian cuisine, especially in Japan in soups, sushi, salads and as a seasoning. Many seaweeds are dried and compressed into sheets, or processed into fine flakes that are used as a seasoning.

types of seaweeds

hijiki   Short, thin sticks of seaweed usually sold dried. Soak before use—it will swell to three times its size. Eat raw in salads, boil and serve with rice or in soups. It is often sautéed, then simmered in soy sauce and sugar.

kombu   Also known as kelp and tangle kelp, kombu is a large, flat, olive-green seaweed. Used to flavour Japanese dashi, a salty stock, or it can be cooked as a vegetable with fish. Sold dried. Often coated with a white salty mould—this gives it flavour and should not be washed off—wipe over with a damp cloth to remove any grit and cut into pieces.

nori (laver)   A marine algae found on the surface of the sea off Japan, China and Korea. It is formed into paper-like sheets, compressed and then dried. Nori is also sold in flakes. Its colour ranges from purple to green. Used for wrapping sushi, shredded into soups or crumbled onto rice. The sheets need to be crisped over a flame or under the grill (broiler) before use. The sheets may also be sold pre-toasted.

wakame   A curly-leafed, dark green or brown algae with a mild flavour and soft texture (after soaking in boiling water). Used in soups, to flavour salads and as a vegetable. Usually sold dried in pieces or flakes—soak in cold water for 5 minutes, or until softened, before use. Use wakame sparingly as its volume increases about 10 times.

Some types of seaweed include (from top): hijiki, kombu, nori sheets and flakes, and wakame.

salmon nori roll with sesame noodles

150 g (5½ oz) soba noodles
1 teaspoon sesame oil
1 tablespoon sesame seeds
10 x 15 cm (4 x 6 inch)
   salmon fillet, bones
   removed
1 nori sheet
1 tablespoon butter
125 g (4½ oz) baby spinach
   leaves (about 4 handfuls)

cook the noodles in a large saucepan of boiling salted water for about 5 minutes, or until they are just cooked, stirring once or twice to make sure they are not stuck together. The cooking time will vary depending on the brand of noodles. Drain the noodles, add the sesame oil and some seasoning, then toss them so they are coated in the oil. Gently dry-fry the sesame seeds in a frying pan until they start to colour and smell toasted, then add them to the noodles. Cover the noodles and keep warm.

cut the salmon fillet in half horizontally and neaten the edges. Cut the sheet of nori in half with a pair of scissors and lay a piece of salmon fillet on top of each half. Season well, then roll up the fillets to make neat log shapes. Trim off any bits of nori or salmon that stick out. Using a sharp knife, cut each roll into 3 pieces.

heat the butter in a non-stick frying pan and fry the pieces of roll until they are golden on each side and almost cooked all the way through. This will take about 4 minutes on each side. Lift out the salmon. Add the spinach to the pan, stir it around until it wilts, then turn off the heat.

serve the salmon nori rolls with the noodles and some spinach on the side. Serves 2.

sushi hand rolls

rinse the rice under cold running water. Put the rice into a saucepan and cover with 200 ml (7 fl oz) cold water. Cover the pan and bring the water to the boil, then reduce the heat and simmer for 10 minutes.

mix together 1 tablespoon of the vinegar, the sugar and ¼ teaspoon of salt. When the rice is cooked, remove it from the heat and let it stand, covered, for 10 minutes, then transfer to a mixing bowl. Add the rice vinegar mixture, bit by bit, turning and folding the rice with a wooden spoon. Continue to fold until the rice is cool. Cover with a damp tea towel and set aside, but do not refrigerate.

using a sharp knife, cut the fish into 16 paper-thin pieces, measuring 2 x 5 cm (¾ x 2 inches). Cut each sheet of seaweed in half. Thinly slice the avocado and sprinkle with a little lemon juice. Mix the remaining vinegar with 3 tablespoons water in a small bowl. Use the vinegar water to stop the rice sticking to your fingers as you form the sushi. Taking 1 tablespoon of rice at a time, carefully mould the rice into oval shapes—you should end up with 12 ovals.

holding a piece of nori seaweed in the palm of your hand, smear a little wasabi over it, put an oval of rice on top, then fill it with a piece of fish, avocado, daikon and cucumber. Wrap the seaweed around the ingredients in a cone shape, using a couple of grains of cooked rice to secure the rolls. Alternatively, put the ingredients on the table for guests to help themselves. Serve the sushi with soy sauce, extra wasabi and pickled ginger. Serves 6.

220 g (1 cup) Japanese short-grain rice
2 tablespoons rice vinegar
generous pinch caster (superfine) sugar
175 g (6 oz) sashimi grade fish, such as tuna or salmon
6 sheets roasted nori seaweed, each measuring 20 x 18 cm (8 x 7 inches)
1 small avocado
1 tablespoon lemon juice
wasabi paste
60 g (2¼ oz) pickled daikon
85 g (3 oz) cucumber, cut into thin strips
Japanese soy sauce, to serve
pickled ginger, to serve

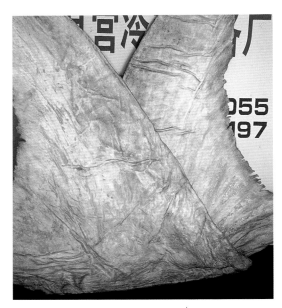
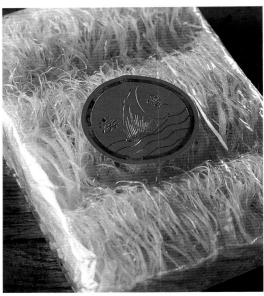

shark's fin

300 g (10½ oz) ready-prepared shark's fin
400 g (14 oz) bacon or ham bones
500 g (1 lb 2 oz) chicken bones
500 g (1 lb 2 oz) beef bones
4 slices ginger
300 g (10½ oz) skinless chicken breast fillet, minced (ground)
1 egg white, lightly beaten
4 tablespoons cornflour (cornstarch)
1 tablespoon light soy sauce
white pepper
red rice vinegar

One of the most expensive and prized of all Chinese delicacies, shark's fin is served on special occasions and at banquets, most famously in shark's fin soup. It is favoured more for its texture than for its flavour. The task of preparing a dried fin takes several days, so using the ready-prepared version, which is sold shrink-wrapped in dried, thin noodle-like strands (above, right), is much easier as it just needs soaking and then cooking.

shark's fin soup

put the shark's fin in a large bowl and cover with cold water. Leave to soak overnight. Strain the shark's fin and rinse gently to remove any remaining sand and sediment. Bring a stockpot of water to the boil. Add the shark's fin, reduce the heat and simmer, covered, for 1 hour. Strain and set aside.

put the bacon or ham bones, chicken bones and beef bones in a large stockpot with the ginger slices and 2 litres (8 cups) water. Bring to the boil, then reduce the heat and simmer, covered, for 2 hours. Skim off any scum and fat during cooking. Strain the stock, discarding the bones. Measure the stock—you will need 1.5–1.75 litres (6–7 cups). If you have more, return the stock to the pan and reduce it further until you have the correct amount.

combine the chicken, egg white and 1 tablespoon of the cornflour. Set aside in the refrigerator.

put the prepared shark's fin and stock in a large clay pot or saucepan and simmer, covered, for 30 minutes. Add the chicken mixture and stir to separate the meat. Simmer for 10 minutes, or until the chicken is cooked.

season the soup with the soy sauce and some salt and white pepper. Combine the remaining cornflour with 125 ml (½ cup) water, add to the soup and simmer until thickened.

serve the soup with some red rice vinegar, which can be added to the soup, to taste. Serves 6.

shrimp

Shrimp are small crustaceans similar to prawns but are members of a different family; in North America, however, both prawns and shrimp are encompassed under the general term of 'shrimp'. There are hundreds of species, which thrive in both warm and cold water. The colour of raw shrimp varies greatly but most will assume a pale to bright pink or brown colour on cooking.

In Asian cooking, shrimp are generally used in their dried form. These are tiny, orange, saltwater shrimp that have been dried in the sun. They come in different sizes and the really small ones have their heads and shells still attached. Dried shrimp need to be soaked in water or rice wine to soften them before use. They may be used in noodle or rice dishes, or as a seasoning, not as a main ingredient.

Shrimp are usually sold frozen or in tins or, if dried, in packets. If buying fresh, they should have a firm shell and flesh and a fresh, slightly sea smell. Store in the refrigerator for up to 2 days or freeze. See also shrimp paste, page 91.

silver leaf

Pista rolls are an Indian sweet that uses silver leaf as an edible decoration. These rolls are made from a paste of ground almonds and sugar and wrapped around a filling of chopped pistachio nuts.

Silver leaf are very thin, edible sheets of silver with no flavour or aroma. The leaf comes in boxes or books between sheets of tissue paper. Apply the silver to the food from the backing sheet, then pull off the backing sheet—if you touch the foil it will stick to you. Silver leaf does not go on in an even layer because it is so fragile. Buy from Indian food stores.

cashew nut barfi

500 g (1 lb 2 oz) cashew nuts
6 cardamom pods
200 g (2 cups) milk powder
2 tablespoons ghee or butter
¼ teaspoon ground cloves

185 g (¾ cup) caster
(superfine) sugar
2 sheets edible silver leaf
(varak)

place a small frying pan over low heat and dry-roast the cashew nuts until browned all over. Cool, then chop in a food processor or with a knife. Remove the cardamom seeds from the pods and crush in a spice grinder or mortar and pestle. Line a 26 x 17 cm (10½ x 6¾ inch) baking tin with baking paper.

combine the milk powder and cashew nuts in a large bowl and rub in the ghee until completely mixed. Stir in the cardamom and cloves.

combine the sugar and 250 ml (1 cup) water in a heavy-based saucepan and heat over low heat until the sugar melts. Bring to the boil and simmer for 5–7 minutes to make a sugar syrup. Quickly stir the sugar syrup into the cashew mixture (if you leave it too long it will stiffen) and spread the mixture into the baking tin (the mixture should be about 1.5 cm/⅝ inch thick). Smooth with a buttered spatula. Place the silver leaf on top by inverting the sheets onto the surface and peeling off the paper backing. Leave to cool, then slice into diamond shapes. Serve cold. Serves 12.

Also known as — varak

Carefully lay the silver leaf on the barfi and pull off the backing paper. If you touch the silver with your hands, it will stick to them.

apricots in cardamom syrup with silver leaf

300 g (10½ oz) dried apricots
3 tablespoons caster (superfine) sugar
3 tablespoons slivered, blanched almonds
1 cm (½ inch) piece of ginger, sliced
4 cardamom pods
1 cinnamon stick
4 pieces edible silver leaf (varak)

soak the dried apricots in 750 ml (3 cups) water in a large saucepan for 4 hours, or until plumped up.

add the sugar, almonds, ginger, cardamom and cinnamon to the apricots and bring slowly to the boil, stirring until the sugar has dissolved. Reduce the heat to a simmer and cook until the liquid has reduced by half and formed a thick syrup. Pour the mixture into a bowl, then refrigerate.

serve in small bowls with a piece of silver leaf for decoration. To do this, invert the piece of backing paper over each bowl. As soon as the silver leaf touches the apricots it will come away from the backing and stick to them. Serves 4.

This Kashmiri speciality is best made from dried kashmiri apricots, which have lots of flavour. They are not as brightly coloured as most Western dried apricots and have a tougher texture. They need to be soaked before use to soften them. The silver leaf makes this a special dessert but can be substituted with thick cream or yoghurt to temper the sweetness of the apricots.

sugar cane

Sugar cane was first cultivated in India over 2000 years ago. In the seventh century, the Persians set up sugar refineries and it is from their word for it, 'sakar', that we get the English name. Sugar, like spices, reached the Western world via the Arab trade routes, and when it first appeared was considered an exotic and prohibitively expensive commodity, often called 'white gold'. Until the eighteenth century, when sugar cane from the West Indies became more plentiful and less expensive, food was sweetened with honey or fruit syrups. Sugar is made by extracting crystals from sugar cane juice. Throughout many Asian countries the juice that is extracted by crushing the cane is sold as a refreshing drink. In Vietnam, the canes are split lengthwise and used as skewers on which to grill (broil) minced prawns (shrimp).

These brightly coloured spice preparations are something of a gamble. They are eaten after a meal to aid digestion and freshen the breath but actual contents can vary greatly. They range from fennel seeds and cardamom pods coated in silver to colourful mixes of split, roasted coriander (cilantro) seeds, sugar balls, sesame seeds, sugar-coated fennel seeds, coconut shreds, bits of betel nut and aniseed. What is worrying, however, are the unknowns, which, some research suggests, may consist of tobacco, morphine, saccharine, colouring agents and other carcinogenic materials. Eating spice mixes is an age-old tradition in south Asia, where paan, a sweet spice mixture, mostly (though not always) flavoured with tobacco and wrapped in a betel leaf, is eaten daily. Dried paan without the betel leaf is known as paan masala and gutkha, and it is the presence of gutkha in supari mixes that is concerning health professionals, as this is where the undesirables enter the mix. As well, because people think they are eating spices, not tobacco, the health concerns of tobacco are not considered. So, if in India and you see a plate of these beside the cash register in a store, take a pinch—but perhaps no more.

supari mixes

Brightly coloured supari mixes, containing spices such as fennel seeds, cardamom pods, coriander seeds, sesame seeds and aniseed.

sushi/sashimi

Sushi is a favourite dish right across Japan and now the rest of the world, consisting of various ingredients served with sushi rice (rice prepared with sweetened vinegar). The rice encloses or sits under fillings such as seafood (usually raw), vegetables (mostly cooked), omelette or pickles.

Sashimi, sliced raw fish, is often served as first course in a sushi bar. The preparation of sashimi is the reserve of highly skilled chefs. Sashimi is usually served with wasabi and a dipping sauce, often with pickled ginger or finely shredded daikon, and is prepared according to the appearance, taste, texture, size and colour of the fish or seafood. If buying fish for sashimi it is very important to find a supplier who sells sashimi-grade fish.

Tuna (maguro) is probably the most popular fish used for sushi and sashimi, but other types include: toro (tuna belly), salmon (sake), ika (both cuttlefish and squid), mackerel (saba), octopus (tako) and prawns (ebi).

some types of sushi

maki zushi There are countless variations of this type of sushi, which is made using a square of nori seaweed, spread with rice and topped with a filling such as fish, vegetables or cucumber. The rice is rolled into a cylinder using a bamboo mat, then sliced into rolls. This type of sushi can also be rolled by hand into a cone shape, when it is called temaki (see recipe, page 229).

inari zushi These are made from sushi rice, sometimes flavoured with pickled ginger or sesame seeds, packed into a deep-fried bean curd pouch. The pouches (aburaage) are slightly sweet and can be bought ready-made.

nigiri zushi Consists of a pillow of rice smeared with wasabi, usually topped with a slice of raw fish or other seafood.

chirashi zushi Meaning 'scattered sushi', this is the easiest sushi to make. Cooked rice is placed in the bottom of a bowl, then topped with raw or cooked fish, vegetables and strips of omelette.

gunkan maki The roe of sea urchin are often used in gunkan maki, meaning 'battleship sushi', where the side of the seaweed is higher than the rice so as to form a little wall. This wall holds in the soft sea urchin roe that sit on top of the rice.

oshi zushi Meaning 'pressed sushi', this is made using a special box. The rice is pressed into the box, then topped with fish. It is then removed from the mould and cut into slices to serve.

maki zushi

rinse the rice under running water until the water runs clear, then drain thoroughly. Place in a large saucepan with 375 ml (1½ cups) water and simmer for 20–25 minutes, or until tender. Cover with a clean tea towel and leave for 15 minutes.

combine the vinegar, sugar, mirin and 1 teaspoon salt and stir until the sugar dissolves. Spread the rice over a non-metallic tray and pour the dressing on top. Mix with a spatula, gently separating the grains of rice. Allow to cool to body temperature.

cut the tuna, cucumber and avocado into thin strips. Put a sheet of nori on a bamboo mat, shiny-side down and with a short end towards you. Evenly spread the rice 1 cm (½ inch) thick over the nori, leaving a 1 cm (½ inch) border. Make a shallow groove down the centre of the rice towards the short end closest to you. Spread some wasabi along the groove. Put a selection of strips of your filling ingredients on top of the wasabi. Lift the edge of the bamboo mat and roll the sushi, starting from the edge nearest to you. When you've finished rolling, press the mat to make either a round or square roll. Wet a small sharp knife, trim the ends and cut the roll into 6 pieces. Repeat the process with the remaining nori sheets and ingredients. Makes 48.

275 g (1¼ cups) sushi rice
50 ml (1¾ fl oz) rice vinegar
1 tablespoon sugar
½ tablespoon mirin

250 g (9 oz) sashimi tuna
1 small Lebanese (short)
  cucumber
½ avocado
8 sheets nori
3 teaspoons wasabi paste

tempeh

Tempeh is a vegetable protein food made from soya beans, which are cooked, inoculated with a starter culture of mould, then left to ferment. Unlike bean curd, the beans in tempeh are still visible, giving it a nutty aroma and flavour. Tempeh is eaten cooked, sautéed or deep-fried, in stews or a salad. It is sold in blocks in sealed packets, often marinated in spices. Keep sealed and refrigerated to prevent mould forming.

Also known as — tempe

tempeh stir-fry

- 1 teaspoon roasted sesame oil
- 1 tablespoon peanut oil
- 2 garlic cloves
- 1 tablespoon grated fresh ginger
- 1 red chilli, thinly sliced
- 4 spring onions (scallions), sliced on the diagonal
- 300 g (10½ oz) tempeh, cut into 2 cm (¾ inch) cubes
- 500 g (1 lb 2 oz) baby bok choy (pak choi) leaves
- 800 g (1 lb 12 oz) Chinese broccoli, chopped
- 125 ml (½ cup) vegetarian oyster sauce
- 2 tablespoons rice vinegar
- 2 tablespoons coriander (cilantro) leaves
- 40 g (¼ cup) toasted cashew nuts

heat a wok over high heat, add the oils and swirl to coat the side of the wok. Add the garlic, ginger, chilli and spring onion and cook for 1–2 minutes, or until the onion is soft. Add the tempeh and cook for 5 minutes, or until golden. Remove from the wok.

add half the greens and 1 tablespoon water and cook, covered, for 3–4 minutes, or until the greens have wilted. Remove from the wok and repeat with the remaining greens and a little more water.

return the greens and tempeh to the wok, add the sauce and vinegar and heat through. Top with coriander and nuts. Serve with rice. Serves 4.

umeboshi

This is a small tart apricot, salted and dried by the Japanese as umeboshi, a name meaning 'dried ume', often erroneously called a Japanese plum. The ume was originally brought to ancient Japan from China. Samurai ate them to ward off battle fatigue and it was believed that they had medicinal, cleansing and curative powers.

Ume are picked before they ripen and soaked in brine and red shiso leaves until shrivelled and wrinkled. It is the shiso leaves that give the ume their characteristic deep-red hue. Umeboshi are used extensively in Japanese cuisine as a condiment, often served with rice or to make bainiku, a tart purée used in some sauces. Ume are also macerated in alcohol with rock sugar to make a liqueur, umeshu.

water chestnuts

The walnut-sized corm of an aquatic plant native to Southeast Asia, water chestnuts have dark-brown skin and a crisp, juicy, white, mildly sweet flesh, eaten raw or cooked. Bought fresh or in tins, water chestnuts add texture to Asian cooking, especially in minced (ground) meat dishes, stir-fries, won tons or sweet dishes. They are usually cooked quickly to retain their crisp texture, for which they are prized. In China, street vendors sell water chestnuts as a snack. They are threaded onto skewers and served warm in winter and cold in summer. Tinned chestnuts keep in a jar covered with water for up to 1 week (change the water daily), or can be frozen. Water chestnut powder or flour is used as a thickener in Asian cooking.

san choy bau

to make the stir-fry sauce, combine the oyster and soy sauces, sherry and sugar in a small bowl and stir until the sugar dissolves.

heat a wok over high heat, add the vegetable and sesame oils and swirl to coat. Add the garlic, ginger and half the spring onions and stir-fry for 1 minute. Add the pork and cook for 3–4 minutes, or until just cooked, breaking up any lumps.

add the bamboo shoots, water chestnuts and remaining spring onion, then pour in the sauce. Cook for 2–3 minutes, or until the liquid thickens. Stir in the pine nuts. Divide among the lettuce cups. Drizzle with oyster sauce, if desired, then serve. Makes 12 small or 4 large lettuce cups.

60 ml (¼ cup) oyster sauce
2 teaspoons soy sauce
60 ml (¼ cup) sherry
1 teaspoon sugar
1½ tablespoons vegetable oil
¼ teaspoon sesame oil
3 garlic cloves, crushed
3 teaspoons grated ginger
6 spring onions (scallions),
  sliced on the diagonal
500 g (1 lb 2 oz) minced
  (ground) pork
100 g (3½ oz) tinned
  bamboo shoots, drained
  and finely chopped
100 g (3½ oz) tinned water
  chestnuts, drained and
  finely chopped
1 tablespoon pine nuts,
  toasted
12 small or 4 large soft
  lettuce leaves, such as
  iceberg lettuce
oyster sauce, to serve (optional)

crisp rubies

Remove the water chestnuts—now resembling shiny rubies—from the pan and cool in cold water.

add the food colouring to 60 ml (1/4 cup) water in a bowl. Add the water chestnuts and mix with a spoon. Leave for 10 minutes until the pieces turn pink, then drain and leave to dry.

put the tapioca flour in a plastic bag. Add the pink water chestnuts and shake the bag to coat them well. Dust off any excess flour. Bring a saucepan of water to boiling point. Add half of the water chestnuts and cook for 1–2 minutes, or until they float to the surface. Lift out with a slotted spoon and put them in a bowl of cold water. Repeat with the remaining water chestnuts. Drain all the pieces.

in a small saucepan, heat 250 ml (1 cup) water and the sugar until the mixture boils, stirring constantly. Lower the heat to medium and simmer for 5–10 minutes, or until the liquid reduces to a thick syrup.

mix the coconut milk and salt in a small saucepan and cook over a medium heat for 1–2 minutes until slightly creamy.

divide the water chestnuts among individual bowls and top with a few spoonfuls each of sugar syrup and creamy coconut milk. Sprinkle with ice and serve cold. Serves 6.

8–10 drops of pink or red food colouring
2 x 225 g (8 oz) tins water chestnuts, drained and each chestnut cut into 10–12 pieces
150 g (5 oz) tapioca flour
250 g (1 cup) sugar
185 ml (3/4 cup) coconut milk
1/4 teaspoon salt
crushed ice, to serve

dumpling wrappers

Made from wheat starch, wheat dumpling wrappers are white and can be round or square. They are used to make dishes such as har gau, steamed prawn (shrimp) dumplings (pictured below), a dim sum speciality. The filling of prawns and minced water chestnuts or bamboo shoots is folded into the wrappers.

Egg dumpling wrappers are yellow and may also be round or square. They are used for Chinese dishes such as siu mai (pork and prawn dumplings), and filled with a mixture of pork, prawns and Chinese mushrooms or water chestnuts.

Dumpling wrappers are found in the refrigerated section of Chinese shops and good supermarkets and can be frozen until needed.

Har gau dumplings are the benchmark dim sum for any Chinese restaurant. Each dumpling wrapper is filled as it is made because the pastry is hard to handle. The wrapper is then pleated and sealed and the dumpling is placed in the steamer. The dumplings turn translucent as they cook, showing their prawn and water chestnut filling.

Wheat dumpling wrappers are also known as — Shanghai wrappers

Egg dumpling wrappers are also known as — egg dumpling skins, gow gee wrappers

jiaozi

to make the filling, put the cabbage and salt in a bowl and toss lightly to combine. Leave for 30 minutes. Squeeze all the water from the cabbage and put the cabbage in a large bowl. Add the pork, garlic chives, soy sauce, rice wine, sesame oil, ginger and cornflour. Stir until combined and drain off any excess liquid.

put a heaped teaspoon of the filling in the centre of each wrapper. Spread a little water along the edge of the wrapper and fold the wrapper over to make a half-moon shape. Use your thumb and index finger to form small pleats along the sealed edge. With the other hand, press the 2 opposite edges together to seal. Put the dumplings on a baking tray that has been lightly dusted with cornflour. Do not allow the dumplings to sit for too long or they will go soggy.

bring a large saucepan of water to the boil. Add half the dumplings, stirring immediately to prevent them from sticking together, and return to the boil. For the traditional method of cooking dumplings, add 250 ml (1 cup) cold water and cook over high heat until the water boils. Add another 750 ml (3 cups) cold water and continue cooking until the water boils again. Alternatively, cook the dumplings in the boiling water for 8–9 minutes. Remove the saucepan from the heat and drain the dumplings. Repeat with the remaining dumplings.

alternatively, the dumplings can be fried. Heat 1 tablespoon oil in a frying pan, add a single layer of dumplings and cook for 2 minutes, shaking the pan to make sure they don't stick. Add 80 ml (1/3 cup) water, cover and steam for 2 minutes, then uncover and cook until the water has evaporated. Repeat with the remaining dumplings. Serve with red rice vinegar or a dipping sauce. Makes 50.

filling

300 g (10½ oz) Chinese cabbage, finely chopped
1 teaspoon salt
450 g (1 lb) minced (ground) pork
100 g (3½ oz) Chinese garlic chives, finely chopped
2½ tablespoons light soy sauce
1 tablespoon Shaoxing rice wine
2 tablespoons roasted sesame oil
1 tablespoon finely chopped ginger
1 tablespoon cornflour (cornstarch)

50 round wheat dumpling wrappers
red rice vinegar or a dipping sauce

Perhaps no other food typifies the hearty characteristics of northern home-style cooking more than these meat dumplings. They are an enjoyable, easy snack to prepare and eat at home.

1 Handle the wrappers carefully so that they don't tear or get too wet.

2 Squeeze the pleats firmly or they will undo as they cook.

1 Put the filling in a corner of the wrapper. Fold over the corner.

2 Roll up the spring roll, folding in the corners as you go.

3 Don't roll them too tightly or they may burst during cooking.

spring roll wrappers

Spring roll wrappers, or skins, are made with egg and are a pale or dark yellow. They are found in the refrigerated cabinets of Chinese shops and supermarkets and can be frozen until needed.

spring rolls

filling

6 dried Chinese mushrooms, soaked in boiling water for 30 minutes, then squeezed dry
3 tablespoons light soy sauce
1 teaspoon roasted sesame oil
1/2 teaspoon cornflour (cornstarch)
1/2 teaspoon freshly ground black pepper
4 tablespoons oil
450 g (1 lb) centre-cut pork loin, trimmed and cut into very thin strips
1 tablespoon finely chopped ginger
3 garlic cloves, finely chopped

140 g (5 oz) Chinese cabbage, finely shredded
140 g (5 oz) carrot, finely shredded
2 tablespoons Shaoxing rice wine
30 g (1 oz) Chinese garlic chives, cut into 2 cm (3/4 inch) lengths
175 g (6 oz) soya bean sprouts

1 egg yolk
2 tablespoons plain (all-purpose) flour
20 square spring roll wrappers
oil, for deep-frying
plum sauce, to serve

remove and discard the stems of the mushrooms and shred the caps. Mix the soy sauce, sesame oil and cornflour with the black pepper.

heat a wok over high heat, add half the oil and heat until very hot. Add the pork and stir-fry for 2 minutes until cooked. Remove and drain.

wipe out the wok and reheat over high heat. Add the remaining oil and heat until very hot. Stir-fry the mushrooms, ginger and garlic for 15 seconds. Toss in the cabbage and carrot. Pour in the rice wine, then stir-fry for 1 minute. Add the garlic chives and bean sprouts and stir-fry for 1 minute. Add the pork and the soy sauce mixture and cook until thickened. Transfer to a colander and drain for 5 minutes, tossing occasionally to remove the excess liquid.

mix together the egg yolk, flour and 3 tablespoons water. Put 2 tablespoons of filling on the corner of a wrapper, leaving the corner free. Spread some of the yolk mixture on the opposite corner. Fold over one corner and roll it up, but not too tightly. Fold in the other corners, roll up and press to secure. Repeat with the remaining wrappers.

fill a wok one-quarter full with oil and heat to 190°C (375°F), or until a piece of bread fries golden brown in 10 seconds. Cook the spring rolls in 2 batches, turning constantly, for 5 minutes, or until golden. Drain on paper towels. Serve with plum sauce. Makes 20.

prawns in a blanket

to make the prawns easier to wrap, make 3 or 4 shallow incisions in the underside of each, then open up the cuts to straighten the prawns.

mix the flour and 3 tablespoons water in a saucepan until smooth. Stir over medium heat for 1–2 minutes until thick. Remove from the heat.

using a pestle and mortar or a small blender, pound or blend the garlic, coriander roots and ginger together.

in a bowl, combine the garlic paste with the prawns, oyster sauce, pepper and a pinch of salt. Cover with plastic wrap and marinate in the refrigerator for 2 hours, turning occasionally.

put a spring roll or filo sheet on the work surface and keep all the remaining sheets in the plastic bag to keep them moist. Fold the sheet in half, remove a prawn from the marinade and put it on the sheet with its tail sticking out of the top. Fold the bottom up and then the sides in to tightly enclose the prawn. Seal the joins tightly with the flour paste. Repeat with the rest of the prawns and wrappers.

heat the oil in a wok or deep frying pan over medium heat. When the oil seems hot, drop a small piece of spring roll sheet into it. If it sizzles immediately, the oil is ready. Deep-fry 4 prawns at a time for 4 minutes, or until golden brown and crispy. Remove with a slotted spoon and drain on paper towels. Keep them warm while deep-frying the rest. Serve hot with a chilli or plum sauce. Serves 4.

12 raw large prawns (shrimp), peeled and deveined, tails intact
1 tablespoon plain (all-purpose) flour
2 garlic cloves, roughly chopped
3 coriander (cilantro) roots, finely chopped
1 cm (1/2 inch) piece of ginger, roughly sliced
1 1/2 tablespoons oyster sauce or, for a hotter flavour, 1/2 teaspoon red curry paste
a sprinkle of ground white pepper
12 frozen spring roll sheets or filo sheets, 12 cm (5 inches) square, defrosted
peanut oil, for deep-frying
a chilli sauce, or plum sauce, to serve

1 Fold the spring roll sheet in half to form a triangle.

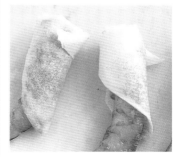

3 Serve the prawns immediately, using the tails to pick them up.

2 Wrap the prawn in the sheet, keeping its tail sticking out.

won ton wrappers

Won ton wrappers or skins are thinly rolled sheets of dough made from flour and eggs—the same dough used to make egg noodles. They are cut into squares. Both won ton wrappers and ready-made won tons can be purchased from Asian supermarkets. Store in their packets in the freezer for several months and defrost as needed.

won ton soup

250 g (9 oz) raw prawns (shrimp), peeled and deveined
85 g (3 oz) tinned water chestnuts
250 g (9 oz) lean minced (ground) pork
3½ tablespoons light soy sauce
3½ tablespoons Shaoxing rice wine
1½ teaspoons salt
1½ teaspoons roasted sesame oil
½ teaspoon freshly ground black pepper
1 teaspoon finely chopped ginger
1½ tablespoons cornflour (cornstarch)
30 square or round won ton wrappers
1.5 litres (6 cups) chicken stock
450 g (1 lb) spinach, trimmed (optional)
2 spring onions (scallions), green part only, finely chopped

put the prawns in a tea towel and squeeze out any moisture. Mince the prawns to a coarse paste using a sharp knife or food processor.

blanch the water chestnuts in boiling water for 1 minute, then refresh in cold water. Drain, pat dry and roughly chop. Put the prawns, water chestnuts, pork, 2 teaspoons of the soy sauce, 2 teaspoons of the rice wine, ½ teaspoon of the salt, ½ teaspoon of the sesame oil, the black pepper, ginger and cornflour in a mixing bowl. Mix vigorously.

put a teaspoon of filling in the centre of one won ton wrapper. Brush the edge of the wrapper with a little water, fold in half, then bring the two folded corners together; press firmly. Put on a cornflour-dusted tray.

bring a saucepan of water to the boil. Cook the won tons, covered, for 5–6 minutes, or until they rise to the surface. Remove with a wire sieve and divide among six bowls.

put the stock in a saucepan with remaining soy sauce, rice wine, salt and sesame oil, and bring to the boil. Add the spinach and cook until just wilted. Pour the hot stock over the won tons and sprinkle with the spring onion. Serves 6.

Fold the wrapper in half, then bring the two folded corners together and press firmly.

gold purses

115 g (4 oz) minced (ground) raw prawns (shrimp)	1 tablespoon oyster sauce
80 g (½ cup) water chestnuts, drained and roughly chopped	¼ teaspoon salt
	¼ teaspoon pepper
1 garlic clove, finely chopped	30–35 won ton wrappers
1 spring onion (scallion), finely chopped	7.5 cm (3 inches) square peanut oil, for deep-frying sweet chilli sauce, or other chilli sauce, to serve

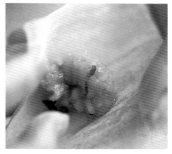

1 Put a small ball of mixture in the middle of a won ton wrapper.

2 Squeeze the edges of the wrapper to enclose the filling.

3 Gently press the corners together, firmly sealing shut the 'purse'.

combine the prawns with the water chestnuts, garlic and spring onion in a bowl. Mix in the oyster sauce, salt and pepper. Put half a teaspoon of mixture into the middle of each won ton wrapper. Carefully gather up, squeezing the corners together to make a little purse. Put on a tray. Continue until you have used up all the wrappers and filling.

heat 5 cm (2 inches) oil in a wok or deep frying pan over a medium heat. When the oil seems hot, drop a small piece of won ton wrapper into the oil. If it sizzles immediately, the oil is ready. Don't have the oil too hot or the purses will burn.

lower 5 purses into the oil. After 2–3 minutes they will start to go hard. Lower another 4 or 5 purses into the oil and deep-fry them all together. To help cook the tops, spoon some of the oil over the tops. Deep-fry for another 3–4 minutes, or until golden brown and crispy. As each batch cooks, lift out the purses with a slotted spoon and add some more in their place. Drain on paper towels. Keep warm while deep-frying the remaining purses. Transfer to a serving plate and serve with chilli sauce. Makes about 30.

subject index

recipe index

Published by Murdoch Books®, a division of Murdoch Magazines Pty Ltd.

Murdoch Books® Australia
Pier 8/9
23 Hickson Road
Millers Point NSW 2000
Phone: + 61 (0) 2 4352 7000
Fax: + 61 (0) 2 4352 7026

Murdoch Books UK Limited
Erico House
6th Floor North
93/99 Upper Richmond Road,
Putney, London SW15 2TG
Phone: + 44 (0) 20 8785 5995
Fax: + 44 (0) 20 8785 5985

Design Concept and Design: Vivien Valk
Editorial Director: Diana Hill
Project Manager: Kim Rowney
Editors: Kim Rowney, Wendy Stephen, Lulu Grimes
Photo Library Manager: Anne Ferrier
Production: Monika Vidovic

Chief Executive: Juliet Rogers
Publisher: Kay Scarlett

National Library of Australia
Cataloguing-in-Publication Data
Asian Kitchen. Includes index.
ISBN 1 74045 274 7.
1. Cookery, Asian
641.595

PRINTED IN SINGAPORE by Tien Wah Press.
Published 2004.

IMPORTANT: Those who might be at risk from the effects of salmonella food poisoning
(the elderly, pregnant women, young children and those suffering from immune deficiency
diseases) should consult their GP with any concerns about eating raw eggs.

acknowledgements

Photographers: Alan Benson, Craig Cranko, Ben Dearnley, Joe Filshie, Jared Fowler, Ian Hofstetter, Jason Lowe,
Andre Martin, Luis Martin.

Stylists: Jane Collins, Carolyn Fienberg, Mary Harris, Katy Holder, Cherise Koch, Michaela Le Compte,
Sarah de Nardi, Justine Poole.

Food Preparation: Shaun Arantz, Rekha Arnott, Ross Dobson, Jo Glynn, Sonia Grieg, Olivia Lowndes, Julie Ray,
Wendy Quisumbing.

Recipe Development: Rekha Arnott, Oi Cheepchaiissara, Ross Dobson, Margaret Grimes, Lisa Harvey, Deh-Ta Hsiung,
Radha Jayaram, Ajoy Joshi, Wendy Quisumbing, Carol Selva Rajah, Nina Simonds, Kuvel Sundar Singh,
Priya Wickramasinghe and the Murdoch Books Test Kitchen.